The Concept
of Representation
in the Age of the
AMERICAN REVOLUTION

The Concept
of Representation
in the Age of the
AMERICAN REVOLUTION

John Phillip Reid

The University of Chicago Press
Chicago & London

John Phillip Reid is professor of law at the New
York University School of Law. He is the author
of twelve books on political thought, including
*The Concept of Liberty in the Age of the American Rev-
olution,* also published by the University of Chicago Press.

The University of Chicago Press, Chicago 60637
The University of Chicago Press, Ltd., London

© *1989 by The University of Chicago*
All rights reserved. Published 1989
Printed in the United States of America
98 97 96 95 94 93 92 91 90 89
54321

Library of Congress Cataloging-in-Publication Data
Reid, John Phillip.
   The concept of representation in the age of the American
Revolution / John Phillip Reid.
      p.   cm.
   Bibliography: p.
   Includes index.
   ISBN 0-226-70898-5 (alk. paper)
   1. Representative government and representation—United States—
History. I. Title.
KF4881.R45   1989
342.73′053—dc20   89-32139
[347.30253]   CIP

for Ann and Susan

CONTENTS

INTRODUCTION

The concept of representation in the eighteenth-century English-speaking world has been extensively researched. The studies of J. R. Pole have said the last word on many political aspects of the subject. The purpose of this book is not to uncover new political, economic, or social data but to examine the same material from the perspective of the history of law. To delineate the contours of the inquiry, it is necessary to draw academic, occasionally pedantic distinctions between legal history and nonlegal history. They are concerned with the same problems but ask different questions.

A difference of perspective separates the political, social, economic, and legal historians of eighteenth-century representation. The political perspective asks who could vote, how ballots were cast, what representation meant to the functioning of society, and—at least until recently—the degree to which representation was democratic.[1] The social perspective asks about the representation of hierarchical classes, the domination of the naturally superior elite, and to what extent eighteenth-century Great Britain and British North America were deferential societies.[2] The economic perspective asks about the representation of interests, the dissemination of the spoils of "influence," and advantages reaped through representation by the West Indian islands over other parts of the empire such as Ireland. Legal history seeks a more technical yet quite practical perspective. It is interested in the political, social, and economic but has another set of queries.

As legal history is concerned with law, a legal history of representation in the eighteenth century has little interest in identifying arguments as "old whig," "commonwealthman," or "country" when origins can be located in constitutional or common law predating any of these political schools. Nor is it of concern to the history of law whether eighteenth-century representation was "democratic." This question becomes especially irrelevant when one turns from twentieth-century histories to eighteenth-century polemical literature and discovers that people in the

1

eighteenth century did not ask if representation was "democratic," "deferential," "oligarchical," or any of the words intriguing historians of a few years past. What they asked was whether the system was "constitutional." If we are to understand their concept of representation rather than judging eighteenth-century representation by our own questions, we must ask why a representative system to be legitimate had to meet the standard of constitutionalism rather than some other standard such as equality, or universality of suffrage, or geographic parity.

For purposes of outlining the objectives of this book, a further distinction should be drawn. This study is less concerned with traditional legal history than with two of its subdivisions, constitutional history and jurisprudential history. To illustrate the distinction, a legal history of representation deals with such matters as the statutes determining who in the population was eligible to vote, the legal mechanisms available to a person qualified to enforce the right to vote, and the writs or processes available to a candidate to have his election certified. A constitutional history of representation, by contrast, deals with the institutional and the operational functions of representation in the day-to-day business of the government. A major *constitutional* theme of this book is that eighteenth-century representation was primarily an institution of restraint on governmental power and that the constitutionality of its elements and programs was judged by how they maintained and served the integrity of that institutional purpose. A jurisprudential history of representation in the eighteenth century concentrates more on theory and philosophy than on function and institutions, probing the meaning of consent, the eighteenth-century belief that interests could represent people, the nature of the representative's trust as an agent of the elector, and the accountability of the representative. A *jurisprudential* question for the twentieth century, a question that has not been answered in the historical literature because it has not been asked and probably has not been understood, is how, in the eighteenth century, all citizens were required to consent for government to be legitimate when few were permitted to participate directly in the process of consent.

There are several reasons why the history of representation in the eighteenth century merits retelling from the constitutional and jurisprudential perspective. One is the institutional role of representation in the old pre-nineteenth-century constitution: the constitution of British government before sovereign, arbitrary authority became the acknowledged constitutional norm. A constitutional commentator had that institutional role in mind when he warned that to give Americans representation in the British parliament "would be taking away from the colonists the grand bulwark of their liberties, whose representatives in these assemblies are their constant support against arbitrary encroachments."[3]

A second lesson derived from the jurisprudential approach is the light that eighteenth-century representation sheds on the nature of law. It is eighteenth-century law that will be discussed—not the law that we have known for the last 150 or 200 years, the law of sovereign command, but, rather, a law of custom. Even the law governing electors was as much a law of custom as it was a law of statutory modification. By the general custom of England, the franchise was determined by local custom. The fee-simple owner of a freehold of a certain type, size, or value might be eligible to vote in one borough, while the freeholder of an exactly similar estate in a neighboring borough would not be eligible. By custom— or by charter granted by the crown with custom growing out of charter—some places had representation and other places did not. The law of representation was less the will and pleasure of a lawmaker than rights proven by past usages exercised from time beyond memory. "The very nature and meaning of law was involved," Bernard Bailyn has observed. "The traditional sense, proclaimed by Blackstone no less than by Hobbes, that law was a command 'prescribed by source superior and which the inferior is bound to obey'—such a sense of law as the declaration of a person or body existing somehow independently above the subjects of law and imposing its will upon them, was brought into question by the developing notion of representation."[4] Bailyn's view is from the familiar perspective of law in the twentieth century, and we may wonder if he did not allow twentieth-century concepts to determine the conclusion. As the evidence presented in this study indicates, a better explanation is that custom came before command, that custom gave rise to representation, and that only with the development of representation—and the nineteenth-century theory of consent to government by representation—did the British acquire a "safe"—that is, nonmonarchical—institutional framework to replace custom as law with the sovereign's command.

A third jurisprudential aspect of eighteenth-century representation is that it was unlike most other areas of British constitutional law. An outstanding characteristic of eighteenth-century constitutional law was its changeless, timeless nature. As the constitution was custom, it had not been ordained and had not been altered over the centuries. It had always been as it was now, the creator, not the creature, of government, the sovereign that was law rather than the law that was the command of the sovereign. This was the notion of the ancient, Gothic, fixed constitution, which soon would be replaced in jurisprudential thought by the acceptance of law as command. Together with prerogative law, representation was one of the first legal concepts to force common lawyers to acknowledge that constitutional law changed over time. In 1716, Parliament had altered what had been regarded as fundamental law when it passed the Septennial Act, abrogating the revolutionary settlement of triennial elections. That statute, changing representation and extending the terms of the members of the House of Commons then sitting four years beyond what they had been elected to serve, had taught a lesson of parliamentary power and foreshadowed the shift of sovereignty from customary right to legislative will and pleasure. When, in the 1770s, reformers began to urge "equal" representation and were told that the right of suffrage was beyond the authority of Parliament to alter, even "constitutionalist" lawyers who thought about the matter had to acknowledge that that argument was no longer "law." With that acknowledgment came the realization of the potential, if not the actuality, of parliamentary power.

A fourth aspect of representation worth restudy also has to do with the fact that disagreements about representation were an anomaly in the general constitutional history of the American Revolution. If there was a given of constitutional law that dominated the revolutionary controversy between the colonies and the mother country, it was that both sides were in basic agreement about the constitution. Americans did not rebel from Great Britain because they wanted a different government. They rebelled because they believed that Parliament was violating constitutional precepts. Colonial whigs did not fight for American rights. They fought for English rights.[5] The reason that they did so is that the constitution they were defending was that of Great Britain. The one clear exception to this general truism was representation. American perceptions of the constitutionality of representation, of the responsibility of representatives to their constituents, and of the constitutional function of consent had departed from British perceptions. This historical fact alone gives the concept of representation in the age of the American Revolution unique significance. To the extent that the imperial controversy was a dispute about a shared, revered constitution, the fact that there was one area of legal theory on which the two sides could not agree contributed to conflict and disharmony. Perceptions about representation may not have led to civil war, but they made constitutional adjustment more difficult.

The suggestion just made should not be misinterpreted by exaggeration. The historical judgment so central to the argument of this book—that American constitutional and political thought had separated quite far from the contemporary British constitutional and political thought about representation—is, owing to the nature of the evidence, more implicit than explicit, and the degree of divergence is quite difficult to measure because few eighteenth-century political theorists commented on it. Indeed, it is a good question whether many American whigs realized how far their constitutional practice had strayed from British constitutional theory. The extent to which they did not realize the differences helps explain why these different perceptions about representation did not contribute in substantive ways to the coming of the American Revolution. The basic constitutional argument between the mother country and her colonies was about the rule of law and government by consent, and, to the extent that representation was an element of consent, representation was, of course, an issue. But representation was not a direct issue because, although colonial whigs thought of representation in the newer, American sense, they still thought of consent in its older, English constitutional sense. Why the difference in concepts concerning representation in the two parts of the British dominions made "adjustment" of the conflict more difficult, if not impossible, is because it made difficult, if not impossible, the most obvious solution. Americans could not have been granted "representation" in Parliament according to American concepts of constitutional representation without raising havoc with British concepts of representation, perhaps even destroying the customary constitutional foundation on which Parliament's authority to govern rested. Colonial whigs, however, could have accepted "representation" in Parliament only on American, not British, constitutional premises.

It would be well to guard against obvious assumptions. Too easily made, they could lead to false conclusions. Students of twentieth-century principles of representation may think that this study gives greater emphasis to eighteenth-century British concepts of representation because colonial American concepts seem fairly "conventional." That would not be an accurate inference. Colonial American concepts of representation were conventional only to the degree that they were closer to twentieth-century concepts of representation than were eighteenth-century British concepts. In fact, except for the importance attached to the right of electors to impose binding instructions on their representatives, the colonial American concept of representation can be said to have had the future before it—in Great Britain as well as in the United States.[6]

Of course, to the extent that the colonial concept of representation corresponds to our concepts, it is less surprising and needs no explanation, and it is, therefore, discussed less. But it will not do to be anachronistic. If we must think in terms of such words as *conventional,* they should be kept in historical perspective. British notions of representation were more "conventional" than were American when examined, not from twentieth-century premises, but from eighteenth-century premises. The gulf of change separating two centuries of constitutional thought may be greater in the matter of understanding the concept of representation than understanding most other constitutional and political concepts. It will be a matter of surprise to most readers to be told that colonial whigs such as John Adams and John Dickinson thought that the doctrines of virtual representation and vicarious consent were reasonable, viable constitutional concepts. A historical fact that is too often misunderstood is that they rebelled not because they objected to virtual representation as a constitutional norm but because they insisted that virtual representation be imposed on them constitutionally. Our problem is that because of twentieth-century constitutional agnosticism we can no longer appreciate how those doctrines could have been "constitutional" to them.

Another word to be avoided is *innovation.* In the eighteenth century, the American concept of representation was an innovation only in contrast to the British. It was not an innovation in the sense that it was a new theory of representation. Americans arrived at their law of representation not by theory but by experiment. It had developed with the colonies by the English tradition of the practice of "customary" constitutional growth. Neither political scientists nor lawyers had had to formulate or direct its course.[7] That is one explanation why much more will be said about the British concept of representation than about the American. Again, it is not because the American was "conventional" by today's understanding but because much more was written in the eighteenth century concerning the British concept. It was both the dominant concept and the concept then coming under political attack. Had the British understood better than they did the democratic aspects of the American concept, it would have generated a much larger literature of criticism. More was written about the British concept of representation because there was more to be said, because it was more clearly understood, and because, being better understood, it was more controversial.

Yet it will not do to oversimplify even the most obvious conclusions of history. Of course the eighteenth-century American concept of representation seems conventional because it is closer to today's law and today's political theory. And the eighteenth-century British concept of representation seems so discredited that we have difficulty comprehending the respect that it once enjoyed. But are the eighteenth-century British doctrines of constructive consent and virtual representation as obsolete in the twentieth-century United States as they are in twentieth-century Great Britain? To what extent has the virtual, vicarious, nonelected "representative" of eighteenth-century Great Britain been reincarnated in the twentieth-century United States in the function of the "public interest" litigator or even the instigator of a class-action lawsuit? The strange twisting of American government by judiciary in the late twentieth century may be lending new respectability to a British constitutionalism that we had thought was discarded in disgrace long ago.[8]

A fifth value to isolating the concept of representation for separate study is what it tells us about the eighteenth-century notion of constitutionalism. It was, after all, the colonial constitution and the British constitution that gave birth to the United States Constitution of 1789. This fact was especially true for the principles of restraint inherited from the old English balanced constitution, a constitutional ideal that, by the eighteenth century, had come to be restrained and balanced largely by the concept of representation. The concept of constitutionalism in eighteenth-century British legal thought had less to do with the mechanism of governance than with restraints on power. Departing from its English inheritance, American constitutionalism, retaining the representative branch of government as one of three equal weights, would seek different institutional ways to maintain constitutional restraint. The British, ironically, would use the representative institution to undo the balance and, as representation in Great Britain through legislative reform became more representative of the general population, would replace the eighteenth-century constitutionalism of restraint discussed in this study with sovereign, arbitrary government. The process of change is less well known than it should be, not because the transformation is not understood, but because we too often have not heeded the former role of representation in the constitutional scheme of balance.

Our problem is that we no longer employ the concept of constitution as it was used in the eighteenth century. *Constitution* in the twentieth century, at least in American law, has a much sharper, clearer meaning than it did in the eighteenth century. One explanation is that in the twentieth century *constitution* is a more technical, more specialized, more "legal" word than it was two hundred years ago, when it was much more part of the popular language of everyday life.

In the eighteenth century, the constitution was not the measure of what was lawful but the standard of what law should be. The British constitution was whatever could be plausibly argued and forcibly maintained. The argument that was plausible was based on custom, precedent, and the existing arrangement of government institutions, and the force was provided by the consensus of the ruling class. The law might be whatever Parliament said it was, but Parliament, when it strayed from traditional ways, was always called back "to the first principles of the constitution." A person believing that Parliament, when enacting a statute, had departed from constitutional norms would think of that statute as both legal and unconstitutional. A person who believed that Parliament had acted constitutionally thought of the same statute as legal and constitutional.

Consider just some of the ways that the term *constitution* was used when eighteenth-century people talked about representation. As often as not, it was a descriptive adjective. Arguing for annual elections in Great Britain, Granville Sharp referred to yearly sessions of Parliament as "the constitutional term." He wanted the constitution "returned to its first principles," and it would have been immaterial to him if it were proven that neither annual elections nor annual sessions had ever been the parliamentary rule. In 1777, Sharp contended that the Revolution could be ended with reconciliation because "the Americans were inclined to a *re-union,* even *under* the *crown,* on constitutional principle," provided the administration adopted "*legal* means of *political reformation.*" Sharp meant changes in parliamentary representation, or what John Almon called putting "the right of election upon a constitutional footing."[9]

To appreciate what eighteenth-century Britons meant by such concepts as consent and representation, we must escape from thinking of a constitution as law and return to the eighteenth-century idea of a constitution as law's imagery. In the twentieth-century United States, the habit of equating law with constitution gets in the way of our understanding of some of the complexities of eighteenth-century constitutionalism. If an action is unconstitutional, Americans think it unlawful. That was, of course, not the eighteenth-century thought. "[T]he *law* and the *constitution* are not the same, nay, . . . they are essentially and necessarily distinct," John Cartwright explained as late as 1797. Pennsylvania's Joseph Galloway had that distinction in mind when, in a speech to the first Continental Congress, he defended as legal Parliament's supremacy over the colonies. "I am free to confess," he added, "that the exercise of that authority is not perfectly constitutional in respect to the Colonies." The reason was that Americans did not enjoy direct representation. Cartwright, asking the question "whether our House of Commons be, or not be, at present, what our constitution requires," agreed that failure of representation could make the legal unconstitutional. "[W]hat may be at this time *law*, respecting our representation and our elections, cannot decide the point at issue," he explained, "for our dispute is not about *law*, but the *constitution*." [10]

We tend to forget that at one time in English and British constitutionalism, in addition to speaking of constitutional and unconstitutional law, it was possible to speak of legal and illegal constitutions. For example, consider how Virginia's Richard Bland tied the concept of representation to the concept of a legal constitution. "If then the People of this Colony are free born, and have a Right to the Liberties and Privileges of *English* Subjects," he wrote, "they must necessarily have a legal Constitution, that is, a Legislature, composed, in Part, of the Representatives of the People." [11] Bland was stating a very British thought perhaps too concisely. The principle was that a constitution became legitimate when the representative element provided a balance to government, checking its authority to an extent sufficient that people were not subject to arbitrary command but were, rather, the opposite of being subject to arbitrariness or, in eighteenth-century parlance, were "free." The *London Journal* had elaborated on the idea when discussing Paul de Rapin's historically nonsensical but constitutionally sound version of the ancient constitution: "[W]hat *Rapin* excels all our other Historians in, is his *just* Notion and *true* Representation of the *Constitution* of *England:* He hath shewn, that we always *had a Constitution;* that our Government was always *Legal;* that the People had their *Rights,* as well as the Kings their *Prerogatives;* and had *Representatives* too, to assert those Rights; that our Kings were not *arbitrary,* nor our Monarchy *absolutely* Hereditary." [12] Representation was constitutional when it performed its constitutional task: checking arbitrary power and securing individual rights. "Our constitution is founded on jealousy and suspicion," Charles Carroll of Carrollton contended; "its true spirit and full vigour cannot be perserved

without the most watchful care, and strictest vigilance of the representatives over the conduct of administration." Carroll was explaining that,
as a constitutional institution, the House of Commons had a constitutional task entailing more than legislation, a task as the earl of Chesterfield said "to examine severely, and judge impartially the conduct and
the measures of those employed in the administration, to represent the
grievances, and watch over the liberties and the properties of the people
of this nation, and to take away evil counsellors from before the king." [13]

The institution of representation as outlined by Chesterfield is the
subject of this book. It is a perception of representation that makes the
concept almost synonymous with that of constitution and constitutionalism. As James Wilson pointed out, whenever the people of Great Britain elected a new Parliament, when they, that is, passed judgment on
members of the House of Commons by asking if they had served their
constituents' interests, the "constitution" was "renewed, and drawn back,
as it were, to its first principles; which is the most effectual method of
perpetuating the liberties of a state." [14]

Wilson, a future justice of the United States Supreme Court, meant
what he said. The *constitution* was what was renewed when representatives were elected. In a manner of speaking, the House of Commons
was also renewed, but that fact was incidental.

The Concept of Consent

In the year of the Declaration of Independence, John Cartwright wrote of "that poor consolatory word, *representation,* with the mere sound of which we have so long contented ourselves." Similar words soothing to the British and their American colonists in the eighteenth century were *constitution, liberty, property, security,* and *consent.* British people on both sides of the Atlantic had enormous pride in their representative constitutional government and in their own remarkable virtues. They were, as they often reminded themselves, "the wisest and greatest people on earth," living under "the safest and best government in the world." The balanced representative government of Great Britain, a Virginian boasted, "formed the wisest system of legislation that ever did, or perhaps ever will exist." "[T]hank GOD, we live under one of the happiest Constitutions in the World," a Massachusetts pamphleteer agreed, "a Constitution that admits of no Law whatever, without the Voice of the People." The British constitution was the happiest, Sir William Meredith explained, because "[i]t distinguishes us, not as Freemen only, but above all Freemen upon Earth. Since it is the Privilege of the Englishman alone, 'To chuse those Delegates to whose Charge is committed the Disposal of his Property, his Liberty, his Life.'"[1]

Other nations of Europe once had possessed elected "Dyets," "Cortes," and "Parliaments," but by the age of the American Revolution only the British, Irish Protestants, and English colonists in North America and the Caribbean still enjoyed the "security" of representative government. "Foreigners," an English political theorist claimed, "in all their writings and observation upon England, on the wisdom of its form of government, the limited prerogative of the crown, and the just liberties of the people, have always attributed these blessings to the constitution of our parliaments; and it is certainly this our privilege of representation, which is not only the origin, but the security of all the rest."[2]

Consent was the word constitutionalists used to describe the constitutional apparatus that theoretically made the eighteenth-century British

11

secure. It was the first principle cited by Americans in their struggle to retain their customary constitutions. In 1764, before Parliament had enacted any of the legislation that precipitated the revolutionary crisis, the Connecticut assembly asserted that, "[b]y the Common Law of England, every Commoner hath a Right not to be subjected to Laws made without his Consent." Fourteen years later, as Massachusetts was debating the elements of its first written constitution, an Essex County convention insisted that "a fundamental principle on which each individual enters into society is, that he shall be bound by no laws but by those to which he has consented." Perhaps the best concise statement of the constitutional doctrine, one that can serve as a summary for hundreds of others, was voted by a meeting of Fairfax County, Virginia, called to protest the Massachusetts intolerable acts of 1774 and presided over by George Washington: "Resolved, That the most important and valuable part of the British Constitution, upon which, its very existence depends, is the fundamental principle, of the peoples being Governed, by no Laws, to which they have not given their Consent, by Representatives freely chosen by themselves; who are affected by the Laws they enact, equally, with their Constituents; to whom they are accountable, and whose Burthens they share."[3]

The doctrine of consent was not a colonial concoction, nor was it a principle championed only by British radicals or American whigs. It was as often embraced by conservatives as by reformers and was favorably discussed by every political catechism printed in the eighteenth century, including Viscount Bolingbroke's.[4] The doctrine was staple to assize sermons and grand jury charges[5] and can be found in judicial pronouncements, including *Ashby* v. *White,* the leading constitutional decision on the right to vote. "[T]his is not a *minimum in lege,*" Chief Justice Sir John Holt said of the concept of consent, "but a noble Privilege, which intitles the subject to a share in the government and legislature: no laws can be made to affect him or his property but by his own consent, given in person if he be chosen, or by his representative if he is a voter."[6] The doctrine was so entangled in the British constitutional consciousness that even administration hacks and anti-American pamphleteers used it when arguing against the claims of colonial whigs.[7] An indication of how tenaciously the eighteenth-century British believed that theirs was a nation of consent can be gathered by considering a boast by Francis Plowden, a conservative common lawyer. "The *free will and consent of a free people* is not only the origin, but the permanent basis of our constitution," he wrote. As a Roman Catholic, Plowden was not eligible to vote and hence should have been the last person to repeat the myth that he could consent to anything. Instead, like almost every other Briton, he gloried in the privilege of consent, boasting "that the British constitution is founded upon a democratic basis, *the free-will and consent of a free-people*," even though that constitution made him less "free" than most other males.[8] It tells us something that a person in Plowden's situation would think not only that the concept of consent was the basis of free government but also that Great Britain was governed by consent. Just what it tells us is the question this book attempts to answer.

ROOTS OF CONSENT

There is a misconception that must be disabused: that the doctrine of consent was a relatively new concept in British constitutionalism, originating with Harrington or Locke or other political philosophers formulating theoretical restraints on royal power. It was rather a doctrine of English common and constitutional law, embedded in the governance of the kingdom as long as it had been guided by the rule of law. During the age of the American Revolution, the accepted teachings of contemporary historical scholarship—more forensic history than an impartial investigation of the past—traced the concept back to the Anglo-Saxons, who had been governed on the Continent by consent and had brought the doctrine with them to Britannia. In eighteenth-century Great Britain, consent was perceived to have been a key element of the Gothic constitution of post-Roman Europe. Generally called the "ancient constitution," it is better thought of as the "timeless constitution," a constitution that contained, without change or transition, constant principles, unaltered over a period to which the "memory of man runneth not to the contrary," and owing their authority not to will, power, or royal creation, but to immemoriality. It was the constitution and, therefore, consent that had created English governments and dynasties, not conquest, divine right, or the iron fist of despotic power.[9]

During the Middle Ages, the concept of consent had often been articulated in official documents, even in statutes of the realm, and associated with both Parliament and the common law.[10] A remarkable portion of the theories on which the constitutionality of consent would be based during the age of the American Revolution had been developed during the centuries before the English Civil War. Sir Thomas Smith explained the representative nature of Parliament as the constitutional vehicle of consent by locating "every Englishman . . . to be there present either in person or by procuration and attorney." Christopher Saint German used the same fiction to explain why statutes bound commoners. Richard Hooker said consent was the ingredient that made government legitimate.[11] Sir John Fortescue, who articulated all these arguments, explained how consent restrained power by delineating actions that the king could not constitutionally undertake, such as altering statutes or levying taxes at discretion.[12]

The reign of Charles I was the proving time for the concept of consent. Although it risks oversimplifying a very complicated political situation, the constitutional controversy that led to the English Civil War could be explained in one word: consent. "The question in dispute between the King's party and us," a future regicide observed in 1642, was "whether the people should be governed by laws made by themselves, and live under a government derived from their own consent."[13] The Petition of Right codified the constitutional requirement for parliamentary consent to taxation, the earl of Strafford was attained and executed for governing the Irish "against their Consents" and advising the king to "lay *Taxes* and *burdens* upon them without their *consent*," and the Levellers argued for the constitutional principle that there is no legitimate authority "but what is erected by the mutual consent of a people."[14] The concept achieved universal constitutionality when Charles I adapted it to his own defense. The king was accused of making war on Parliament "and the people therein represented" in order to maintain "a Personal Interest of Will, Power, and pretended Prerogative to himself and his Family."[15] Earlier, Charles had attempted to turn the consent complaint around by saying that his authority had been vested by "God, the Law, the Custome and Consent of this Nation" and that the House of Commons, by acting "without & against my Consent," was subjecting the English to "lawless Arbitrary power and Government."[16] He refused to recognize the jurisdiction of the court trying him, partly because he had not consented to its creation, and partly because it did not have the consent of the people. "[Y]ou manifestly wrong even the *Poorest Ploughman*, if you demand not his free Consent," Charles had intended to say had he been allowed to speak, "nor can you pretend any colour for this your *Pretended Commission*, without the Consent at least of the *Major Part* of every Man in *England*."[17] We may recognize the king's constitutional hypocrisy and admit that a desperate man was seeking to salvage something from the ravages of total defeat, yet it is striking that what he tried to save was a semblance of legality through constitutional consent.

Charles was not making a political plea for his prerogative or a constitutional claim of divine right. In his desperation, he had turned to the
same legality that his enemies professed to champion, the common law
of Sir Edward Coke, John Hampden, and Sir John Eliot.

In the years between the English Civil War and the American Revolution, there would be disagreement about the meaning of consent, but
with the words of Charles I on the constitutional record the concept of
consent was entrenched in constitutional theory. The judges of common
law made it part of constitutional rhetoric: a lord chancellor boasted that
throughout their history the English had been "subject only to the laws
made by their own consent in their general assemblies"; and a lord chief
baron wrote that "Humane Laws have their Force and Authority from
the Consent and Agreement of Men." [18] Across the Atlantic, governance
of the colonies was, from the time of the first settlements, based on consent, at least in theory and quite often in practice.[19] The concept helped
force a constitutional crisis when New Englanders rebelled against Sir
Edmund Andros and his cohorts, who ruled without an elected assembly, charging that "they made what Laws they pleased *without any
consent of the People, either by themselves or representatives,* which is indeed
to *destroy the Fundamentals of the English,* and to *Erect a French Government.*" [20] By the age of the American Revolution, the concept was such a
constitutional commonplace that clergymen invoked it as often as lawyers did, making it a set piece of their sermons. "It is a mix'd Government," the pastor of Rutland told the Massachusetts General Court in
1758. "All our Laws are made by the common Consent, as in the famous
Commonwealths of *Athens* and *Rome.*" Just a short time later, these words
were echoed in the mother country by the bishop of Worcester, praising
common lawyers "who constantly and uniformly speak of the *English,* as
a mixed and limited form of government, and even go so far as to seek
its origin, where indeed the origin of all governments must be sought,
in the free will and consent of the people." [21] Consent was so obviously
constitutional that there was no need to explain what it meant.

MEANING OF CONSENT

There has been much written about how the idea of consent changed in
the eighteenth century. It is sometimes said that there are older and
newer concepts of consent. The older was summed up by Edmund Ludlow's reply to Oliver Cromwell's question, "[B]ut where shall we find that
consent?" "Among those who have acted with fidelity and affection to
the public," Ludlow answered, implying that consent would be estab-

lished by paternalistic authority earning consent by knowing what is best for the governed. The newer theory in the age of the American Revolution was expressed in James Burgh's comparison of the people's right to consent with the voting of stockholders in a company or James Wilson's contention that "consent was given with a view to ensure and encrease the happiness of the governed."[22] Perhaps there were shifts in the political uses of consent, but it is difficult to find anything original in eighteenth-century jurisprudential theories explaining the concept of consent. The reasons stated in the eighteenth century as to why consent was necessary for law or for government can almost be traced back to earlier common-law doctrine or writers of political theory.

Some legal theorists, not many, just a few, in the age of the American Revolution and even before denied that the concept of consent was either constitutional theory or constitutional practice. They asked when freeholders had ever consented to laws depriving them of the right to hunt game on their own land or when Catholics had consented to laws disenfranchising them and subjecting them to double taxation?[23] Indeed, the case against consent could be so persuasive that the wonder might be that so many eighteenth-century commentators not only utilized the theory but seemed to believe the fact. Necessity explained why. Real or theoretical, British constitutionalism needed the concept of consent. To question or doubt the concept entailed risks that tories as well as whigs did not care to run.[24]

Agreement that consent was an essential element of British constitutionalism was not the same as agreement about what it meant or why it was constitutional. Richard Wooddeson, Oxford's Vinerian professor of English laws, located consent's authority in government coercion, a power that had had a beginning sometime in the immeasurable infinity of immemorial history. "That which originally *constitutes* a nation, is common consent, tacit or express," Wooddeson argued, "for every state must have had some origin, before which it did not exist as such, however uncertain or remote the period." Another theory located the authority of consent in natural law, but not just in the natural law familiar to American scholars of eighteenth-century political history and of Lockean thought—the law that was "natural" because it was found in existing governmental institutions. Theorists of the eighteenth century tended to locate natural law either in God's direct ordinance or, more commonly, in the dictates of observable nature.[25] "All men are, by nature, equal and free," James Wilson explained, "no one has a right to any

authority over another without his consent: all lawful government is
founded in the consent of those who are subject to it."[26] More fundamental and much more frequently cited than natural law was the constitutional explanation that the people possessed the right of consent
because their consent had created government. When the younger Pitt
argued that the concept of consent "makes no part of the Constitution
of England," a barrister of Lincoln's Inn answered that "this principle
was acted on at the Revolution, and is therefore a part of the Constitution of England." It was, he said, "the principle of the Sovereignty of the
People."[27] The legal theorem was that "the original of all power and
government, is and ought to be in the PEOPLE," or, as a Bury St. Edmunds grand jury was charged, because the people have "a Power to
chuse their own Government, so consequently have They the same
Power to frame and make such Laws as They think most conducive to
the Support and Maintenance of the Government They have made
choice of."[28]

The idea may sound whiggish, and so it is. But it would be misleading
to think of it only in that way, for it was a familiar notion long before
the emergence of whiggery, employed by common lawyers to explain
the sources of law and by the House of Commons to justify the trial of
Charles I. There were at least two explanations in the eighteenth century for a government's right to command. One was authority—naked
force, conquest, usurpation, the patriarchal analogy. The other was consent of the people.[29] In truth, the theoretical bases for the authority of
consent were never developed as thoroughly as we might expect, and
one reason is that English constitutional thought had never been recep-
tive to martial or hierarchical justifications of ultimate authority. As a
result, consent had few theoretical alternatives, and it may be said with
only some exaggeration that consent preempted doctrine and was as
much presumed as rationalized as the source of the right to govern by
command and to punish the breach of command.[30]

It was a matter of conferring legitimacy on government. First, consent
provided command with general concurrence. Although not everyone
agreed with John Trenchard "that the whole people, who are the Publick, are the best Judges" or "often judge better than their Superiors,"
the premise does seem to have been accepted that "*the people* (that is,
such as shall be successfully chosen to represent the people) *are the best
keepers of their liberties.*"[31]

Second, consent created obligation. Consent "is the parent of all good

Laws, and just obligation to obey them." In fact, the Massachusetts House of Representatives argued, "the People must consent to Laws, before they can be obliged in Conscience to obey them." "[T]he Law derives its Being and Efficacy from common Consent," Sir Joseph Jekyll, a barrister and future master of the rolls, told the House of Lords when opening the articles in the impeachment trial of Sacheverell in 1710. Then he made as extreme an assertion as one could expect from a law-yer who had been chief justice of Chester as well as a king's serjeant. "And to place it on any other Foundation than common Consent, is to take away the Obligation this Notion of common Consent puts both Prince and People under to observe the Laws." In other words, if it were not for the concept of consent, there would be no moral obligation to obey law, only fear of coercion.[32]

The third element of legitimacy, but a shade different from the last, was that laws received "their binding Force from the Consent of the People governed." That is, Chief Justice Matthew Hale explained, the binding force of law depended on the consent of those to be bound by those laws. "If any doubt remain amongst you with respect to the force or efficacy of whatever laws you now, or hereafter make, be pleased to consider that all power is originally in the people," Richard Henderson told the House of Delegates of his short-lived colony of Transylvania. The laws they made would be binding, he concluded, because "it is prob-able, nay certain, that the laws may derive force and efficacy from our mutual consent." Henderson's political judgment was erroneous; Vir-ginia and North Carolina would not permit the new colony. But his theory of law claimed stirps running back beyond Locke and Hooker to the writers of the common law, Glanvil, Bracton, Fleta, Fortescue, and Coke.[33]

CONSTITUTIONALISM OF CONSENT

The concept of consent was the operative element of eighteenth-century British constitutionalism, the element, a Bury St. Edmunds grand jury in 1716 was told, that made "the best of Governments under the Sun, a mix'd limited Monarchy, where the supreme Power is divided between the King and the People."[34] It was therefore the basic check making British constitutionalism a rule of restrained government, the source of much of the vocabulary used in the eighteenth century to describe the uniqueness of the fabled constitution: bringing the "mix" to mixed government, furnishing the "balance" of balanced government, and placing the "limit" on limited government.

A twentieth-century word that would help us to understand the eighteenth-century concept of consent is *constitutionalism*. Had the term *constitutionalism* been current then, it would have embraced the dual principle, long well established in common-law legality, that law was restraint on authority and that there could be no authority without consent. The prerogative, for example, was said to be limited by laws established by consent, and those laws could be exceeded only by consent.[35] To prove the constitutional status of the doctrine of consent, there should have been no need to go back further than the Glorious Revolution, when James II lost his crown after threatening arbitrary rule of government without the restraint of consent.[36] In fact, the historical record of consent as restraint on power was traced back to the ancient Germanic constitution, when law was sovereign and the government could promulgate innovations only with the assent of those whose rights were affected.[37] By the age of the American Revolution, when law was less *the* sovereign than commands of *a* sovereign, it might seem that new concepts would have had to have been introduced. There had been no need. "It is a Maxim," the Massachusetts General Court asserted in 1776, "that, in every Government, there must exist, Somewhere, a Supreme, Sovereign, absolute, and uncontroulable Power; But this Power resides, always in the body of the People, and it never was, or can be delegated, to one Man, or a few." Neither the problem nor the solution was new. "Unlimited power must be in some to make and repeal law," William Pierrepont had told the House of Lords 135 years earlier; "nature placeth this in common consent only." Pierrepont was addressing the Lords in the impeachment trial of Robert Berkley for his judgment in the ship money decision, that is, for departing from fundamental law by sanctioning taxation without consent.[38]

The restraint of consent was on government, but owing to the dynamics of British constitutionalism, discussions always focused not on checking general state power by withholding consent of the people but on a crown checked by the consent of Parliament. In a 1643 tract, a Netherlander had asked if the English king was absolute. "In no wise," an Englishman answered, "for kings are limited by laws, so that they can make no laws, nor lay any impositions on their subjects, nor go to war with any, without the consent of the parliament, else the inhabitants are not bound thereunto." He was saying that the constitutional restraint of consent was institutionalized and that the institution containing it was Parliament. "In the true sense of the term *people*, they form one of the three estates," Baron Rivers of Stratfieldsaye explained. "They have, by their legal Representatives, their ample share in the government of the nation, and, consequently, of themselves." What they had is today thought of as the power to make laws, but in the old constitutionalism before the American Revolution a better description was the power to prevent law being made: prevention and protection against arbitrariness. "Will any man shew a Law that was ever made by any King of *England?*" Daniel Defoe once asked. "All our Laws are made by the King, Lords and Commons, and by their joint Consent and Authority. . . . [I]f the Consent of any one is wanting, no Law can be made." That is, the right to consent checked arbitrary decision, will, and power—no small role, as the essence of constitutional rule in the eighteenth century was to be free of arbitrariness.[39]

In twentieth-century constitutional law, the concept of consent restraining government might be explained as an aspect of the legislative check and balance against executive power. In the eighteenth century, it was analyzed as a private right: property inherited by each citizen at birth and held both personally and concurrently. It was a right making government accountable and providing security of life and property to the individual owner.[40] In the constitutional parlance of the day, to be governed without consent was to live in slavery. "I have no other notion of slavery, but being bound by a law to which I do not consent," Richard Price and many other observed. "What, my lord, is the definition of a slave?" an Irish barrister asked Lord North in 1780. "Is it not where a man is bound by laws, to which he never assented, and lies at the mercy of a power over which he has no controul?" North and every other political leader in Great Britain or the colonies would have answered yes.[41] They also generally agreed that for liberty to prevail people had to consent to their government and to the laws with which their government governed them. What was disputed was whether consent had to be individual and direct or (to say that the British people were the freest in the world because they consented to their government and laws) whether it was enough that they consented only in an attenuated, constructive, or vicarious sense, that is, consented as the word *consent* was defined in constitutional law.[42]

Disagreement was not that *consent* had a constitutional rather than a popular meaning. Disagreement was over what *consent* meant in constitutional law. One answer, that we today may think we understand, was asserted by "Providus" in the *Boston Evening-Post*. "The constitution," he contended, "frees me from obedience to the edicts of one or more absolute despots; let them pretend divine right, virtual representative right, ministerial representative right, or what right they please, underived from the free consent of the people, the alone natural source of all legislative and executive right whatsoever." Providus may have said nothing controversial. Contemporaries who wrote on legal and political theory did not quarrel with the notion that the concept of consent was synonymous with "the constitution." If, however, he was suggesting anything akin to popular sovereignty, Providus had little support. Most likely he was not; by "consent of the people" Providus probably meant the constitutional "consent" of the constitutional "people."[43]

"Government is (certainly) an institution for the benefit of the people governed, that is for the whole people," an anonymous London pamphleteer wrote in 1776, "but the whole of people have not a right to model Government as they please, because . . . the greater part of them have no right to interfere in matters of Government at all." There was, however, another definition of *people*—"those who are essentially necessary to constitute the State, and who represent the whole people." The constitutional "people" then, another anonymous London pamphleteer had explained six years earlier, were the enfranchised. "Their authority and character, as electors, are derived from the people, in the very same sense, in which the legislative authority of those whom they elect, and indeed every other civil authority has that origin." Both powers—the authority of the electors and of the officials whom they elected—were derived from sources that the author describes with the same word, "the people." Whether one or two "people," it came from the same source, "from a higher source, from the constitution; of which too these very electors are the instruments and creatures merely."[44]

Consent was both the most fundamental principle of the eighteenth-century British constitution and a term without precise meaning. It was less a constitutional definition than an explanation of ancient and current constitutional law. It was a constitutional truth rendered undeniable by the circuitousness of English constitutional reasoning: British government was the world's best because it was based on consent, and because it was government by consent it was best. Consent not only established the obligation of the citizen to obey law; it also gave to law and hence to government its legitimacy. As every common-law barrister could prove, consent had been the essential constitutional right of the English since at least the age of the Anglo-Saxons, and, throughout the nation's history, consent had been the operative constitutional doctrine preventing the development of a sovereign, omnipotent monarch autonomous from and superior to the ancient constitution, the law, and the people. For American whigs, the concept of consent in the age of the American Revolution would serve the same constitutional function against the British Parliament—the constitutional expression of consent for the British people—when it claimed to be autonomous from and superior to the ancient constitution, the law, and the American people.[45]

Mechanics of Consent

To a person in the twentieth century who thinks of consent in terms of participatory democracy, it might appear that in the age of the American Revolution the concept of consent was entirely substantive or theoretical, having no procedural incidents or rules for specific application. Indeed, from the perspective of two centuries, the concept of consent has the aura of being more a passive condition than an act and, to the extent that it was an act, more an act of political submission than one of legal participation. Perhaps it was easier to accept the reality of constructive consent in the eighteenth century, a time when much common-law procedure was secreted in fictions.[1] William Knox, the ministry's expert on colonial rule and former agent for Georgia, called consent "one of those Fictions, those nicer Principia of the Laws of Society."[2] But these terms could be misleading if we think of fictions masking reality.

"Consent is the essence of legislation, but this consent may be given by overt sign, by proxy, or by representation, or by implication," the theologian Richard Hooker explained in the sixteenth century, stating the constitutional theory still prevalent two hundred years later. In a literal sense, consent was impossible, William Jones noted in 1768, but, in an "appropriated and political sense, it is perfectly clear and intelligible. Though it cannot be understood to mean the *express* and positive consent, it may . . . mean the *implied* consent of every man." The range of implication was carried far by the eighteenth-century legal imagination. "[E]very man has . . . some mode or other of *actually consenting* to, or disapproving of the institutions and measures of government," "Regulus" asserted in 1775. How? "By his vote, if he has any; if not, by the press; by freedom of speech; by interest and connections; but above all, by an appeal to the laws against every institution, and every act of government which may affect either his property or personal freedom."[3]

We may think Regulus sophistical, and so he was, but not by the norms of eighteenth-century political writers with their felt need to convince themselves that British government ruled by consent. By constitutional norms, however, he was out of line. At common law, the concept of consent by implication had a loose but normative meaning; it was constructive but not fictive if one accepted the premises that underlay British constitutional authority.

IMPLIED CONSENT

When considering eighteenth-century theories explaining consent by implication, it is well to keep in mind what was consented to. Generally, it was nonlegislative law, not the kind of law discussed in this book, that is, statutory law, enacted law. One theory was consent to law by inheritance. "[M]y Ancestors did presume to Consent for me, that I should be subject to all the Laws which they Enacted," William Sherlock, a leading whig divine, wrote. John Shute, first Viscount Barrington and a barrister of the Inner Temple, had a better explanation. He theorized government's authority "not to the consent of Men in former Ages, but to those of the present time, who generally have the veneration for the Wisdom of the Ancestors, as to follow the example they have set them."[4]

A less passive theory implied consent from current citizenship. Every member of society, as well as "majority and minority" political groups, has "consented to be of one political society or community," or, put another way, persons by accepting a nation's protection "consent to be bound by its laws." The theory had the endorsement of some of the most distinguished writers on common law as well as John Locke and may have been most concisely summarized by the Scottish poet Thomas Blacklock. "Any man who is born in a particuliar country, or who, after his arrival in it, continues to claim its protection, to adopt its manners and customs, to obey and approve its laws, to enter into its interests and concerns, is effectually engaged in the political compact; because his consent, though never verbally expressed, is unquestionably and sufficiently implied in his conduct." Consent was tacit, to be sure, but it also could be proved by overt action. For, and this was especially true if people were free by law to leave the country, by remaining and enjoying the benefits of government they gave their consent to it and to its laws.[5]

Today we can fault as misconceived the contention that consent is found in the acquiescence of our ancestors, for we prefer to think of that acquiescence as evidence of the legitimacy of authority from prescription or custom rather than from direct consent.[6] Such analysis would have been misdirected in the eighteenth century, when lawyers equated consent with custom and found implied consent in the usages of customary law. "For what gives any legislature a right to act, where no express consent can be shewn?" Richard Wooddeson, Oxford's Vinerian professor of law, asked. "[W]hat, but immemorial usage? and what is the intrinsic force of immemorial usage, in establishing this fundamental or any other law, but that it is evidence of common acquiescence and consent?"[7]

Wooddeson's questions had already been answered by Thomas Rutherforth, who lectured on law in Cambridge. "For the general consent of the society binds each of its members," he had explained, borrowing from Grotius. "[A]nd any rules, which arise out of such usage, as has continued for time immemorial without being interrupted by any act of the public, become laws to all, whom the society intended to include within those rules." The argument had far-reaching potential and was one of the most controversial legal theories of the common law. For what Wooddeson was saying was that custom—that specialized area of jurisprudence known only to those trained in the technicalities of common law—was democratic. "[L]ong and uniform custom bestows a sanction, as evidence of universal approbation and acquiescence, [of] having been approved by the experience of ages," he claimed.[8] This explanation of the popular basis of immemorial custom infuriated Jeremy Bentham on one side of the Atlantic and that intransigent foe of common law, Thomas Jefferson, on the other.[9] The argument is usually attributed to Sir William Blackstone and to James Wilson, but the notion that the uninterrupted flow of custom proves its acceptance by the legal consciousness of the community, that it is the people's law, was staple stuff in both traditional common law and in what the eighteenth century understood to have been the ancient constitution of the European continent.[10]

Consent by Representation

Eighteenth-century constitutional theorists did not have to imply consent. They located its direct expression in the institution of parliamentary representation. Whether ultimate power was theorized as vested in the whole people or in the sovereign government of which the people held a tripartite share, consent was manifested by representation or delegation. It was a necessity dictated by numbers. As the entire population could not come together to vote consent, delegates consented for them.[11]

We must not let the word *represent* mislead us. Like *consent*, it had attenuated, legalistic meanings far removed from the concepts and images of popular usage. Just whom Parliament represented and what *represented* meant were matters of wide dispute. The "better" view, in the sense that it was the most frequently articulated, was that the entire Parliament, not just the House of Commons, the elected or what we would call the "representative" part of Parliament, but the king and lords as well, expressed the consent of the collective nation. The "constituent power" of Parliament, the theory explained, was received from "every Englishman, from the prince to the peasant, and of whatever state, dignity, or quality, possessing the right of being present in parliament either in person or by procuration or attorney; and the consent of the parliament is understood to be every man's consent." Yet, owing to the peculiar logic that shaped eighteenth-century constitutionalism, representation was not the same as consent. All three branches of the legislature had to consent to the enactment of law, but only the Commons could propose or alter money bills. There may have been several explanations for this rule, but one universally accepted by constitutional experts, aside from established custom, was that the House of Lords did not represent the people. Parliament constitutionally could tax commoners because the Commons were the representatives of the commoners of the nation. Until Parliament attempted to impose the Stamp Act on the North American and Caribbean colonies, territories of the realm that did not enjoy representation in Parliament—the Isle of Man, Jersey, Ireland—had not been taxed by Parliament for purposes of raising revenue. And, according to the accepted understanding of English constitutional history, some places—Chester, Durham, Wales, Calais—had been given representation so they could be taxed constitutionally.[12]

We are considering doctrines of the immemorial British constitution, based on English customs and usages, whose origins are lost in time but whose principles contained the rules of governance for the nation. We must not expect that a theory for these rules be logical, only that it be legal. The practical, indeed the sensible explanation of how consent was established by representation in one-third of a legislative body that was not representative in any of its three branches was that the sovereign power decreed it was. If the sovereign promulgated that the unrepresented had consented through representation, then there was both constitutional consent and constitutional representation. But that meaning of sovereignty belonged to the nineteenth century. Eighteenth-century legal theory could not tolerate the thought of will and command superior to customary right, which was, after all, the constitutional safeguard against arbitrary power. Because they could not contemplate ultimate sovereignty, commentators on the constitution groped for a theory explaining institutions that had developed over centuries in response to forces that were not planned, related, or consistent. The paradox is that there was agreement in disagreement, there was consent through representation even though the instrument of consent was not actually but only constitutionally representative.[13]

There was consent of the people whenever the houses of Parliament consented because members of the House of Commons were constitutionally delegated the representatives of the people, Henry Goodricke acknowledged, "but in that strict sense of consent, either *personal,* or by a *representative of one's own choice,* . . . it is a very false, absurd, and licentious doctrine." Why was this consent even without representation, and why was it representation even without the consent of those supposedly represented? The best and most frequently stated answer was unsatisfactory. Admitting that there was little direct consent through representation in the Commons, this answer avoided acknowledging supreme sovereignty by assuming a second consent, the delegation by the people of the right to consent for them, a delegation assumed in the constitution and proved by acquiescence in parliamentary rule.

> Though there is no *distinct* representation, yet, the subjects of Great Britain are neither bound by laws, nor is their money taken from them, without their *own consent* by their representatives: *the King, Lords, and Commons, are their representatives,* for to them they have delegated their individual rights over their lives, liberties, and property; and so long as they approve of that form of government, and continue under it, so long do they consent to whatever is done by those they have intrusted with their rights. This is the *British Constitution.*

The constitutional conclusion was that "[t]he consent of the whole, must, in the British government, be included in that of a part, because, by the constitution, only a part have votes for representatives."[14] It was not necessarily a matter of an imperfect institution, one that was currently defective and would not operate properly until brought to some ideal stage of full representation. Because of the constitutional function of consent as a check on government power, any degree of representation was a positive constitutional good. "[I]t is one of the highest recommendations of such governments," Richard Price pointed out, "that, even when the representation is most imperfect, they have a tendency to give more security than any other governments."[15] Price was a master of political

platitudes, and this statement could have been just one more platitude—
depending on the substance of that security and how it was affected.

Purpose of Representation

The initial and most frequently articulated purpose of representation
was to preserve the people's role in government in a population too large
for direct participatory democracy. The first task of representatives was
to express the people's consent and act for the whole people.[16]

Another purpose of representation was institutional, "to be an exact
balance to the prerogatives of the other branches of the legislature."
Representatives were "a check to insolent, licentious ministers; a terror
to ambitious statesmen; a defence against corruption in high offices; and
against the violent temper of a prince aiming at arbitrary power."[17] As
their job was "to take care, that all the executive Powers of Government
are kept within the Limits of the Law," representatives were called "inquisitors" in Parliament and "watchmen and guardians" in the Massachusetts General Court. Bolingbroke, who developed this constitutional
theory as much as did any eighteenth-century statesman, described parliaments as "the true guardians of liberty" and the Commons as "the
grand Inquest of the Nation." It was for this purpose "principally they
were instituted; and this is the principal article of that great and noble
trust which the collective body of the people of Britain reposes in the
representative."[18] This was, of course, the talk of opposition spokesmen.
But the fact that Bolingbroke would not have been stressing the theory
had he been in administration is too obvious to merit discussion. What
deserves attention is the bifarious location of Bolingbroke's constitutional stance. Intending to describe eighteenth-century law, he reached
back to an earlier theory that may already have been passe, although
possibly presaging future constitutional practice. In the seventeenth
century, during Stuart times, the constitutional role had belonged to the
House of Commons as an institution. In the nineteenth century, with
the emergence of responsible government and cabinet rule, the constitutional role would be transferred to the political opposition.

The other great purpose eighteenth-century constitutional commentators assigned to the people's representatives was also one that had
flourished in the seventeenth century and was now of declining significance. It was to formulate and redress the grievances of the nation.
"[T]he business of this House," Watkins Williams Wynn told the Commons, "is to represent to his Majesty the grievances of the people, to
inform his Majesty if any of his ministers or officers makes an ill use of

the power he delegates to them, and to impeach and prosecute such evil minsters." George II's ministers had him welcome a newly elected Parliament as "an opportunity of knowing the more immediate sense and disposition of my people in general, from their representatives." The Commons in return, Thomas Carew said, should "represent to our sovereign the sentiments of our constituents."[19] By the age of the American Revolution, the theory was still being articulated, but practice had become reversed. In the House of Commons, grievances were used to argue for annual elections and frequent parliaments: to learn their grievances the people should be polled yearly and to redress them the Commons had to be in session. Other bodies such as London's Common Council were petitioning not against the crown as in centuries past but to the crown, praying that not Parliament but the king redress grievances. The grievances, in the guise of grievances of the people, were against the House of Commons, the supposed representatives of the people. But the old practice was not transferable. The constitution had bypassed the king; he no longer could protect rights or redress grievances. The constitutional irony is difficult to credit, but once the two houses of Parliament became supreme there appeared to be no formal mechanism for redressing the grievances of the nation. The explanation is that as the Commons grew independent and believed itself "representative" it became the "nation," and grievances were redressed by legislation rather than by impeachment, attainder, or confrontation with the crown.[20]

In North America, the old constitution still operated. Elected representatives voiced the grievances of the localities, never more significantly and effectively than during the revolutionary controversy against Parliament, when the colonial assemblies promulgated the whig constitutional program in large part by reciting the grievances of the colonies.

American constitutional theory was generally the same as British constitutional theory. Americans thought of their representatives as checks on executive authority and as the voices of grievances. The Pennsylvania Assembly was described as "the only Barrier the People have to oppose against arbitrary Power," and in New York "the representatives of a people" were elected "to be the guardians of their sacred rights and liberties, and to secure them in the full enjoyment of their property."[21] There was, however, a remaining distinction between eighteenth-century descriptions of representation in the colonies and in the mother country. British constitutional commentators seldom mentioned legislation. One reason is that most legislative business that Parliament dispatched was private, local, and facultative. A more relevant explanation is that eighteenth-century British people thought that the House of Commons performed more important tasks than lawmaking, or, as Edmund Burke expressed the notion, "It was not instituted to be a controul *upon* the people. . . . It was designed as a controul *for* the people." When things were put in this light, Parliament's job of enacting statutes just had to seem secondary.[22]

Colonial assemblies pursued a wider variety of legislative activity than did the eighteenth-century Parliament. They made law, settling by legislation many problems that Parliament would not take up until the nineteenth century.[23] For that reason, it may be assumed, American political commentators were more likely to stress legislation than were eighteenth-century British observers. The words "Rusticus" wrote in New England, asking Massachusetts legislators to pass laws discouraging purchase of foreign luxuries, would have been unfamiliar stuff in the contemporary British press. "It is the Business of the *Legislature*," he argued, "to put a Stop to these Extravigancies, and preserve, as much as possible, the Stock of the Community, whereby the *greatest Good* of every Individual, is preserved; *which is the End and Design of appointing the Legislative Body.*" Once the purpose of legislation became the greatest good of each citizen, something was added to the traditional constitutionalism that represented people by guarding their liberty and redressing their grievances.[24]

Concept of Representation

B efore 1765, the constitutional theory of representation had a much clearer focus in the American colonies than it had in Great Britain. Colonial assemblies had for decades been arguing with the imperial government about elections, the franchise, the regularity of sessions, the power to convene or prorogue, and the authority to extend representation to newer areas of settlement. Battles occurred frequently enough, in so many colonies, and were so well publicized that Americans had the concept of representation thrust on them to an extent unknown in the mother country before 1768. They might not have asked which social classes could vote, how democratic the system was, whether it was representative, oligarchic, or deferential, or any of the other questions that were once the primary interest of historians. But owing to the concept of consent and the eighteenth-century consensus that legitimacy was based on consent of the governed, both sides of a political controversy concerning colonial representation knew that they were debating questions lying at the heart of power, obligation, and obedience. Throughout the period of colonial British rule, local American leaders sought to strengthen local government, not only by cementing the loyalties of the people, but also by increasing the weight of the representative assembly vis-à-vis the governor appointed by the crown. London in turn hoped, by vetoing extensions of the franchise or increases in representation, to preserve the weight of prerogative against the erosive force of popular politics.

In Great Britain, there were far fewer occasions for public reflection, leaving the perception of the concept of representation much less sharp than it was in North America. In truth, the concept was remarkably fuzzy and was the subject of basic disagreements among writers who professed to be constitutional experts. In 1791, for example, George Rous, a barrister and former member of Parliament, claimed that "the modern improvement of representation has given order to democracy, divested it of all its terrors, and enabled it to debate every question of public interest with all the wisdom, and knowledge, and ability, of every species, which the nation can boast." It was a wild assertion, far wide of any mark except continual rule by the oligarchy, and could have been written only by someone defending the constitutional status quo against reformers seeking a more extensive representation. Such was also the purpose of Arthur Young, the famed agriculturalist, who published a number of works against constitutional change on grounds directly opposite Rous's. Three years after Rous's pamphlet, Young took 256 pages to argue that the representation of people was not part of the constitution, that representation of people was not desirable, and that the House of Commons should not be representative of people. The rule in British and English law, he insisted, had always been that representation "was of property, never of persons."[1]

The fact may be hard to credit, but possibly a majority and more likely a plurality of those who wrote about and commented on constitutional representation believed that representation in Great Britain was "a representation of property, not of numbers." The most famous, perhaps the most extreme statement of the doctrine was pronounced by one of the leading jurists of the period, Lord Camden. "[T]here is not a blade of grass growing in the most obscure corner of this kingdom, which is not, which was not ever, represented since the constitution began," the chief justice of Commons Pleas, who was soon to be appointed lord chancellor, told the House of Lords during the debate on repeal of the Stamp Act; "there is not a blade of grass, which when taxed, was not taxed by the consent of the proprietor." If today we are amazed that a discerning common lawyer could espouse such an extreme position, we may be even more surprised that there were many in the eighteenth century who thought Camden made sense. "And why?" the earl of Abingdon asked. "Because the Interest of that Land whence the Grass grows, and not the Owners of the Grass, was the Object of Representation." Abingdon even distinguished between representatives of different types of property: "the Members of Counties being the Representatives of all the Land of England, for the Interest of that Land, whilst the Members of the Cities and Boroughs are the Representatives of all the Money and Trade of England." It is worth emphasizing what Abingdon did not say. He did not say that the members represented the owners of that land or the plyers of that trade. They represented the land and the trade, not the proprietors. Eighteenth-century constitutional theory did not stop there. Even members of the two universities were, it was said, "the Representatives of a supposed Property in *Literature,* and the Propertiers of the Rights thereunto belonging."[2]

REPRESENTATION OF PROPERTY

There may have been no other point of law about which British and colonial constitutional and political values were so divergent than the theory that representatives who gave consent to legislation represented property rather than people. American legal thought simply did not cotton to the notion. True, after the Revolution some of the new state constitutions proportioned representation on wealth, but it was people, not property, being represented. Colonial opinion was committed to the proposition that for representation to confer legitimate consent it had to be elected directly by the people for whom it consented.

Some British constitutionalists may have been surprised that American theory was so different, especially in view of the fact that Camden formulated his blade-of-grass argument in defense of American rights. After all, if it was property that was represented, it followed that there was no American representation in Parliament as there were no blades of American grass sending representatives to the House of Commons. Taxation was one explanation why property not people was represented. Government had the authority to tax property because property consented to the tax. If there was no American property represented in Parliament, it followed that Parliament could not tax Americans.[3]

A second explanation for the representation of property rather than people was security of property. "[P]roperty would become the most precarious and insecure thing in the world" if subject to laws made by representatives of people with no stake in that property. At the very least, Edmund Burke contended, property could not be safe "unless it be, out of all proportion, predominant in the representation. It must be represented, too, in great masses of accumulation, or it is not rightly protected."[4]

Third, the nature of property in society is such that, as Robert Robinson, a dissenting clergyman, explained, it "is the ground of power, and power will always follow property." Another way to put the proposition was that every citizen's power and influence in a state should be, ceteris paribus, in proportion to the amount of that citizen's property. Not only did the maxim seem to be undeniable in the eighteenth century, but it was also believed to be morally right. "[T]hough it is true, that what concerns all, should be judged by all," the Scots advocate, Sir John Dalrymple, explained, "yet it is equally just, that those who have the largest share of the property, should likewise have the largest share of that legislature, which is to dispose of it."[5]

In the eighteenth century, English social and constitutional historical scholarship described as irrefutable doctrine the inevitability with which possession of property sought out political power. In early times, the property of the nation had been largely possessed by crown and barons, and power had been balanced between them. In Tudor reigns, with a general redistribution of ecclesiastical and hierarchical wealth, a shift in the ownership of property occurred, commencing the alteration in political influence—to the representative of the transferred wealth—that eventually led to the constitutional domination of the House of Commons. "By these *Facts* and *Reflections*," one of Robert Walpole's newspapers proclaimed, "it plainly appears, that *Power* is founded in *Property;* and that the *Liberty* of the People grew with their *Possessions.*"[6]

From the perspective of twentieth-century political values, the argument cuts two ways. To say that property, not people, should be represented has an undemocratic component, yet to say that political power should reflect property, which was preponderately in the hands of commoners, was an argument against prerogativism and hierarchical oligarchy. Indeed, one constitutionalist in 1780 feared that "to say, that the power of the House of Commons ought to be proportionable to the property of the whole commons [i.e., the people], is saying that the other branches of the legislature ought to be annihilated." With the coming of the American Revolution, the concept of representing property rather than people began to lose respect, but for a time it had the odd role of what is by today's standards an undemocratic argument justifying what by eighteenth-century standards was a democratic result, the dominance of the House of Commons.[7]

A fourth reason for representation of property rather than people was democratic from the perspective of the social values of the eighteenth century. "The Owners of the Land," someone argued, "are properly the *Body* of the Nation." "These, in this Island, are strictly the *People* of *Great Britain.*" What was meant was not that "the people" owned all the wealth and that representation of property meant representation of "the people" but that ownership of a certain kind of property—real estate—was characteristic of that part of the population whose representation assured stable, constitutional government by sturdy people of the better sort.[8]

Those who wanted representation limited to landed property expressed both a preference and a prejudice. The preference was for owners of land because they were "the principal bulwark of English freedom," men of civil virtue attached to things native, fixed, and local—not like "lawyers," "coach-makers," or "hair-dressers," but "a robust, well-limbed, healthy, useful race of men; men who in time of war shall recruit your fleets and armies with strength, vigour, and activity."[9] The prejudice was against owners of other types of property, men such as those of whom Chatham spoke when he warned the House of Lords of "little paltry, peddling fellows, vendors of twopenny wares, and falsehoods, who under the idea of trade, sell every thing in their power—Honour, Trust, and Conscience." One perception was that, just as land made its owners resolute and independent, property in the form of stocks, interest, trade, and species made the owner and those serving him suppliant and dependent. "Multitudes of such men live upon the publick spoil," the Baptist minister Robert Robinson warned in the year of Yorktown. "Solomon's Rabbi flatters him, his solicitor glosses for him, his attorney puzzles, and . . . his tradesmen and servants all contrive to please him for the same glorious reason . . . because they gain by doing so."[10]

Americans generally shared these perceptions, but the substance of their mistrust was not quite the same. After all, merchants in the colonies made up a large slice of the respectable, solid gentry, and land in the New World was as much an instrument of speculation as was stock-jobbing in the mother country.

PROPERTY OF REPRESENTATION

In Great Britain during the age of the American Revolution, not only was property "actually" represented, but property determined who could be a representative. A writer for the *London Magazine* summed up the constitutional rule when saying that no one should be "a member of the house of commons, who has not in his own right an estate for life, sufficient for his subsistence as a gentleman." An extreme version of the theory argued that there was no need for representation of localities or for representatives acquainted with the circumstances, interests, or attitudes of their constituents. To obtain the best representatives and best representation, "every Member of the *House of Commons* should be qualify'd by a *certain Proportion of Land*," that is, "have an Estate descendable to *Posterity*." Considering that protection of property was the end of government in eighteenth-century Great Britain, it would have been contrary to constitutional policy for a man without property "to assist in the making of laws, concerning the disposal of the property of other people." For representatives to own "a stake" in society, Arthur Young remarked, "is the best pledge against their embarking in designs dangerous to the public repose."[11]

Land, the type of property that was represented, was also the property that set the prerequisite for the representative, and for the same reasons: it gave its owner a fixed, permanent stake in the well-being of society. The ideal was not just land but great estates, for the "large proprietors of land, have one general interest; and, as their property is of a permanent nature, this bond of union never changes."[12] There were several purposes for this test of representation; the chief two were the stability and security of property and the independence of the House of Commons. The objective may strike us as odd, that the standard for selecting representatives was less representation itself than the integrity of the representative body, but it followed from the institutional definition of constitutional liberty in the eighteenth century. Because membership was "accessible to men of large fortunes, and to those alone," William Paley boasted in one of the most widely read textbooks of the age, "such men are engaged in the defence of the separate rights and interests of this branch of the legislature as are best able to support its claims." In other words, independent representatives were the constitutional prescript to make the Commons independent—even though mere independence did not make them more representative. Members, therefore, were not what were usually meant "by the words *citizens* and *burgesses*." Representing the commoners of Great Britain, they were hardly plebeian. In most other countries of Europe, perhaps a majority of the British House of Commons would have been members of the assembly of nobles.

> A very few considerable merchants, . . . men of large moneyed property, mixed . . . with those who, from their birth, and education, and landed possessions, have every title to be ranked in the patrician order: a few ambitious rising lawyers, a great many sons and younger brothers of peers; country gentlemen of decent fortunes, with some few men of parts, of little or no fortune, introduced by the influence of individuals: all these together form that medley which composes the house of commons.[13]

The patrician cast of representation was codified policy. An act of 9 Anne, "for securing the Freedom of Parliaments, by the farther qualifying the Members to sit in the House of Commons," may or may not have secured the independence of the Commons, but it made certain that the House would in no way represent an economic cross section of the population. Those sitting for counties needed estates of £600 per annum, and to represent a borough a member had to own an estate of £300 per annum. Even more revealing, the act excused "the eldest son, or heir apparent of any peer" from meeting these qualifications, assuring that the two houses of Parliament would draw members from the very top of the dominant class. Alan Ramsay might complain that the statute transmuted the Commons from the wise men of England to the rich men of Britain, but most commentators praised the act as necessary for constitutional liberty. Even London's Common Council, often said to have been the nation's major voice for radicalism, boasted to its representatives that they had been elected because "we considered all of you to be possessed of Fortune sufficient to render you independent." That was the security of liberty—independence from the crown and ministry. "The Independence of our Representatives is the only Security of those Rights and Liberties, which our Ancestors have deliver'd to us," the electors of Gloucester told their representatives.[14]

The political theory may seem oversimple today, but it was uncontestable in the eighteenth century. Property was independence; lack of property was servility, even servitude. A man of substance could not be bought or bribed. A man without independent wealth could easily be bought and bribed. A man of property had a will of his own. A man of poverty had a purchasable will. "[M]en of property may be influenced to do good," Young explained, "but does it therefore follow that they would be influenced to do evil? To sell the fee simple of their own importance? While the government of the kingdom is in the hands of those who have property, tempered as it is on one side by popular election, and on the other by the legal rights of the Crown, all must be safe."[15]

There were few—very few—commentators in Great Britain who did not stress independence as the reason that only men of substantial property should be representatives. Matthew Wheelock was almost a lone exception in 1770 when he noted that the act of 9 Anne gave "honour to wealth, and had the appearance of computing the abilities and integrity of the English, by their possessions." A better reason, Wheelock argued, "for making riches a qualification" for representatives would be that "they may be able to employ their whole time and attention in the discharge of their public duty, and that their estates may be a sort of security to the publick in case of misbehaviour." Wheelock had lived in the colonies, an interesting and perhaps not irrelevant fact when it is realized that his argument was much closer to contemporary American than to British constitutional theory. Colonial writers sometimes warned against electing "Slaves, Sycophants and Coxcombs" and urged choosing representatives with independent spunk to stand up to royal or proprietary governors. But their emphasis was not on wealth; it was on character. Once, when an American commentator made a connection between money and the elected representative, it was to make a constitutional proposal quite the opposite of what was being suggested in Great Britain. He wanted less than well-to-do representatives given some support "out of the Publick Treasury." The purpose was not to guarantee legislative independence from royal bribery but to "make it a thing feasible for them, to spend a convenient part of their Time, in Reading and Study that they may serve the Publick better." [16]

The quality that colonists—clergy as well as laity—most wanted in a representative was not substantial income but intelligence. Men of "superior wisdom," discretion, and integrity were the ideal, with emphasis on knowledge of the British constitution, the provincial charter, "public affairs," the operation of government, the laws, and the circumstances of the community in which the representative lived. [17] There was a great deal of boasting in the eighteenth century, especially in Connecticut, that American representatives were local men, "from among our selves, well known in our Towns, and not Strangers; they are of our own choosing, and have the same common Interests with us, so interwoven, that they can't be separated." That qualification—the local connection—was a commonplace in the colonies, but it was seldom mentioned in the mother country. [18]

In both countries, a goal was to elect men of religion, but that was an attribute much more likely to be mentioned in New England than by British theorists. In the northern colonies especially, the ideal representation was of "experienc'd Probity," "steady Conduct," governed "by natural Principles, and the fixed Rules laid down in the Constitution." The similarities and differences between American and British standards of representation were summed up in a question asked by a Massachusetts election pamphleteer who believed that the first task of representation was to shield property from the will and pleasure of arbitrary power, most notably the property rights that a master possessed by contract to the services of an indentured servant: "Whether the Men of the best Knowledge, Reason and Vertue, as well as Estates, are not more likely to serve us in the General Court, and less liable to be tempted from their

Trusts, with Posts of Honour and Profit, than Men of different Characters?" The pamphleteer was aware of the same dangers to liberty that concerned his British contemporaries and knew that one way of getting representatives with the grit to guard liberty from royal power was to elect men of "Estates." But if we construe his words loosely, it appears that he put the attributes of knowledge, reason, and virtue before the security of wealth.[19]

THE PROPERTY OF ELECTION

There was a second function to the representation of property in the eighteenth century. Just as property determined the qualifications of representations, it also determined who elected representatives—and who did not. There was a property qualification for electors, and the purpose was not to limit the franchise to the rich. "The true reason of requiring any qualification, with regard to property, in voters, is to exclude such persons as are in so mean a situation that they are esteemed to have no will of their own," Sir William Blackstone wrote. "If these persons had votes, they would be tempted to dispose of them under some undue influence or other." Blackstone's explanation is a remarkable example of eighteenth-century legal reasoning: admitting that all adult males have a constitutional right to vote but saying that even a universal right cannot be universally enjoyed as most men cannot be trusted to exercise it constitutionally.

> Upon the true theory and genuine principles of liberty, every member of the community, however mean his situation, is entitled to a vote in electing those delegates, to whose charge is committed the disposal of his property, his liberty, and his life. And this ought to be allowed him in every free state, provided it be probable that such a one will give his vote freely, and without influence of any kind. But since that can hardly be expected in persons of indigent fortunes, or such as are under the immediate dominion of others, (whose suffrages therefore are not so properly their own, as those of their superiors, on whom they depend;) all popular states have therefore been obliged to establish certain qualifications; whereby some, who are suspected to have no will of their own, are excluded from voting.[20]

The rule was a constitutional contradiction. It seemed to limit the franchise to property owners, yet the ostensible justification was to curb the influence of the great landowners with numerous tenants and dependents. The purpose was not (as is sometimes stated) that the choice of representatives should be limited to freeholders as "they were the repository of virtues not found in other classes." Political theory may have valued virtue; constitutional law knew better than to seek it out. The legal principle had two constitutional goals. The first, stated by Henry Ireton at the Putney debates of the 1640s, but with respect to the "local interest" little cited in the age of the American Revolution, was that "no person that hath not a local and permanent interest in the kingdom should have an equal dependence in election with those that have." The expectation was much the same as why a representative had to own property: owning property made an elector a more stable citizen, one who voted with concern for a permanent fixed interest. "[B]esides his life and liberty," Christopher Keld would argue in 1785, "an elector should have some property to defend."[21]

The main constitutional theory explaining why electors had to be independent had also been debated at Putney. The Levellers pleaded for a broad franchise but would have excluded "apprentices, or those that take alms," saying that "they depend upon the will of other men and should be afraid to displease [them]." By the eighteenth century, there was no disagreement about the goal: only independent men should vote. What argument occurred was over the criterion. As the object was to identify electors independent of the large magnates, the test had to be free tenure of some ascertained value. An estate of substantial freehold made the owner autonomous, and, interestingly enough, in the scale of British values of the eighteenth century, landed property was prized for just that reason, not as capital or for economic benefit, but for "Independency," allowing possessors to function as uninhibited citizens. "Without property," Keld observed, "men are, if we may say so, but half-citizens."[22]

Theory did not determine practice. The ideal was independent electors, but often the result was dependent representatives. Some of the boroughs sending members to the Commons were so small that great lords controlled the votes of their electors and, being able to name the representative, controlled his vote in Parliament. By the age of the American Revolution, a large percentage of the members of the House of Commons were created by the nobility. In theory, they represented "the people," but practice was quite often the reverse of theory.[23]

As time passed, law in Great Britain also fell behind theory. The law restricted the franchise to freeholders, a tenurial status that in the eighteenth century still did not include copyholders. This exclusion was a carryover from medieval times, when owners of unfree tenure were dependent on the lord of the manor. By the age of the American Revolution, copyholders—and even leaseholders—were as politically autonomous and as secure in their possessions as were socage-tenure freeholders, yet this immense portion of English and Welsh taxable land wealth remained unrepresented. The same was true for the emerging forms of nonlanded property. A rich man who invested all his money in trading companies or was himself a merchant and lived on leased or copyhold real estate, owning no freehold, could not qualify to vote no matter how "independent." New forms of property had been introduced, but the constitution and statutory law were not altered to accommodate them.[24]

In the colonies, matters had taken a remarkably different turn. Where in Great Britain the law ran behind theory, making the electorate a decreasing portion of the expanding pool of independent men,[25] in America practice ran ahead of theory. The franchise was widely distributed in the colonies, extending in practice to many more males than those who were substantial freeholders. Yet American constitutional theory almost, although not quite, mirrored the British. Intending like the British to enfranchise independent voters, colonial legal theorists seemed also to have expected that property owners, in addition to being independent and having greater "Political Attachment" than nonproperty owners, would be wiser persons, who, in John Adams words, would be "acquainted with public affairs" and attached to both the cause of liberty and the public good. "[T]here must be some restrictions as to the right to voting," James Iredell of North Carolina, a future justice of the United States Supreme Court, wrote; "otherwise the lowest and most ignorant of mankind must associate in this important business with those who it is to be presumed, from their property and other circumstances, are free from influence, and have some knowledge of the great consequence of their trust." The idea, he concluded, was "to regulate the right of election, as that it may be presumed the choice of the voter is free and able."[26]

Although it cannot be said that American theory was more democratic than British theory, historians have shown that practice was more egalitarian. Equality meant not that more people should be able to vote but that people in similar positions or comparable circumstances should be equal. Colonial whigs did not contend that they were not bound by parliamentary statutes because the House of Commons, elected by property to represent property, was unrepresentative and undemocratic. The constitutional argument concerned not democracy but equality within inequality. If British law provided that "independent men" or "free agents" possessing freehold worth forty shillings per annum were entitled to vote for those who made their laws, Alexander Hamilton argued, than Americans of comparable wealth were entitled to the same right. "It is therefore evident to a demonstration, that unless every *free agent* in America be permitted to enjoy the same privilege, we are entirely stripped of the benefits of the constitution, and precipitated into an abyss of slavery. For, we are deprived of that immunity, which is the grand pillar and support of freedom. And this cannot be done, without a direct violation of the constitution, which decrees, to every *free agent*, a share in the legislature." Hamilton did not overstate his case for he did not mean "every" independent man or free agent. He meant the constitutionally independent, the legally enfranchised. American whigs were defending constitutional rights, not natural or ideal rights.[27]

Theories of Representation

The concern of this study is representation, not the American Revolution, yet the revolutionary controversy cannot be ignored because it was the constitutional debate leading to the Revolution that focused the eighteenth century's closest attention on the meaning, the scope, and the theory of the concept of representation.

It is a striking fact about the revolutionary debate that the people who quarreled over whether the colonists had representation in Parliament were generally British. Most Americans, imperial loyalists as well as militant whigs, seem to have agreed, as one Connecticut writer expressed it, that "we are not in any intelligible Sense, represented in Parliament." They were not, the voters of Braintree, Massachusetts, elaborated, "represented in that Assembly in any Sense, unless it be by a fiction of law." There were people in the mother country who concurred. Some were lawyers, one of whom, not surprisingly, was Lord Camden. Camden contended not only that under British constitutional law property was represented in the House of Commons but also that the authority to tax could not be separated from representation. Previous schemes for taxing North America had been rejected, he claimed, "[b]ecause the colonies had no representatives in parliament to give consent." That was Camden's theory of representation, direct representation or what was then called "actual" as contrasted with "virtual representation." [1]

The different extremes in constitutional perspectives can be summarized, at the risk of oversimplification, by two sentences, one by Camden in the Lords, the other by George Grenville in the Commons. "Taxation and representation are inseparably bound," Camden asserted. "Taxation is a Part of that sovereign Power," Grenville replied, denying in every respect Camden's doctrine; "it is one Branch of Legislation; it is, it has been exercised over those who are not, who were not represented." It would be wise to avoid hasty conclusions. The fact that Camden was one of the most distinguished common lawyers of the century and Grenville, although a bencher of the Inner Temple, had not practiced law does not mean that Camden's reasoning was based on more knowledgeable legal premises or on sounder constitutional principles. Had a poll been taken of contemporary British lawyers, a solid but not overwhelming majority would have endorsed the thesis that the authority for taxation was derived from sovereignty, not representation. Three of the leading common lawyers of the era can be cited. Sir William Blackstone was one. He supported Grenville during the Stamp Act debates precisely on that ground. Another was Sir Charles Yorke, who would succeed Camden as lord chancellor. He took direct issue with Camden's representation argument on the floor of the Commons. At most, Yorke argued, "[t]he want of representation carries with it the ground of equity and caution," providing Americans with a claim to being represented in Parliament but in no way limiting Parliament's sovereign authority to legislate and tax. That was the principle—the principle of sovereignty—endorsed by Lord Chief Justice Mansfield, among others. Summed up by a contemporary pamphlet writer, it was that "[r]epresentation has nothing more to do with the right of taxation, than with every other right enjoyed and exercised by the superintending power."[2]

The questions in contention were not new. The constitutional controversy raised by Charles I's levy of ship money had turned on the legality of taxation without the consent of those taxed. Everything Americans would say against the Stamp Act had been said before. Arguing on behalf of the Commons in 1610 against the constitutionality of import duties that James I had promulgated by letters patent, Sir James Whitelocke contended, "[T]he question is, whether the King's Patent hath the force and power of the Law, or not; for if it be not maintained that it hath, it can never be concluded that he can transfer the property of his Subjects goods to himself, without the assent of them." If the king's command was not sovereign, then the patent was not "law." One hundred sixty years later, if Parliament's command was not sovereign, then its tax on those not represented in the Commons might not be law. What Whitelocke had said in 1610, Thomas Walpole repeated in 1776. "The only benefit which has resulted from our unhappy contest with America, is, that by it we have been led to revert to the first principles of civil polity," he told the House of Commons. "[B]y the most solemn provisions of our government, the consent of those from whom money is wanted for national services, is made indispensably necessary."[3]

We might think that British constitutionalists, appealing to parliamentary sovereignty, would have dismissed this argument. They would do so eventually, of course, for sovereignty would be the ultimate legal justifi-

cation for declaring the colonies in rebellion and waging the Revolutionary War. But first British legalists sought to make their case on traditional constitutional grounds, contending that the Americans were
bound by parliamentary decrees not only because Parliament was sovereign but because, in constitutional fact, the colonists were represented
in the House of Commons. Although they elected none of the members
of the House, Americans enjoyed constitutional safeguards that guaranteed that their rights would be protected even by a body possessing
arbitrary, sovereign power. Their condition was constitutionally the
same as if they were electors because the electors in Great Britain, those
who did the actual electing, shared with them the same interests and the
men elected, those who voted the laws, shared with them the burdens
that Parliament's laws imposed. In the language of eighteenth-century
constitutional law, the Americans were *virtually* represented.

DOCTRINE OF SHARED INTERESTS

The more a twentieth-century historian studies the eighteenth-century
concept of representation, the more that concept seems remote from
popular notions and hidden in attenuated meanings. The doctrine of
shared interests is a case in point, removing us yet another dimension
from our own ideas of what representation constitutes. The doctrine
was that members of the House of Commons represented the legitimate
economic, social, political, and local interests of the realm, such as land,
trade, manufacturing, the armed forces, the courtiers, the country
gentleman, and the professions.[4] It was on "this Identity of Interests,"
Sir William Meredith asserted, that "the first Principle of Representation
is founded." The doctrine of interests explained why people could commit their governance to representatives who, in most cases, were strangers. "Reason, justice, & equity never had weight enough on the face of
the earth to govern the councils of men," John Adams told the Continental Congress. "It is interest alone which does it, and it is interest
alone which can be trusted." That same principle formed the foundation
of the eighteenth-century British concept of representation. Owing to
the mutuality of interests, the Scottish divine and historian Thomas
Somerville explained, people who were not electors suffered no harm
from Parliamentary legislation because, in the Commons, "[t]he interest
of the body represented has been precisely the same with that of the
body unrepresented." The doctrine of interests, therefore, provided yet
another definition of "representatives" in the eighteenth century. John
Lind, an administration pamphleteer, wrote the best apologia:

[R]epresentation means something different from what it has been by many understood to mean. The term "body of representatives" has by many been understood to mean, a body of men chosen by the *whole*, or by a *majority* of the community. But it appears that there is no such body; the term therefore appears to mean a body of men chosen by a *part* of the community; but so circumstanced and related to the rest, that they cannot have or *think* they have any separate interests of their own to pursue, to the prejudice of the rest.

"Their interest and that of the People is the same," William Pulteney concluded; "they cannot betray the People without at the same time betraying themselves," a fact equally true for Americans, the loyalist Martin Howard insisted. "[T]hey have no reason to complain" about representation, he said of his fellow colonists, "tho' they are not in fact represented, yet their properties and interests are equally regarded with those of their fellow subjects in Great-Britain."[5]

Considering the importance attributed to the doctrine of shared interests by eighteenth-century constitutional theorists, it is surprising how few interests they identified. One was the commonalty itself. "It is this common interest, this common tie between parliament and the people, that constitutes the security of the whole," Pulteney claimed.[6] The boast was unrealistic, of course. That interest was too diverse to be a common denominator, and, besides, the average member of Parliament had so little in common with most people that he could hardly be said to represent by shared interests even that small part of the population who were electors. What members of Commons did in fact represent was landed wealth. Just as in constitutional theory land was represented, so in constitutional practice the House of Commons most consistently expressed the representation of the landed interest. Yet it does not do to think of a unific land interest. In 1763, to relieve heavy tax burdens on the favored landowners, Parliament had enacted an excise on cider and perry, putting the burden on smaller landowners living in the arboricultural counties. The interest served was not just landed, but the gentry, the country gentlemen, the larger landholders. In their case, the representation of shared interests was truly representative because the interests were truly shared.[7]

The cider and perry growers had been given no chance to state their interest against the excise. The tax was enacted on the sly, before they heard of it or could instruct the representatives of their counties. The doctrine of shared interests had worked as it should, at least in part.

The legislature had responded to the needs of the represented interest but had done so at the expense of a weaker interest—weaker, that is, than the favored represented interest but stronger than any American interest could ever be in the British Parliament. Although they were found in only a few counties and were, at most, a small minority among electors, it cannot be said that cider producers were unrepresented, at least by eighteenth-century terms. Americans, by contrast, were unrepresented in Parliament, certainly by twentieth-century definitions, and even by eighteenth-century American standards.

The British interest that Americans had the most reason to watch was the mercantile/monied interest, another interest frequently mentioned by contemporaries as being underrepresented in the Commons. "It was owing to a want of merchants in the House, that the Bill for restraining paper-credit in America was brought in," a Dublin magazine argued in 1774. If that was true—if the British trade interest in the House of Commons was too impotent to represent American trade in Parliament—what could be expected when the British trade interest conflicted with or felt threatened by the American trading interest? The American trade would have no more representation than Irish trade traditionally enjoyed. Lord North once wrote the lord lieutenant of Ireland hoping the Irish would not seek changes in the trade laws. "The representatives of the trading towns and manufacturing counties," he pointed out, "are fully apprised of the sentiments and wishes of their constituents."[8]

The extreme version of the shared-interests theory, stated by a former attorney general of Quebec, argued that Americans shared such "an immediate common interest" with Great Britain that it was "a moral certainty that the Parliament will never venture to exercise such an authority over them in an unjust or oppressive manner." Both "the landed and commercial interests of both Houses are a perfect security to the Americans," it was argued. "Any interruption to the commerce of America must soon increase the tax upon the landed possessions; and the commercial interests would necessarily fail, was the trade of our Colonies diminished, or destroyed."[9] Colonial whigs knew better. They not only appreciated, as did North, that members of Parliament heeded the interests of their mercantile constituents over trading interests of other parts of the empire; they also had the precedent of the Sugar Acts, passed for the benefit of the Sugar Islands at the expense of northern trading colonies. These two acts constituted a clear case from the past in which a political interest located in the House of Commons overwhelmed the economic interest of New England, and they constituted an even clearer lesson for the future: if North Americans could not depend on the interests they shared with the British to help them against the special interests of rival colonies, what could they expect when the competing interest was British? "Whatever may be said about representation," the Middle Temple barrister Richard Hussey told the Commons, "it cannot be said that the interests of North America are so interwoven with the representatives as the interests of this country are." James Wilson, the future United States Supreme Court justice, not only thought that "Americans cannot avail themselves of that check, which interest puts upon the members of parliament"; he also realized that, in situations of intraempire competition, the doctrine of interests meant that the colonists would always lose. "A candidate may recommend himself at his election by recounting the many successful instances, in which he has sacrificed the interests of America to those of Great Britain. A member of the house of commons may plume himself upon his ingenuity in inventing schemes to serve the mother country at the expense of the colonies; and may boast of their impotent resentment against him on that account."[10]

DOCTRINE OF SHARED BURDENS

The doctrine of shared interests, a New Yorker pointed out in 1732, was based on the assumption that the representatives' "Interest is so interwoven with the People's, that, if they act for themselves, (which every one of them will do as near as he can) they must act for the common Interest." The doctrine of shared burdens—a second explanation of how people were represented by representatives for whom they could not vote—was based on even tighter interwoven interests. "Representatives must be affected by the laws of their making equally with their constituents," freeholders of a Virginia county resolved, stating the doctrine of shared burdens as briefly as it could be stated. Legislators "represented" nonelectors by sharing with them the consequences, costs, and hardships of the statutes they enacted, the taxes they imposed, and the penalties they decreed. "A *British* Constitution," the western Massachusetts lawyer Joseph Hawley assured his fellow colonial whigs, "knows of no laws binding upon its subjects but what . . . the legislators themselves are subject to, in common with every individual in the community." If they were to "impose any burthen upon the subject, in which they do

not share themselves," William Paley exaggerated, it would be "a partiality too flagrant to be endured."[11]

The doctrine of shared burdens was one of the most significant principles of British constitutionalism guaranteeing liberty and security.
"The unrepresented Inhabitants of *Great Britain*," Edward Bancroft
wrote of British nonelectors, "are secured in Life and Property, because
they pay no Tax and are governed by no Law, which does not equally
affect the Legislators themselves and their Constituents." That constitutional condition, he added, was a "Circumstance from which they acquire an effectual Barrier against Oppression." It is remarkable how
much constitutional stock was invested in this speculative doctrine. Hawley termed it "a grand security, a constitutional bulwark of liberty." The
Swiss constitutionalist J. L. De Lolme called it "a complete security." And
the Irish barrister, Francis Dobbs, thought it the mechanical basis for
"the boasted freedom of a subject of Great-Britain."[12]

A few writers—William Pulteney was one—implied that the doctrine
of shared burdens secured "the whole empire," giving "unrepresented
persons . . . the same security as those who elect, or those who sit in
parliament." But in fact the doctrine did not work well even in Great
Britain. Joseph Priestley warned that despite shared burdens "persons
of lower rank, and especially those who have no votes in the election of
members, may have reason to fear, because an unequal part of the burden may be laid upon them." The game laws were evidence of how little
security they had. Americans looking at the same doctrine from the imperial perspective had to feel even less secure. Burdens placed on them
by Parliament quite likely would not be shared either by the representatives or by those who elected them in Great Britain.[13]

The colonial predicament deserves more attention than it has received from students of the American Revolution. The doctrine of
shared burdens was important in British constitutional law because it
made legislators the representatives of people they otherwise would not
have represented. London assumed it applied to colonists as well as to
British nonelectors, and whether it did is a question that sheds light on
the coming of the revolutionary controversy. It is worth recalling John
Wilmot's warning that the doctrine of shared burdens offered Americans even less protection from unequal legislation than it offered the
nonelectors of Great Britain. At least in Britain the "unrepresented . . .
submits to no tax but what the represented equally submit to." The unrepresented Briton could expect the legislators "will lay no unnecessary

burden, for if they did, all must equally bear a share of it. But this was by no means the lot of the American: he must have submitted to taxes, not only which he was not concerned in imposing, but which those who did impose them did not bear any share of." [14]

VIRTUAL REPRESENTATION

The explanation most accepted by constitutionalists of how people not qualified to vote were "represented" in the eighteenth-century Parliament was the doctrine of virtual representation. Stated in its most simple form, the doctrine held that although nonelectors were not *actually* represented in the British legislature they were represented *virtually;* that is, they were not represented just in contemplation of constitutional law but were in fact, not fiction, represented. The doctrine applied to nonelectors both in Great Britain and in the American colonies.

It may be that virtual representation was, in the first part of the revolutionary controversy, the chief legal argument made by imperialists contending not only that the colonists were bound but also that they were represented in Parliament. A point too easily overlooked is that this very contention, consistently and persistently made from 1765 to about 1772, that the Americans were virtually represented, lent substance to the colonial whig assertion that Americans were not bound by legislation to which they had not consented through representation. There may be no more salient proof of the perceived constitutional requirement of consent than that many of the strongest advocates of Parliament's authority to tax and to legislate for the colonies justified that authority on the principle that the colonies were virtually represented in Parliament. At the very least, the doctrine of virtual representation acknowledged that some form of consent by representation was constitutionally necessary. [15]

The doctrine was uncomplicated. "The Parliament of Great Britain virtually represents the whole Kingdom," George Grenville explained to the Commons. "There can be no doubt," Lord Chief Justice Mansfield expanded in the House of Lords, "but that the inhabitants of the colonies are as much represented in parliament as the greatest part of the people of England are represented. . . . A member of parliament, chosen for any borough, represents not only the constituents and inhabitants of that particular place, but he represents the inhabitants of every other borough in Great Britain. He represents the city of London, and all other the commons of this land, and the inhabitants of all the colonies and dominions of Great Britain, and is, in duty and conscience, bound to take care of their interests." A writer in the *Gentleman's Magazine* summed up the doctrine:

> [T]o be legally represented in a British parliament, it is not nec-
> essary to have a vote immediately, or remotely for [a] member
> of parliament, or [a] great part of the inhabitants of *Great Britain*
> are not legally represented. . . . But if by a parliament chosen as
> our constitution prescribes, *i.e. by persons of a particular class only,*
> all *British* subjects are legally represented, then he that lives in
> *Pennsylvania* is, to all intents and purposes, as effectually and
> legally represented by a parliament so chosen, as he that lives in
> *London*.[16]

There were several theories, four minor and one major, explaining how virtual representation operated in practice. The minor explanations are not important enough to merit analysis and can be summarized merely by being stated. One was that Americans were represented by the king: "as no Part of the Property of the People can be taken from them, but by Laws which receive the assent of the Sovereign, who has no Interest distinct from the general Interest of all his Subjects, the Apprehensions of the Colonists on this Head, if we suppose them real, must be groundless." A second was that Americans were virtually represented by "the provincial Agents." A third was that there were at least three American-born members of the House of Commons. Together with members born in the West Indies, not only did they represent the colonists; they integrated the colonists into the nation actually as well as virtually. "Seeing therefore, that the Americans are capable of sitting in parliament, they must be part of that society, over which the parliament presides." The fourth was that the colonists were represented by men with whom they were associated by commercial ties: "[t]heir connection with the merchants of this kingdom, many of whom, depending entirely on the commerce of America, are also members of the House of Commons, and as it were the particular representatives of that country, and knit to the interests of it by the firmest of all ties, mutual advantage." Repeal of the Stamp Act was said to prove the last argument: despite opposition of the landed interests in Great Britain, repeal had been effected by merchants and manufacturers who "had become advocates for the Americans, as much as if they had been chosen to represent them: and by this means the inhabitants of America would be nearly in the same condition with the unrepresented, or non-electing, inhabitants of Great-Britain itself."[17]

The major theory explaining the doctrine of virtual representation was based on British practice rather than American considerations. Although most of the citizens of England, Scotland, and Wales were not eligible to vote for members of Parliament, they were nonetheless constitutionally represented—virtually, not actually.[18] Their ranks included not only such obvious groups as women and children but also a majority of the adult male population, among whom were the owners of land held in copyhold tenure rather than freehold, the inhabitants of large boroughs such as Leeds, Manchester, Halifax, and Birmingham that had not been accorded the franchise, investors in personal rather than real property, and merchants, manufacturers, and other individuals engaged in commerce who might be quite rich but whose wealth was of a type that did not qualify them to be electors.[19] Although no precise figures were agreed on owing to the nature of eighteenth-century statistics, most estimates were that as many as nine-tenths of the people of Great Britain were excluded. Perhaps 250,000 voted, Arthur Young thought, but John Gray put the number at 300,000, and someone else said 500,000.[20] Everyone, at least, agreed that there were 6–8 million citizens in the country. No matter how the sums added up, the conclusion was that most people in the mother country were virtually, not actually, represented, that is, "represented by persons chosen by Freeholders and Freemen of Corporations, who alone are . . . immediately represented by them." The constitutional explanation was that "the Right of Election is annexed to certain Species of Property, to peculiar Franchises, and to Inhabitancy in some particular Places."[21] The political question was not just who was represented but whether political representation existed in Great Britain.

> [H]ow is the whole Nation represented by King, Lords, and Commons? The Lords sit in their own Right. The Commons are elected by Virtue of the King's Summons; the Knights [of the counties] by the Freeholders who have forty Shillings a Year; the Burgesses from Cities and Towns whose Privilege is to send them. But how is every Man suppos'd to have chosen these, and consequently to have given Consent to their Statutes?

The legal answer for British nonelectors was the same as it was for Americans. They were represented virtually, "that is, according to the constitutional customs, usages, and rights of this kingdom."[22]

A perspective from which the doctrine of virtual representation was often viewed with respect to Americans was that of equality. The colonists were said to have "no cause to complain when they are in the same condition as *many* of the natives of G. Britain," that is, "the same situation as the people in these great towns [Birmingham, Manchester, and others without borough members], and all the villages, and open country, which contain thousands, and tens of thousands of people, in Great Britain, who have no power of election." There were, after all, "more millions of subjects unrepresented in England, and yet taxed, than there are inhabitants in British America."[23]

The ultimate constitutional justification for virtual representation, therefore, was that it was a constitutional standard that treated Americans the same way it treated those Britons who were nonelectors. The British thought that this customary standard constituted constitutional equality. The Americans did not.

INTEREST AND VIRTUAL REPRESENTATION

William Pitt was among the first members of the Commons to ask whether the doctrine of virtual representation in Parliament could be constitutionally applied to Americans. The analogy equating British nonelectors with colonists, he concluded, was not persuasive. "The Gentleman," Pitt said in reply to an argument by Grenville, "tells us of many who are taxed, and are not represented—The India Company, merchants, stock-holders, Manufacturers. Surely many of these are represented on other capacities, as owners of lands, or as freemen of boroughs. It is a misfortune that more are not actually represented. But they are all inhabitants, and as such, are virtually represented. Many have it in their option to be actually represented. They have connections with those that elect, and they have influence over them."[24]

We must give attention to what Pitt said because to understand the concept of representation in the eighteenth century it is necessary to look closely at the debate about American virtual representation, for it was on this issue that almost all the discussion centered. Virtual representation of British nonelectors did not come under sustained criticism until after the Revolution. As Pitt says, the imperialist case that Americans were virtually represented in Parliament depended on an analogy that was not very analogous. All analogies that imperialists cited to support their case for the virtual representation of the colonies in Parliament could be—and were—refuted or distinguished by American whigs and their British allies. "It has been alledged," John Scott pointed out, "that many parts of England are no more formally represented than the colonies: but the allegation is a falsehood; every county in England send representatives to Parliament, and every man more or less, by some means or other, is concerned in their election." The very fact that every British county elected two knights meant that one of the most frequently drawn analogies equating Americans with nonelectors in Great Britain—equating colonies without parliamentary representatives with those boroughs in the mother country that did not enjoy the privilege of electing any member of the Commons—was not persuasive. British nonelecting boroughs might not have had a member of the Commons exclusively representing them, but, along with all the other boroughs, towns, and villages in the county, they might have freeholders who could vote for the two knights who represented the county. "The town of *Leeds* has its freeholders for the county of *York*, *Manchester* for *Lancastershire*, and *Birmingham* its electors for the county of *Warwick*. . . . These are the towns that are compared with the colonies—these are the people in *Britain* that are said to be as little represented as the people in *America*." Those nonelector boroughs, the Massachusetts House insisted, could "not be deemed reasonable Precedents for taxing all America, when it is considered that all counties in England return Members, and all Freeholders have a Vote in their Election, and so in Fact are represented." They also had a right to instruct their representatives and to lay their grievances before the Parliament, and, if even that was not effective, "there are always great numbers of voters for the surrounding counties, or for other towns which send members, who communicate protection to the rest, and the whole representatives of England, are to them a protection, against exorbitant taxation." As a result, Price concluded, Americans were by no stretch of comparative logic or political reasoning virtually represented in the same degree or manner as were nonelector burgesses of Great Britain. "*Here* all freeholders and burgesses in boroughs, are represented. *There*, not one freeholder, or any other person, is represented."[25]

The word deserving emphasis is *freeholder*. In a small way, it summarized the colonial whig case against the doctrine of virtual representation. American freeholders, unlike British freeholders, had little likelihood of becoming parliamentary electors. A British freeholder was not qualified to vote if the value of his estate was below the statutory qualification; an American freeholder was peremptorily barred from voting for members of the House of Commons no matter the value of his estate. Male residents of substance in Great Britain could always become electors by purchasing sufficient freehold in most parts of the nation.

Lessees for Years, Copyholders, Proprietors of the Public Funds, Inhabitants of *Birmingham, Leeds, Halifax,* and *Manchester,* Merchants of the City of *London,* or Members of the Corporation of the *East-India* Company, are, *as such,* under no personal Incapacity to be Electors; for they may acquire the Right of Election, and there are *actually* not only a considerable Number of Electors in each of the Classes of Lessees for Years, *&c.* but in many of them, if not all, even Members of Parliament.

The factual argument was that, even if proprietors of funds or investors in the East India Company were not eligible to vote "in that capacity, they may have it in another character as freeholders, *&c.*"[26] The factual assumption was that the conversion from nonelector to freeholder was a step that politically "independent" males in the eighteenth century could easily accomplish.[27] From those suppositions, two legal conclusions could be drawn. The first was that the virtually represented in Great Britain not only consented to legislation as a matter of law but actually consented as a matter of fact. The explanation was that *"every man* that has almost any degree of property *may* acquire a voice in the legislature if he pleases, and if he does not, he *consents* in fact to what is done by others, and cannot therefore with any propriety be said to have his property disposed of *without his consent,* for he really *gives consent.*"[28] As a result, the only people in Great Britain who did not consent directly but only virtually were women, children, and males without property.[29] The second legal conclusion was that, even accepting as valid the doctrine of virtual representation, Americans, whether legislated for or taxed by Parliament, would not be virtually represented to the same degree and in the same "actual" sense as their fellow citizens in Great Britain and, therefore, could not be equal to them.[30] They could, in fact, be equal only by moving across the Atlantic and taking up residence in the mother country.[31] That inequality made constitutionally absurd any comparison between British nonelectors and Americans or any theory that they could be protected equally by the doctrine of virtual representation.

It is comparing the circumstances of men who are *denied* the liberty of *exercising* their *rights,* with those who *are* allowed,—or by the nature of our constitution *supposed* to *exercise* them.—For . . . there is *no man* in England, who though he it not *qualified* to vote, is not *supposed* to be *qualified,* because he is not *prevented* from *qualifying himself* when he pleases; and therefore the *consent* of *every* individual, is supposed to be *given* to those *laws* by which he is bound. But the case of America is totally *different,* their consent is not given, or supposed to be given, either in a manner express or implied; and therefore *they only* are the *multitude,* who under the British empire *"have not votes."*—Wherefore the English parliament, has not "the *same* right to tax them, as to tax *any other* English subjects" . . . ; since *all other* English subjects *are* immediately *represented,* or supposed *to be* so, and are *taxed* either with their expressed or *implied* consent.[32]

There was one final factual consideration cited to prove that Americans were not constitutionally comparable to any of the nonelectors in Great Britain with whom they were often analogized. Many British nonelectors enjoyed actual or virtual representation by consequence of the ownership of property that was not related to their incapacity. "Proprietors of the funds," for example, that is, investors in the East India Company and other commercial enterprises as well as many manufacturers and merchants, were said to be not qualified as voters because of the nature of the property that they owned. The answer was that "Proprietors of the funds, &c., tho' they have no right to such vote, *as proprietors,* &c., may yet have it under another character, *as freeholders,* &c." Of course, "When acting *as freeholders,* &c. they may take care of their interests *as proprietors.*" A somewhat similar distinction was made about copyholders and other nonfreeholders, including "freeholders within the precincts of boroughs, or within the counties or cities, [who,] not being freemen or burgesses in such boroughs, have no vote" even though the borough itself had representation. "For the property of the copyholder is represented by it's [*sic*] lord; and the property within the borough or city, is actually represented by the corporation, or body of freemen in such borough or city, who chuse the member of parliament." It was even contended that British nonelectors were not an analogy for the authority to legislate for Americans because their property in Great Britain was physically mingled with property that was represented: "[T]hey are indirectly or *virtually* represented," a clergyman explained, "by the several members that are chosen for the respective counties or boroughs in which their property lies. . . . The non-voters here, can point out their *virtual* representatives, as clearly as the voters can point out their *direct* representatives. But who are the specific *virtual* representatives of America?"[33]

Another argument why parliamentary legislation, especially taxation of Americans by virtual representation, was not constitutionally comparable to taxation of British nonelectors by virtual representation in Parliament was the peculiar knowledge possessed by the representatives.

British legislators virtually representing Americans could not, in any practical way, be equated with British legislators virtually representing nonelectors in Great Britain. As the Pennsylvania Assembly asserted, their knowledge of the conditions and circumstances of the people whom they represented would simply not be the same: members of Parliament, "at the great Distance they are from the Colonies," could not "be properly informed, so as to enable them to lay such Taxes and Impositions with Justice and Equity, the Circumstances of the Colonies being all different one from the other."[34]

A third argument by American whigs was based on the proposition that a fundamental, irreconcilable difference existed between the reality of virtual representation in Parliament of British nonelectors and the theory of virtual representation in Parliament of people who did not live in Great Britain. That difference arose from the fact that, although British nonelectors might not actually be represented in the same way as were British residents who enjoyed the right to vote, the difference between them was not absolute but a matter of degree. Not only were they virtually represented; they were actually represented, at least more actually represented in Parliament than Americans ever could be. "[T]hese nonelectors are in *fact*, represented," James Otis explained. "They have all fathers, brothers, friends, or neighbors in the House of Commons, and many *ladies* have husbands there. Few of the members have any of these endearing ties to America. We are as to any personal knowledge they have of us as perfect strangers to most of them as the savages in *California*." The chief constitutional defect, the reason Americans and British nonelectors could not be virtually represented in the same manner, was stated by Benjamin Franklin when he observed that "the Members of the British Parliament . . . cannot be supposed competent Judges of the Ability of the Colonists to bear Taxes; whereas, they are Judges of the Ability of their Fellow-Subjects resident in Britain." The member of Parliament was a competent judge of the ability of British nonelectors to bear taxation because "he is an eye-witness of their condition, he can judge of their abilities, he can be wounded at the sight of their distresses. But he cannot see our misery, he cannot judge of our abilities." Or, as Samuel Adams asked, if the people imposing taxes on the colonies "cannot be adequate Judges of our Ability, where is either our Honor or Safety, as Subjects?"[35]

The concept best explaining why virtual representation made constitutional sense to the eighteenth-century legal mind is one already discussed: interests. As it was not individuals but interests that were rep-

resented, and as legislators were to reflect not the political wishes but
the interests of their electors, all who shared those interests were virtually represented.

> [T]he Commons of that Nation [Britain], cannot faithfully serve
> their Constituents as legal Delegates, without favouring Non-
> Electors as virtual Representatives, and must still promote the
> Interest of those which have no Vote, by serving them well that
> gave them a Seat in the House, because the Interest of both Par-
> ties, throughout the Kingdom, are very nearly related, and
> mostly inseperately connected. Thus English Non-Electors are
> and ever must be virtually represented and favoured, while
> Electors themselves are faithfully served.

Edmund Burke got carried away. "This is virtual representation," he
exclaimed of the representation of interests. "Such a representation I
think to be in many cases even better than the actual. . . . The people
may err in their choice; but common interest and common sentiment
are rarely mistaken."[36]

Three theories explained how the representation of interests constitutionally propped up the doctrine of virtual representation. One was
the interest of the state: all people were equally citizens, and the interest
of each individual was involved in "the general Interest." A second was
the interest of the representatives elected to legislate. "[T]hose to whom
the people intrust the care of their interests," it was believed, "cannot
separate their own interest from that of the people." The third came
from the interests that nonelectors had in common with electors: although nonelectors might share no interests with members of Parliament, they could nonetheless expect that their interests would be represented through interests shared with the electors. Examples were
women and children. "Women have not a share in government, but yet
by their strict connexion with the other sex, all their liberties are as amply secured as those of the men, and it is impossible to represent the
one sex, without the other."[37]

Americans were also said to be virtually represented through interests
that they shared with members of Parliament. Because "the American
Colonies are . . . the capital spring of British wealth, all the members of
parliament have a particular, tho' indirect concern in the prosperity of
the Colonists." True, "the colonies, if taxed by the British parliament,
would not have had the same *degree* of security against oppression" as
subjects resident in Great Britain, "yet they would have had a very great,

perhaps a sufficient degree of security, from the very circumstance which gives us security, their manifold connexions of interest with the members of the legislature." As a result of those connections, there was a "community of interests" between Americans and members of Parliament "arising from their trade, by which a great number of people in Britain, both electors of members of parliament and others, are deeply interested in preventing them from being oppressed." Put more strongly, the assumption was that the British Commons had "an interest in preserving to the Colonies whatever freedom and immunities they can enjoy, consistently with their dependence on the Mother Country." As a result, "the Colonies have a virtual, though not a special representation in the Parliament of *Britain;* that is, they have the force, and power, the benefit and effect of representation." [38]

Finally, it was contended that Americans were virtually represented in Parliament because they shared interests with British nonelectors. Again, the common factor was property, particularly "the intercourse between the trading towns in *Britain* and *America*." Because of it, Hans Stanley told the Commons, "The Commercial and landed Int[ere]sts [are] concerned in the Welfare of America." Not only had Parliament "shewn them always Attention," but the British copyholder and manufacturer, both nonelectors yet virtually represented, were "represented no more than the Americans." [39]

As they did of most other theories saying that they were represented in the British Parliament, American whigs and their supporters in Great Britain thought the argument of virtual representation by shared interests rather easy to refute. One avenue of attack was provided by the assertion that the imperialists had the burden of proof and that the sharing as well as the unity of interests had to be established by uncontrovertible evidence. After all, as Governor George Johnstone reminded the House of Commons, the acknowledged constitutional principle was that legislation could be enacted only by consent, and virtual representation was by necessity a deviation from that principle. "[B]ut the deviation from a rule too nice for practice is safely borne, because the interest of every particular member remains as a pledge that no individual can be overburthened: when this security is removed, there is no longer any safety for those to whom the fact does not apply." To any degree that American interests did not match those of either members of Parliament or British electors, Johnstone was saying, there was that much less a "pledge" and hence less "security" and less "safety." [40]

Johnstone's argument reached only the surface of the American whig case against the constitutionality of virtual representation. His distinction could be carried much further: the interests of Americans and of British electors might not only be different; they could be conflicting and competing. That possibility was especially striking in taxation, for American interests were apt to be the opposite of British interests. "The laws made here to tax the Americans," Benjamin Franklin wrote in the *Gentleman's Magazine*, "affect them as a distinct body, in which the law makers are in no manner whatever, comprehended; whereas the laws made to tax Great-Britain, affect alike every member who gives his concurrence to such law. And hence arises the essential differences between *real* and *virtual* representations." A second contributor to the *Gentleman's Magazine* that year thought it

> *self-evident* that the virtual *representation* which it is contended the American is in possession of, is very different from the virtual representation which the Birmingham man possesses; because the virtual representative of the American, can put his hand in the American's pocket, and take out what sum he pleases, . . . without affecting himself . . . ; but the virtual representative of the Birmingham man must contribute shilling for shilling with the Birmingham man, and must likewise be himself subject, in like circumstances, to all the incapacities which he may think fit to impose upon him.[41]

That last given—that when "the virtual representative" taxed the nonelector he also taxed both the elector and himself—was the pragmatic safeguard of British constitutional theory, the doctrine of shared burdens, adding its mite to virtual representation, providing it with constitutional respectability even for theorists who regarded virtual representation as an exception to the doctrine of consent. "The great provision made by the constitution for securing the property of the people," an anonymous pamphleteer elucidated in 1774, "arises from their representatives being made to bear their due proportion of the burthens they impose, in common with the people on whom they are laid: and when the member that has given his voice for making of a law—for granting a supply, comes without the door of the assembly, he must bear his part and submit to the law he has assisted to make." The idea was expressed in popular terms by the metaphor that the representatives' "property was placed as an hostage for their conduct"; representatives were "being exposed to suffer any inconvenience in common with the people they represent." The thesis was especially attractive to the eighteenth-century legal mind because of the value that eighteenth-century constitutionalists placed on security, and the apparatus of shared burdens promised some security from the unequal application of state power. "Our security," John Lind told his fellow British subjects, "is not that our *consent* is given to every tax, but that our interests and those of the *taxers* are so involved, that in general *we* cannot be taxed without *their* being taxed with us."[42]

An affinitive concept, adding persuasiveness to the thesis, was security in property. "The security an Englishman has in his property," Sir William Meredith told the Commons, "consists in this, that no tax can be imposed upon him but by the very Members of Parliament who pay the tax themselves, equally with all those on whom they impose it."[43] As with every other eighteenth-century argument, the maxim that those imposing taxes had to share the burden they were imposing could be stated as a constitutional principle. It was "the Birthright Privilege of every British subject," members of a Virginia association resolved, "not to be taxed" except "by Persons chosen by the People and who themselves pay a part of the Tax they impose on others."[44]

Standing alone, the maxim of shared burdens would not have guaranteed the security of property. It was supplemented by a second constitutional rule. That rule, or "fundamental law," was "the *usage* of Parliament" that "imposes all taxes in a general manner, so as not to tax any particular district or part of the kingdom, while other parts of the kingdom are not taxed."[45] Just as every section of the nation should be treated equally, so should every type of property; nonelecting copyhold was not to be taxed differently from freehold held by electors. The rule meant that there could be no taxes enacted in Great Britain and imposed on virtually represented nonelectors that were not equally imposed on members of Parliament and on their electors.[46]

The constitutional purpose of these two doctrines—the principle of shared burdens and the maxim of equal assessments—was legislative restraint. One of the most frequently used words to explain why restraint was desirable was, again, *security*. The "Restraints" imposed by the two doctrines, the council and burgesses of Virginia insisted, were "the greatest Security against a burthensome Taxation."[47] The theory was that "He, who does not tax himself, taxes others without feeling." Another word used frequently was *oppression*. British nonelectors, knowing that those who tax them "always tax themselves at the same time," had "no reason to be apprehensive of partiality or oppression."[48] Daniel Dulany employed both words when he summed up the theory of restraint.

"The security of the non-electors against oppression is that their oppression will fall also upon the electors and the representatives."[49]

The relationship between American colonists and the British Parliament, no part of which they elected, exposed Americans in a constitutional position almost the opposite of that enjoyed by British electors and nonelectors alike. There were no shared burdens—no one in Great Britain shared the burden of the Stamp Act or of the tax on tea—and therefore no security.[50] The situation of the colonists when taxed by Parliament was much worse than that of British nonelectors; not only did they lack the security of shared burdens, but they were in the precarious position of relieving the burdens of Britain's electors and representatives.

It is important to realize what was being said. The point may seem familiar, but it has not been made before. The security of shared burdens had two aspects. To share the burden was one aspect; to be relieved of the burden was another. Sir William Meredith, referring to the security of shared burdens, argued in the House of Commons that, no matter what security it provided to British nonelectors, it gave none to Americans. "We shall tax them in order to ease ourselves," he said of the colonists. Because members of Parliament not only did not share the burden but also had their "property . . . eased thereby," "they would not tax, but *untax* themselves."[51] From the point of view of interests, the Americans would be placed in a hopeless constitutional position; as the voters of Salem, Massachusetts resolved, "if in any sense we are supposed to be represented [in the British Parliament,] most certainly it is by such only as have an interest in laying *burthens upon us for their own relief.*"[52]

Responsibility of Representation

E very householder almost having a vote in elections," a London pamphleteer wrote of Connecticut and Rhode Island, "the idea of virtual representation was entirely estranged from them." He exaggerated, of course, but not by much. There were differences of substance between representation in the New England colonies and in the mother country. The eighteenth-century House of Commons, J. R. Pole has noted, "represented a federation of oligarchies." The Massachusetts or New Hampshire House of Representatives represented a federation of towns. The local, corporate town meetings "were the constituencies whose representatives formed the General Court." New Englanders had a different definition of "representative" than did Britons and sought different qualities in the men they elected. "[Y]ou ought to choose Representatives, whose Interests are at present the same with your own," Massachusetts electors were told, and Connecticut election sermons boasted that such men were exactly the ones elected in that colony. Connecticut voters "choose from among our selves, of our Fathers and Brethren," "native sons, chosen by their free suffrages," and not "Strangers nor Children to Rule over us."[1]

Differences extended to what was expected of the representatives. In the colonies, representatives were instructed to "have a special regard to the Morals of this People," to "the Virtue of the People," or "to look to the Health of your Constituents." Their first attention should be for the "Towns from which you come: and seek the Welfare of those Societies." In Great Britain, instructions to representatives were more likely to concern issues of institutional integrity. There were occasional demands for "such laws as may strengthen the barriers of public liberty" or for "a fair and equal land-tax," but legislative programs were generally secondary to parliamentary reforms such as limiting placemen, excluding pensioners, and restoring triennial parliaments.[2]

American voters told their representatives to consider themselves part of their communities. The British told their representatives to consider themselves part of an independent institution, with their primary duty to the preservation of institutional independence. "Consider yourselves as part of the representative body of a free people," the freeholders of Devon instructed their members of Parliament in 1756; "continue to preserve your own, and promote the independency of parliament, by which alone the great blessing of liberty . . . can be secured to this nation in the present and future ages." The representatives' duty was not so much to defend the rights and interests of their constituents as to "defend the rights and interests of the Commons against the power of the crown and nobility." If that was done, if the integrity of the institution was maintained inviolable, the representatives' constitutional mission was fulfilled. "The principle of the *British* government is, An independent house of commons," James Burgh insisted. "If that be safe, all is safe. If that be violated, all is precarious."[3]

The contrast of old and New England was complicated by two differing perceptions of two different responsibilities. One was the perception of the representative, the other the perception of the institution in which the representative served. Americans wanted representatives who represented. Britons wanted representatives who were independent. Americans wanted their assemblies to be both representative and independent of the imperial government. Britons wanted the House of Commons to be both independent and a check on arbitrary power. From these two varying concepts of representation came differing theories of the responsibility of representatives. Americans expected their representatives to be responsible to the voters in particular and to "the people" in general. In Great Britain, the expectation was more complicated. If constitutional theorists thought of responsibility at all, it was likely to be the representative's responsibility to his constituents. But the representative was to be responsible not to the wishes or material needs of his constituents but to their constitutional liberty by maintaining the independence of the House of Commons. Consider, for example, what was on the mind of Sir John St. Aubyn when he told his fellow members of the Commons that they should be responsible to their constituents. "The influencing powers of the crown are daily increasing," he warned, "and it is highly requisite that parliaments should be frequently responsible to their constituents; that they should be kept under the constant awe of acting contrary to their interests." St. Aubyn was arguing for the restoration of triennial elections, a measure to strengthen the independence of the Commons against domination by the crown. The responsibility owed to the constituency was a responsibility to Parliament itself and to the constitution: to maintain the independence of Parliament and the balanced constitution. Ironically, that independence would be preserved by resisting equally pressure from either the crown, the constituencies, or the people. The constitutional doctrine may seem inconsistent in this age of democratic representation, but eighteenth-century members of the Commons both maintained the independence of their House and were responsible to their constituents by being independent of their constituents. What constitutional responsibility and accountability of representation meant in the age of the American Revolution is the question discussed in this chapter and the next.[4]

EXPECTATIONS OF REPRESENTATION

There are two facets to the issue of responsibility that must be kept separate. One is the weight that the representative element of the constitution exercises in daily affairs, that is, in British constitutional terms, the distribution of power between the branches of the mixed government. It was on this matter that existed the most striking contrast between the constitution of the mother country and those of the colonies. The differences have frequently been marked by historians, especially by Jack P. Greene, and are not the concern of this book. To summarize, in eighteenth-century Great Britain, because of the limited nature of the franchise and the representation of property, the element of the population giving consent to government was not democratic. In North America, more than anywhere else in the world, the popular element was the wielder of political power through the instrument of representation.[5]

The facet of representational responsibility we are considering concerns the constitutional duty of representatives to be responsible to the interests and/or the wishes of those for whom they express consent. The measure of that duty in the eighteenth century is both elusive and contradictory. Theory was often articulated but never agreed on. It is necessary to be careful interpreting what we read. The twentieth century can easily intrude on the eighteenth and even on the seventeenth. "I beseech you to consider the meaning of that word representative," Lord Mulgrave pleaded in 1692. "Can representatives do anything contrary to the mind of their constituents[?] It would be absurd to propose it."[6] Mulgrave knew that it was not absurd for members of the House of Commons. It cannot be said to have been the normal practice, however, for the general rule was that the representatives did not know the minds of their constituents. The question for constitutional historians is whether they thought they should care or had a duty to care.

Maurice Moore seemed to have thought that representatives in North American colonies should care. "A representative," he wrote of North Carolina in the year of the Stamp Act, "is to act in every respect as the persons who appointed him to that office would do, were they themselves present." We cannot be certain we understand Moore correctly, but he seems to be saying that representatives were the alter egos of those who elected them. Those representatives would be a much broader, perhaps even a more representative sampling of the population of North Carolina than of contemporary Britain, but the question still remains how Moore would have determined how the electors would have acted.[7]

One answer was by election. John Adams appeared to be making a stronger statement for responsibility than Moore did when he said that a representative assembly "should be in miniature an exact portrait of the people at large. It should think, feel, reason, and act like them." If we read Adams loosely, it would seem that he was for universal manhood suffrage. He was not. He wrote of "an exact portrait of the people at large," but what he meant was an exact portrait of the interests in society. Yet there can be no doubt that he, and all other Americans who commented on the responsibility of representatives, had a quite different idea in mind than did most British writers.[8] With the electorate more democratically distributed, smaller populations, and the representatives' life-styles much closer to those of the general population, the concept of responsibility did not have to be more popular in theory, but it did have to be more direct in practice.

In Great Britain, the concept of responsibly was so confused that it would not be unfair to say that there was no constitutional theory. Certainly, there was no agreement on theory. John Brewer's appraisal comes closest to summarizing attitudes about the responsibility of representatives. The issue, he wrote, "was less whether or not one exercised the right to vote than whether or not elected representatives were responsive to importunate groups of constituents." The notion was vague, much more vague than we would expect for a vital concept of constitutional law. Ideally, the "Sense of Parliament," at least in great, controversial issues, should be "influenced and changed by the Sense of the Nation." People who believed in the process had one example that they always cited to prove it worked: repeal of the Jew Bill. "It was the Sense of Parliament, that this was a salutary Law." It was not, however, the sense of the nation, and, "when the Sense of the Nation came to be known, not a Day beyond the Recess of Parliament was suffered to intervene, between the Enacting and the Repeal of that Law."[9] This level of public outcry raising the sense of the nation to the point of arousing Parliament occurred four times during the eighteenth century: the defeat of Walpole's excise in 1733, the Jew Bill, the repeal of the cider excise of 1763, and the repeal of the American Stamp Act. Four occasions may not seem many until we recall how few statutes were enacted during the century.

There is another misconception we should avoid. It would be a mistake to equate expression of the sense of the nation with twentieth-century lobbying or pressure politics. It could be seen in those terms, of course, but in eighteenth-century terms it was a constitutional mechanism helping an otherwise aristocratic House of Commons to function as the democratic branch of the constitution. When George Grenville, attempting to prevent repeal of the Stamp Act, moved an address to the king that the tax be enforced, Edmund Burke warned the Commons that the "People" were "now at your doors with anxious trembling," demanding repeal so that they might be saved from bankruptcy. To retain its constitutional role as representative, he argued, the Commons had to respond to the sense of the nation. "The people will think we do not draw our rights from them if we seem to have so little sympathy for their distress, if those people in whom we live, move and have our being are neglected. Nothing can hurt a popular assembly so much as the being unconnected with its constituents."[10]

Burke's constitutional attitudes demonstrate the difficulty of formulating a general theory of responsibility. History credits him with terminating the movement to have representatives bound by their electors' instructions. He insisted that representatives must remain independent of the electorate, that they vote their best judgment without obeying demands from their constituents. Yet he wanted the "public" or "people" heeded. Burke voted for a bill in 1772, "not because I approve of the measure in itself, but because I think it prudent to yield to the spirit of the times. *The people will have it so; and it is not for their representatives to say nay.*" That was a revealing argument from a man who would disrupt his parliamentary career to defend the right of a representative to ignore the instructions of his constituents. But Burke was not inconsistent. In Great Britain, so few citizens voted that the representative's responsibility was to the "people," not the voters. The House of Commons, Burke contended, was "of a middle nature between subject and Government." Its constitutional mystique was to "feel with a more tender and nearer interest every thing that concerned the people." That constitutional "character"—he might have used the word *responsibility*— "can never be sustained, unless the House of Commons shall be made to bear some stamp of the actual disposition of the people at large."[11]

John Adams would have agreed. Most Americans would have, perhaps adding only that Burke's argument could have gone a bit further, that a representative should be responsible to the reasonable constitutional aspirations not just of "the people" but of the constituency that elected him. By contrast, had the question been put to British constitutional theorists, there would not have been anywhere near a consensus. The ways that people in the mother country perceived the institutional role of Parliament were so varied that there could be little agreement about the responsibilities of the representatives. The debate was whether they were responsible to the people, to the county or borough for which they stood, to their electors (in some cases, to their patrons), to the institution of Parliament, to their oath or duty or whether they were responsible only to the constitution.

Autonomy of Representation

All the theories about the responsibility of representation had some support, but none enjoyed the backing of a majority of critics. A distinctly minority view, but one of great influence that appeared to be growing at the time of the American Revolution, was that the legislature should be autonomous. There were two aspects of autonomy that must be separated. One was the representative's autonomy from the electors, the subject of the next chapter. The second, the matter discussed here, was Parliament's autonomy, that is, whether Parliament was responsible to no exterior force except the law, the constitution, and its own institutional integrity.

It was all of Parliament, in its three branches, not just the House of Commons, that was autonomous, but because the Commons was the only elected branch theorists concentrated attention on the responsibility of the lower house. Electors with the right to vote for members of the Commons, Baron Rivers pointed out, had only one constitutional function, to exert their "best" judgment in that choice. Once elected, the representatives "acquired a separate and distinct interest from the body of the people." They became what a Mr. Downley called "gods of our own creating," not what the people of Salem, Massachusetts, said they expected of representatives, "creatures of our own making." [12]

The dispute was constitutionally cosmic. It was about the nature of legislative power, the source of governmental authority, and the responsibility of elected representatives. When Viscount Bolingbroke claimed that the peers were accountable to no one except God and their own consciences but that the Commons were accountable also to their constituents, he was postulating a doctrine of legislative responsibility to those who consented to government. The trouble was that it was just as reasonable to compare the two houses and draw the opposite conclusion. The Commons were constitutionally analogous to and not representatively different from the Lords, William Knox contended. That is, they were "not elected as representatives of the people, but commissioned by them in like manner as the Lords are commissioned or appointed by the Crown. If the Commons were the representatives of the people," he warned, "the people might control them, and the instructions of the electors would be binding upon the Members." It was an argument about constitutional theory, not logic; hence, what appeared logical depended on how one thought about legislative responsibility. The electors could not vest in the Commons the powers and privileges of legislators as they did not possess those powers and privileges themselves at the time they voted, Arthur Young reasoned. It seemed logical to him, therefore, that "the members when elected, and in combination with the other branches of the legislature, assume, and possess, and give themselves such powers and privileges, which those did not possess who sent them." Capel Lofft thought it illogical. "It would seem," he protested, that "the merit of the representatives of the commonalty depends . . . upon their not representing the commonalty," that the "house of commons owes its whole efficiency to being no longer the representative of those from whom its very name is received." [13]

Lofft was a common lawyer and should have known that the logic of autonomous representatives was constitutional logic, not reasoning based on popular meanings. The constitutional "people" to whom a representative was responsible could as easily be his fellow representatives as the electors, the constituencies, or all commoners. "Each member of the house of commons," Nathaniel Forester explained, "is, in the eye of the constitution, completely his own master. Amenable for his conduct, not to his particular constituents, but to his own body only: that is, to the whole body of the people, in the person of their representatives."

The "people" then were the members of the Commons, and the constitutional responsibility was owed to the institution. From this theoretical perspective, the Commons were not the "Creatures of the People" because "the Powers and Privileges which belong to Members of Parliament, belong to them by Virtue of the Constitution, their Constituents do indeed give their particular Members a Right to them, but then they can neither lessen nor increase them." It was the duty of the electors "to chuse us," Charles James Fox told the House of Commons; "it is ours to act constitutionally, and to maintain the independency of Parliament. Whether that independency be attacked by the people or by the crown, is a matter of little consequence." The constitutional mission was to guard the people from themselves as much as from prerogative abuse by being responsible not to them but to the House of Commons. "[W]e are chosen the delegates of the British electors for salutary not for pernicious purposes; to guard, not to invade the constitution; to keep the privileges of the very freemen we represent, as much within their proper limits, as to controul any unwarrantable exertions of the Royal authority. We are bound to promote their true interests in preference to the dearest desires of their hearts, and the constitution makes us the sole arbiters of those interests." Fox was addressing the House on the matter of the London magistrates arrested for contempt of the Commons after committing to prison agents sent by the House to apprehend printers who had published parliamentary debates. "I stand up for the constitution, not for the people," he announced, "if the people attempt to invade the constitution, they are enemies of the nation." The independence of the House had priority over the wishes of the people because on the independence of the House depended the liberty of the people.[14]

How constitutional theorists answered the question whether Parliament was autonomous often determined whether they thought Parliament sovereign. Although the two concepts were not related, they went together. The concept of an autonomous Commons fit the notion of a sovereign Parliament. Both doctrines were alien to American constitutional thought, explaining why some colonists when encountering the doctrine of autonomy reacted with surprise. Jared Ingersoll was a Connecticut lawyer, yet while serving as agent for the colony during the Stamp Act crisis he felt obliged, when reporting to Hartford, to explain in great detail the theory of autonomy that proponents of the Stamp Act cited to justify taxing the unrepresented Americans.

The House of Commons, say they, is a branch of the supreme legislature of the Nation, & which in its Nature is supposed to represent, or rather to stand in the place of, the Commons, that is, of the great body of the people. . . . [T]his house of Commons . . . is a part of the Supreme unlimited power of the Nation, as in every State there must be some unlimited Power and Authority; and that when it is said they represent the Commons of England, it cannot mean that they do so because those Commons choose them, for in fact by far the greater part do not, but because by their Constitution they must themselves be Commoners, and not Peers, and so the Equals, or of the same Class of Subjects, with the Commons of the Kingdom.

The constitutional theory must have been incognizable to New Englanders, whose representatives were selected from neighbors by vote of town meeting. The Commons, by Ingersoll's understanding, did not represent the people; they substituted for the people. And they represented commoners not because commoners elected them but because they, the representatives, were commoners and not lords.[15]

British constitutional commentators were also disturbed by sovereignty, but not for the reasons we might think: not because it made representatives independent of those whom they represented but because of the implications of sovereign, arbitrary power. "In England," an Irish author complained, "our members do not hold themselves responsible to their *constituents*, but to the *house*, and the house to the *prime minister*. Thus the people, who ought to be all, are *nothing*." The House of Commons, Alan Ramsay agreed in 1771, "from being deputies in a state, formed upon the common rights of mankind, are now become principals; and control the creative power from whence they derive their authority."[16] These writers may have thought they were complaining about the Commons' lack of responsibility and the consequence of arbitrary government. They were, and they were doing more besides. They were describing what Parliament would become in the nineteenth century— a representation possessing sovereign discretion to a degree American constitutionalism would never accept.

INDEPENDENCE OF REPRESENTATION

There was a specific case of autonomy so much in point it must be considered in detail. The House of Commons expelled John Wilkes, member for Middlesex, for offensive publications insulting to the king and to a member of the upper house but not insulting to or involving the dignity of the Commons. The next day, Wilkes announced he would stand for reelection, warning the Middlesex electors that, "[i]f ministers can once usurp the power of declaring who *shall not* be your represent-ative, the next step . . . is that of telling you, whom you *shall* send to parliament, and then the boasted constitution of England will be en-tirely torn up by the roots." Wilkes's prediction proved true. He was reelected, expelled again, voted to be ineligible for that session of Parlia-ment, was reelected a second time, and his opponent, who received about one-fourth Wilkes's votes, was by decree of the House of Com-mons declared elected in his place.[17]

It was during the ensuing political uproar that more was written about the right of voting and the concept of "freedom of election" than at any other time during the eighteenth century. A study of what people thought of the importance of elections to constitutional government, the rule of law, and British liberty could be written entirely from literature generated by the Wilkes affair.[18] No other incident, not even the Stamp Act and the debate whether Americans were virtually represented in Parliament, focused so much attention on the constitutional concept of representation and on the unrepresentative character of the House of Commons.[19]

As he was the principal actor in the drama, it is best to let John Wilkes sum up the constitutional issue. "The question is," he told the Middlesex electors, "Whether the people have an inherent right to be represented in parliament by the man of their free choice, not disqualified by the law of the land?"[20]

The dispute concerned the workings of the current constitution. No one was arguing for universal suffrage, more equal suffrage, or even for a representative suffrage. The Wilkes controversy might cause people to think about these issues more deeply than they had before, but they were not in contention. What was in controversy was whether the cur-rent small electorate, limited to a few substantial freeholders, had a right to the representative of their choice or—should the House of Com-mons, the representatives of other British localities, interests, and prop-erty, rule that choice objectionable—whether the electorate had to ac-cept the member "elected" by the other representatives.

Contemporaries discussed the controversy in terms of freedom of election because that was the issue as they saw it. But also at issue, although generally not recognized, was the autonomy of the representative branch of the British constitution. Two fundamental constitutional rights were in conflict: the right of electors to an uninhibited franchise and the privilege of the Commons to discipline its own members, a privilege that had developed over the centuries protecting the integrity of the House against the crown, the peers, and even the courts of common and prerogative law. Today we might think that the conflict would have been an ideal occasion to test whether the representation of the people existed separately from and was superior to the institutional rights of the embodiment of that representation. But the question in the eighteenth century could not be presented in terms of twentieth-century law. It may come as a surprise, but owing to the constitutional dynamics of that day, the stronger, better documented, more convincing, and more emotional arguments—what in the eighteenth century were called the more "constitutional" arguments—were on the side of parliamentary privilege.

The privileges of the House of Commons were constitutional mechanisms for maintaining its independence as an institutional check on prerogative power. Among the most fundamental of the privileges was the exclusive jurisdiction of the House to judge the qualifications of its members. Only the Commons, not the crown, the House of Lords, or the law courts, could investigate and determine matters of election. A reporter of common law described that privilege as "this great Palladium of the Constitution, and of the Independency and Freedom of the House of Commons." Without it, the best legal theory of the day believed, the Commons "could not exist as an independent body." Just one year before the Wilkes affair, the speaker of the Commons, insisting that "The freedom of this house is the freedom of this country," reprimanded officials of Oxford for interfering in parliamentary elections. Supporters of Wilkes's right to sit—or, more accurately, the right of Middlesex electors to be represented by him—stressed the irony that the privileges of the House, acquired to protect subjects from arbitrary government, were now "brought into a contest with its constituents." But many contemporaries did not think this the correct legal perspective. So dominant was the institutional integrity of the Commons in current constitutional values that the concept of the House as "representative" outweighed the rights of localities to representation or the rights of electors constitutionally entitled to representation. The House of Commons was in constitutional fact "the people of England," George Onslow assured that body with words less amazing at the time than they would be today. "The present dispute will then appear to be not between the House of Commons and their electors, but between almost the whole people of England, and a very small portion of them called the freeholders of Middlesex." In the eighteenth century, one did not have to be a lawyer to intuit that the argument had sense. After all, in constitutional parlance, the privileges of the Commons were the privileges of the people.[21]

Of course, there was another, less constitutional, more political perspective, one that we, in the twentieth century, can more easily appreciate than we can theories of institutional integrity. In fact, arguments that we would be comfortable making today were made in the 1760s. Members of the Commons had confused their legislative selves with "the people," London's government complained to the king. John Wilkes even sounded like a twentieth-century American lawyer. "There can be no representation," he contended, "but when the greater number to be represented have freely chosen a person who is legally qualified."[22] The argument would have been persuasive in the colonies and probably was for those Britons who thought of Middlesex's representative as the choice of Middlesex's electors, but it ignored one constitutional meaning of representation. Wilkes said that the elected representative had to be "legally qualified," and, owing to the Commons's privilege of guarding its own integrity, that was just what Wilkes had not been. "No one disputes their right," Jeremiah Dyson, a "king's friend" in the House of Commons and a barrister of Lincoln's Inn, wrote of the Middlesex electors. "All that is contended is, that they have exercised their *right* INEFFECTUALLY." To maintain its own independent integrity, the Commons had to possess power to expel, and power to expel implied power to qualify. The electors' right was "to vote for whom they please, *being duly qualified,* to represent them." Otherwise, the House would not be independent because the Middlesex electors would "in effect over-rule" its resolutions.[23]

Of course politics determined the outcome: most members disliked Wilkes, and there was a general understanding that the king wanted him excluded from the House. But the fact remains that two constitutional doctrines and two concepts of the meaning of "representation" had come into conflict, and what little "freedom of election" existed in eighteenth-century Great Britain was diminished. A constitutional innovation had been established, William Dowdeswell warned: an innovation vesting in the members of one house of Parliament "the power of *chusing their associates,* and erecting the worst of tyranny, that which can exist only by the perversion of its authority to the *oppression* of those very persons from whom it is derived." For, instead of preserving the constitutional independence of the Commons, the purpose of that independence had been extended. By implication of constitutional precedent, the institutional integrity of the Commons might now mean that its independence should be maintained against that part of the people who were electors as well as against the crown. If true, some critics warned, the House of Commons "will no longer represent the people, but dwindle into a separate body altogether independent, self-existing, and self-electing."[24]

The Middlesex election did not become a constitutional precedent. John Wilkes would be the last candidate declared disqualified for election by a political vote of the Commons, and his opponent would be the last member of Parliament "elected" by his fellow representatives. But, at the time it was in contention, the Wilkes affair gave British constitutionalists their most difficult questions concerning the meaning of *representation,* questions that would have to be answered if the controversy with the colonies was to be resolved on constitutional principles. Even more, it forced American whigs to ask if Parliament could ever be representative of them—even if it was agreed that the doctrines of shared interests, shared burdens, equal assessments, and virtual representation sufficiently protected their constitutional rights so as to make the members of the Commons their *constitutional* representatives. Although the expulsion of Wilkes would not become a precedent for similar expulsions, the innovation of seating his opponent presaged a drift toward sovereign arbitrary law—the constitution of nineteenth-century Great Britain—that Americans could not accept.

We must concede to the opponents of Wilkes the sincerity of their views. The attorney general, William De Grey, intended to defend the integrity of the Commons when he urged his fellow members to vote against Wilkes to "preserve the independence of our own body, as involving the liberty of the people, and defend it against the people themselves misguided and inflamed by faction and self-interest, with no less activity and perseverance than against the Crown or the Lords." It was a matter of the people's liberty, but again it was that special constitutional, constructive meaning of liberty, not a liberty that could include American rights. It was the institutional liberty maintained by the independence of each branch of Parliament, but at the cost of departing from the rule of existing law. American whigs thinking about how the Commons dealt with John Wilkes could not help but agree with a pamphleteer who told the duke of Grafton that "the implied consequences of that vote would resolve all right into power, and leave the use of that power to the casual impulses of occasional policy and prejudices." He was warning about the future: government by ministers rather than by representatives.[25]

Accountableness of Representation

There were two explanations for the autonomy of Parliament. One was that the people as a group did not constitutionally exist separately from the members of the Commons. "The Legal Authority, that is, the Authority vested by the Constitution in the People, resides, while they are sitting, in them." What was vested in the members was a collective power, not a mass of individual powers.[1] Another argument was that the legislators were autonomous from the people because of their oaths to the constitution. They were not empowered to violate the constitution even to suit their constituents and therefore were independent of them.[2] Any way it was theorized, autonomy implied parliamentary sovereignty, and that was why it never had a chance of becoming the majority position in British constitutional theory until the next century. The eighteenth-century constitutional mind could not accept the possibility that Parliament's command should alter fundamental law. Certainly, it could not alter the terms under which it sat as the nation's legislature. If it wished to promulgate a new Magna Carta or change the mode of representation, it had to return to the people, or else it might become that constitutional monstrosity the British dreaded above all others, arbitrary power.[3]

What was the rationale for the majority view against autonomy? There were several explanations, none better than that representation did not receive its autonomy from the constitution or natural law. In other words, rejecting the "autonomous" argument that parliamentary authority could not be conferred by electors as they could not give what they did not possess, espousers of parliamentary accountableness invoked the authority of the people. Parliament was accountable because, Lord Mulgrave pointed out, the people, when delegating their power, "do always retain to themselves more than they give; and, therefore, the People do not give their Delegates an absolute Power of doing what they please, but do always retain to themselves more than they confer on their Deputies, who must, therefore, be accountable to their Principals."[4]

Mulgrave's theory was not as controversial as we might think, not even the notion of legislative accountability. After all, there was near universal agreement that civil rights were not grants from government but the property of the people, and among the people's privileges was the right to be governed by the rule of law and not by the arbitrary caprice of an unrestrained sovereign.

It is important not to jump to conclusions. An eighteenth-century constitutionalist did not have to be a democrat to endorse this theory of delegated power: to acknowledge an ulterior authority superior to the will and pleasure of the legislature whether it be the Parliament or a colonial assembly. It was an explanation of the customary constitution, and even constitutionalists who were monarchists had no difficulty with the constitutional implication that "the people" retained a residue of authority, making their representatives accountable to them.[5] The matters about which there was disagreement were in what manner they were accountable and to whom accounting was due.

As with the theory of autonomous representation, the theory of accountable representation could be overstated. Constitutional commentators described representatives as "*created* by" the "people at large" and said that Parliament was "the *meer creature* and *dependent* of the people at large," but none developed a jurisprudential explanation of how the creatures accounted to the creators. The reason was largely a matter of implication squeezed from certain descriptive designations: at best, law implied by normative titles. "The COMMONS are the *Counsellors,* the *Trustees* and *Guardians* of the People, their *Representatives,* and *stipulated* Servants," a barrister of the Middle Temple wrote in 1750.[6]

We must assume that these terms were intended to mean something as so many constitutional theorists repeated them in the eighteenth century. Representatives were called *attorneys,* a word often joined with another such as *advocates, servants, factotums, proxies, stewards,* and even *plenipotentiaries;*[7] *trustees,* perhaps the most frequently repeated appellation, was used to suggest that representatives were bound by a trust relationship to secure the well-being of the beneficiaries and, especially, to prove that the representation was not autonomous;[8] *delegates,* was employed quite often to accentuate the fact that representatives were "not *principals*";[9] and *agents* was used to emphasize that representatives served as an agency conducting the people's business.[10] The nomenclature must be accorded some significance as form, but it had none in substance.

The designations of "attorneys" or "agents" or "trustees," as Sir William Yonge complained, were "artfully brought into the debate, as if the members of this House were nothing more than the attornies of the particular county, city, or borough, they respectively represent." The words themselves were interchangeable. When a writer on political liberty asserted that representatives "are Trustees, not Proprietors, to do their Constituents, the People's Will, not their own," he might as easily have said that representatives were "servants, not masters" or "agents, not principals." To say that they were trustees acting "under a *trust* which the constitution of this country supposes *may be abused*" was the same as saying that they were agents acting under a fiduciary relationship for which they could be held accountable. It is, therefore, less words than issues that we should heed, and the constitutional issues to be explored in this chapter are to whom representatives were accountable and how?[11]

UNIVERSAL REPRESENTATION

The answer most commentators favored, with great shades of differences, was that representatives were accountable to all the British people—a universal representation—in a loose, unenforceable way. The House of Commons was viewed as a unified, single body in which each member represented the general collective good. It was not a congress of individuals sent to speak for particular places. At its most extreme, the theory of universal representation limited the representative to furnishing information concerning the condition or wants of the people or property that elected him, but he was not to know the interests of the constituency if those interests came into conflict with the general interest of the whole people.[12] The premise was that in Great Britain, where (it was often pointed out) legislators were "not stiled the *Representatives of the People,* but the *Commons in Parliament,*" each member, no matter where from or by whom elected, represented all the people, not a locality or the interests of that locality alone. After all, each member of Parliament voted on every issue, not just on questions of local concern. Should the general good or interest clash with the particular good or interest of the electoral district, the "representative" supported the general over the particular.[13]

The arguments that elected representatives were "guardians of all British commoners, wheresoever dispersed," might have been so much theoretical speculation, of no practical consequence, except for two important implications. One was an extension of the concept of consent.

The maxim that "the Consent of the *Parliament* is taken to be every man's consent" was certainly strengthened by the notion that a member of the House of Commons represented every citizen and not a single constituency.[14] Indeed, some supporters of the "universal representation" theory went further than saying that all Britons were represented by each member, contending that, "[i]f, by the local situation of any part of the kingdom, representation is rendered impractical, each member of the state is bound to give a more immediate attention to that part of it, than to any other."[15]

We should not be amazed at such an incredible conclusion—that the representative was obliged to represent the unrepresented more than the represented. It was typical of the strange twists to constitutional reasoning of which the English were so fond until the nineteenth century. What deserve attention are the conclusions that could be drawn. One was that reform was that much more unnecessary. If "every Member of Parliament is a representative of all the Commons of Great Britain," what difference did it make if representation was unequal or that there were "rotten boroughs" with few or no electors? Another was that virtual representation was more plausible, as was the doctrine of constructive "representation" or constitutional "consent." If the constitution decreed that the individual representative represented everyone in the empire and not just his electors, it followed that everyone was virtually represented and that everyone gave constitutional consent to legislation. And why not? Thomas Blacklock asked about the representative. "Is it not his business to adjust the interest of subordinate communities with the general interest of the whole society? . . . Why then should not the same delegated powers virtually extend to the continent, which is a part of the British empire, as well as to those in Britain, who have no vote?"[16] The answer was that it did extend to North America, that, just as the member of Parliament elected by London "represents London and all the commons of the island, he represents the colonies; and is in duty and conscience bound to consult their interest." We cannot be certain that he believed it himself, but Rhode Island's Martin Howard thought it plausible to argue that the theory of universal representation—if the representatives accepted and acted on it—meant that Americans were as well represented as were British electors. "That the house of commons consider themselves as representatives of every British subject, wherever he be; and therefore to every useful and beneficial purpose, the interests of the colonists are as well secured and managed by such a house, as if they had a share in electing them."[17]

It is worth making distinctions so that the fine points of the argument are not missed. Howard was saying that the colonists were either actually or virtually represented by the House of Commons under the doctrine of universal representation. It was a different contention than that Americans were bound by statutes enacted by the three branches of Parliament because of the doctrine of sovereignty. That was the principle James Otis conceded in his famous answer rejecting Howard's constitutional law. "Will any man's calling himself my agent, representative, or trustee make him so in fact?" Otis asked. "At this rate a House of Commons in one of the colonies have but to conceive an opinion that they represent all the common people of Great Britain, and according to our author [Howard] they would in *fact* represent them." A sounder reason was sovereignty, Otis thought, and, like most commentators who discussed the question, he based the right on the sovereignty of the three branches of Parliament rather than on the universal representation of one. "The supreme legislative indeed represents the whole society or community, as well the dominions as the realm," he wrote; "and this is the true reason why the dominions are justly bound by such acts of Parliament as name them. This is implied in the idea of a supreme sovereign power."[18]

The second implied consequence of the universal representation doctrine was that there were no specific groups to whom a representative was accountable. This is not the same in theory as saying that the legislature was constitutionally autonomous, for universal representation postulated representational accountableness to the "people" rather than to the integrity of the institution or to the constitution. The reality was, however, that, if the elected representative was in theory accountable to all the people of Great Britain, he was in practice accountable to no one. As "[e]very Englishman, of every rank, has a claim to his services," Baron Rivers pointed out, he was, in the words of Sir William Yonge, "at full freedom to act as he thinks best for the people of England in general." If that were not true, Rivers thought, the peers in the House of Lords would be better representatives of the people than the elected commoners in the House of Commons because they would be the only ones able to "pursue the real welfare of the people, without any private reason for studying, or indulging their inclinations." Rivers even had the fantastic idea that it was the elector and not the representative who might be accountable. At least he said that the elector "is answerable for the choice of his representative to the whole community, from the King to the child of the peasant in the cradle," but because of the doctrine of universal representation it was absurd to think of the representative "rendering account solely to his constituents." Perhaps Rivers did not mean this too seriously, but we can never be certain of eighteenth-century constitutional epicures. Then, too, Horace Walpole thought Rivers "half-mad." [19]

LOCAL REPRESENTATION

A pragmatic reason why universal representation made sense in the eighteenth century was that representatives did not have to be residents of the boroughs or counties from which they were elected. Thomas Carew thought that there were members of the Commons "who never saw the borough that sent them hither, nor knew any thing of its constitution or interest, perhaps could not recollect its name," and Judge Spencer Cowper told Watkins Williams Wynn that "he had never been in the borough he represented in parliament, nor had he ever seen or spoke with any of his electors." Little wonder that some constitutional experts insisted that each member represented the whole nation, not just the electors of his district. From the facts of constitutional reality it seemed logical.[20]

There were, however, just as many students of the constitution insisting on the opposite. "A member of parliament is certainly a joint *legislator* for the whole kingdom," John Cartwright wrote, "but it is absurd to call him the *representative* of any but the community who sent him to parliament." This constitutional reality made sense to John Joachim Zubly, the Swiss-born pastor of Savannah, Georgia. "[N]o member can represent any but those by whom he hath been elected," Zubly pointed out; "if not elected, he cannot represent them." From this constitutional perspective, the *"Elective"* were "bound to promote the Interest and Welfare of their *Constituents*," to preserve and secure their persons and property; they were "dependent" on them and, by implication, accountable to them at least to the extent of owing them "a proper regard."[21]

It cannot be said to what degree the doctrine of local representation was supposed to make representatives accountable. Few eighteenth-century commentators discussed the question in the abstract as they were much more interested in detailing the limits and implications of the mechanics of accountability such as the constitutional nature of instructions and the constitutionality of consulting with constituents. In these cases, responsibility to the local constituency rather than "the people" was assumed as there had to be a constituency to instruct or with whom to consult. Perhaps the only clear statement of the abstraction was a caricature: Nathaniel Forester's criticism of Sir William Meredith's explanation of accountability. It was, Forester complained, "the most servile court to his constituents; avowing his total dependance upon them, and very humbly declaring himself to be nothing more than the mere channel of their inclinations and opinions to the house. His rights are their rights, his privileges their privileges, his voice the mere eccho of their voice; nay, his very heart, and mind, and soul, connected by some secret bond of indissoluble union with theirs."[22]

From what will be said in the next chapter, it may be supposed that Forester's caricature fit American attitudes, that the colonists wanted representatives accountable to their constituents' wishes. That fact is true and is another contrast with contemporary British representational theory. But when Americans spoke in the abstract about why representatives were responsible to the local electoral district rather than to the whole people, they were less interested in stressing obedience or accountability than knowledge. Only local representatives, locally elected, Virginia's legislators pointed out in a typical appraisal, "are acquainted with the Circumstances of their Constituents" well enough to legislate for or to tax them fairly and constitutionally. The Virginians tried to pass off this localism of representation as British custom, but it was generic American theory. "[T]he Taxation of the People by themselves, or by Persons chosen by themselves to represent them, who can only know what Taxes the People are able to bear, or the easiest Method of raising them, and must themselves be effected by every Tax laid on the People, is . . . the distinguishing Characteristick of *British* Freedom, without which the ancient Constitution cannot exist."[23]

It was easy to apply this test to imperial legislation. The information on which Parliament acted when legislating for the colonies, the freeholders of Fairfax County, Virginia, contended, "must be always defective, and often false," because, Israel Mauduit explained, "being at a great Distance, they [the members of the Commons] will, for Want of proper Information, be ignorant of what the Colonies are able to bear. This may occasion great Injustice, and perhaps the most pernicious political Blunders."[24]

Although the benefit of localness could be most graphically expounded in the context of the imperial controversy, American theory had always favored local representation. The doctrine was not devised to resist parliamentary legislation; it was the pragmatic explanation of American constitutional conditions. It has been expressed in earlier chapters and will be again. Here we need only quote a typical instance published in the *New York Gazette*. "It is essential to the character of a representative," a correspondent wrote, "that his interest shall be consistent with that of his constituent, and that he shall have an exact knowledge of his circumstances & all his concerns. Without these no reasonable man would choose a representative." It was an ideal of representation quite different from what was said in the mother country. There was no need to mention accountability. It was implicit in the requirement of knowledge.[25]

Authority of Consultation

I n Great Britain during the eighteenth century, there were always just enough constitutional arguments about the responsibility of representation to imply that some right of accountability was vested somewhere. Whether it was owed to all the people, just to the electing constituency, to the electors, to the electors who voted for the representative, or to some other group was a question seldom raised in the abstract as it generally was submerged in the more practical question of the mechanics of accountability—to whom could a representative be held accountable and how?

The hard line of British constitutional theory against the concept of accountability was formulated by Robert Walpole's hacks responding to the excise crisis of 1733. It was primarily a matter of partisan politics that both sides attempted to wrap in the respectability of constitutional doctrine. The opposition fought the excise with petitions and instructions to representatives. The government sought to defuse popular expression by denying its constitutional relevance to parliamentary decision making. That reason was why the excise crisis was the occasion for the case against representative responsibility (or for parliamentary autonomy) to be stated at its most practical extreme. The fact to note is that it was by no means as extreme as we might expect. There was a Lockean qualification to the Walpolean denial of accountability. "[T]he People have *no Authority* nor *Power,* after a Government is *settled,* and the *Legislature* chosen," Walpole's *London Journal* asserted, laying down what appeared to be a categorical principle, only to follow it immediately with a large exception: "as long as the Constitution is preserved, and such Laws made as are *not inconsistent* with the *fundamental* Principles of just Government." The right of resistance, a principle inherited from the old English constitution, was still viable in the mid-eighteenth century, providing a legal basis for the argument that Parliament could not exceed its constitutional powers and implying that it was somehow accountable if it did.

Walpole's *Journal* gave several reasons why representatives were not accountable. One was that because the sense of the people could not be known representatives were better off trusting their own good judgment than worrying about the people's expectations. A second was that the sense of the people was not worth knowing, certainly not their sense about excise taxes, "for, what is *this whole Body of the People* . . . but only *Dealers in Tobacco* and *Wine,* of *London, Bristol,* and *Liverpool,* influencing the smaller Tradesmen, who depend upon them, throughout the kingdom."[1]

The lesson is not that Walpolean politics missed an opportunity to alter the constitution by anticipating a principle that would become dominant in the nineteenth century. It is, rather, that the constitutional rights of resistance, consent, representation, and election contained a residue of accountability that the doctrine of parliamentary sovereignty was as yet not strong enough to dismiss. At the very least, there was still the belief that there were unconstitutional actions that Parliament could not undertake. At the most, it was potentially much more, as Robert Walpole perhaps acknowledged when he bowed to public reaction and withdrew the excise bill.

Mechanics of Consultation

The doctrine of accountability was as old as it was vague. During the age of the American Revolution, commentators often cited Lord Coke to prove that the opposite rule—that representatives were not obliged to obey their constituents—was "a novel doctrine." Coke had asserted as "the custom of parliament" that "when any new device is moved for in parliament, on the King's behalf, for his aid, or the like, . . . the Commons may answer, They dare not agree to it without conference with their counties."[2]

Eighteenth-century students of representation cited Coke for the right of electors to instruct their representatives how they were to vote. If Coke's words are heeded closely, it appears that he also was talking about the doctrine of consultation. That was a process of accountability somewhat different than instructions and much more an American technique than a British one. Patricia U. Bonomi has noted that in New York "Assemblymen frequently expressed the wish to 'consult their Constituents,'" suggesting that this wish was a "remarkable responsiveness to public opinion."[3] In other colonies, consultation was more often a technique to marshall public opinion in support of some political objective or to add the weight of public opinion to the representative branch of the legislature in its constitutional balance against the prerogative branch.

There were several consultations in Massachusetts legislative history, one of which is worth considering in detail. In 1728, William Burnet arrived as governor and within less than a month addressed his first session of the General Court, demanding on behalf of the imperial government that the colony confer on him a permanent salary. The timing is important because there could be no political animosity. There had been no time for factions to develop. Burnet enjoyed the good feelings that greeted most new governors. The salary issue, therefore, involved constitutional principle. What interests us is that, when the House of Representatives refused to vote a permanent salary, granting only an annual one, it based its reasoning on the doctrine of the balanced constitution preserved in the institutional integrity of the representative branch. A permanent salary, the legislators replied, "has a direct tendency to weaken if not destroy our happy Constitution, by our giving away the great and almost only Privilege that gives weight to the House of Representatives, which is the making Grants of Moneys as the Exigence of Affairs requires, and which being once given up, the Governour will be too absolute; whereas . . . We humbly apprehend that no Part of the Legislature should be so independent." The Massachusetts argument was a classic statement of eighteenth-century representational independence, one of the fundamental principles structuring constitutional checks and balances. A permanent salary, making the governor independent of the other two branches, would have "a direct tendency to weaken our happy Constitution" by lessening "the Dignity and Freedom of the House of Representatives . . . and consequently cannot be thought a proper Method to preserve that Balance in the three Branches of the Legislature."[4]

Burnet professed puzzlement how a permanent salary could jeopardize the representative branch's institutional independence. In Great Britain, the king was granted a permanent civil list by Parliament, and the independence of the House of Commons was not diminished. By analogy, why should not the governor, the king's representative in the colony, enjoy the same security? Because, the House of Representatives answered, constitutional situations were not analogous. Massachusetts legislators could not confide in a governor to the same degree that they or Parliament could confide in a king. The prosperity and welfare of his people was the king's interest. "Whereas it is most obvious that commonly neither the Prosperity nor Adversity of a People affect a Governour's Interest at all, when he has once left them." Besides, in the colonies, the executive held stronger checks on the houses of representatives than the king did on the House of Commons. Not only did governors frequently veto colonial bills, a power no longer exercised in Great Britain against parliamentary legislation, but, in addition, the crown itself, acting through the Privy Council in London, could disallow colonial acts that had inadvertently received a governor's consent. As a result, the colonial constitutional balance was more heavy on the executive's side, justifying the counterbalance of a representational check over an annual salary.[5]

Burnet persisted. Instructed by London to accept only a permanent salary, he refused to adjourn or prorogue the General Court until it gave in. After some weeks of stalemate, several representatives "desired to know the Minds of their Principals." The House complied. Telling the governor that it "did not dare to come into such an Act, without the special Orders of Our Constituents," it drafted an "account" of the dispute for each member "to send to his Town for their *Orders either the one way or the other.*" Put in constitutional terms, the representatives sought consultation with their constituencies.[6]

We need not assume that the representatives were seeking instructions. They may have been using consultation to rally public opinion, even to create it. Although ostensibly asking their constituents for guidance as to how they should vote as representatives, the better view is that they, in political fact, were letting people know what they thought were the constitutional exigencies. What is worth marking is not the strategy but the terminology. The representatives defined their relationship to their electors in rather explicit language, using words not commonly heard in Westminster Hall such as *principals* and *orders* from constituents. It is tempting to speculate that the phraseology reflects the way the relationship was seen in New England if not in all the colonies: principals legally competent to order their representatives how to vote. There is no certainty, however, for the newly arrived Burnet adopted some of the same language, referring to the House's constituents as "*your Principals.*"

It is important to understand that Burnet was both a lawyer and a man of constitutional principles who understood the issues at stake. We may be impressed, therefore, that he not only embraced the concept of consultation but carried it as far as it could go. "[I]t opens a Door to *your Constituents to give you special Orders* to comply," he told the representatives, adding that "Orders" would be binding: "that you may be lawfully *compelled* by your *Constituents* to [d]o a thing, though it should be against *your own declared Judgments.*" That statement is a remarkable as well as surprising theory of constitutional law, so extreme for the eighteenth century that it cannot be said to represent even American thought. It was certainly contrary to everything that would be said in Great Britain when the arguments in favor of consultation reached their height during the age of the American Revolution. To hold elected representatives "lawfully *compelled*" to obey their constituents would never be British constitutional law and would be American constitutional custom only in isolated situations. Burnet's theory illustrates the constitution as it might have become but never did.[7]

Radical as Burnet seems to have been in retrospect, his constitutional strategy was by no means as extreme as that of a later eighteenth-century governor who asserted the authority to initiate a consultation. In 1754, Massachusetts was at war with France, and the government badly needed revenue. Following one of the most bitter taxation debates in the General Court's history, the House of Representatives enacted a bill imposing an excise on all liquor produced in the province, even on the output of stills located in private residences. The bill may have been an attempt by the agricultural districts of the colony to throw the costs of the war onto town dwellers and innkeepers, but, as with the controversies surrounding the British excise bill of 1733 and the cider excise of 1763, the debate was constitutional, not economic. The amount of the tax was not what upset people; it was the government's intrusion into the home. "[B]y obliging every Freeholder in the Province to give a publick Account upon Oath of his private Consumption of Spirituous Liquors," it was charged, "[t]his Bill, of which a Parrallell cannot be shewn in any Age or Country, shock'd all who considered the Nature and Tendency of it, and had any Affection for Liberty." The bill was "condemn'd *as grievious and unconstitutional*, both by the G[o]v[erno]r, and the Voice of the People." The governor was William Shirley, who said that the bill violated the "natural rights of every private family." To dissipate some of the legislative bitterness, he hit on a scheme, to which he tried to give a color of legality by saying it had been "frequently us'd by the General Assembly [the General Court] in Cases of the like Nature." It was to withhold his consent to the legislation until the representatives consulted with their constituents. "I think the least that you can do in Justice to your Constituents upon this Occasion, will be . . . by ordering the Bill to be printed, that your Constituents may be fully acquainted with the Contents of it during the Recess of the [General] Court, and your selves informed of the general Sentiments of the Country concerning a Matter of this Importance, and Difficulty, which so nearly touches the natural Rights of every individual Member in his private Family." If, following adjournment, the representatives "continue of the same Opinion, after having informed your selves of the Sentiments of your Constituents upon this Bill; I shall think my self more at Liberty to pass it, and shall have all due Regard to the general Voice of the People, in a Matter which purely concerns their own just Rights."[8]

Shirley may have hit on a clever device to calm a political storm, yet it is difficult to believe that he did not realize that he was proposing a remarkably drastic departure from conventional British constitutional theory. It is possible that Massachusetts legislators thought the consultation standard practice, but it would have been controversial at home. True, Shirley justified it on the grounds that the people's rights were involved to a very unusual extent, and he did not say that his decision, as the chief executive, would be influenced by public opinion. He would, rather, be guided by how the representatives judged public opinion. He did, however, want the representatives themselves guided by the consultation, that is, to give up their independent judgments.

The House of Representatives agreed. It resolved that the proposed statute be printed in the newspapers and that the towns of Massachusetts meet and discuss the legislation so "that this House may know the Minds of their Constituents with Regard to said Bill." The representatives gave themselves four months, ample time to consult. The towns met, and most responded by instructing their representative. When the General Court reconvened, the party opposed to the excise, confident it had carried a majority of towns, moved the question, "Whether the said Returns should be considered?" The motion was defeated and the excise reenacted.[9]

Opponents of the excise and some subsequent historians thought that the people's right to representation had been treated with contempt. "No one suspected, that the Representatives of a Free People would dare to act contrary to the declar'd Sense of their Constituents," one pamphleteer complained. They had been elected "by you to represent your own Sense," he added, stating the extreme theory, and instead "trample upon you with Impunity." "Are the People appeal'd to, only to be insulted," another asked; "the Voice of the Freemen of this Province is not so much regarded, as the Murmurs of Slaves are wont to be in Countries of Tyranny?"[10]

But the procedure was not without legal doubt. Massachusetts representatives were selected by town meetings, generally one representative for each town. When a town voted views on the excise, it could be said, in constitutional law, that it was instructing its own representative, the only one it could legally address, and that the House of Representatives was constitutionally correct when it refused to tally the returns. It is indicative of how uncertain both law and theory were that the constitutional logic of the one-representative/one-town theory was no more convincing than the opposite conclusion, that the collective vote of the towns was binding. "Some may indeed dispute whether a single R[e]pre[sentativ]e who acts for the Publick, is oblig'd to follow the Instructions of his own single Town," an observer explained. "But will any one assert, that the H[ous]e have a right to act contrary to the united Voice of the whole C[o]mm[u]nity which they repr[ese]nt, in an Affair that concerns all; and that has been formally submitted to the Judgment of the People"? That argument made as much sense as the other, although it might be asked whether it was the representatives or only the governor who was being informed by the collective "Judgment of the People." [11]

Many instructions are no longer extant, and it is not possible to survey the returns, but those that are available indicate that the towns addressed their own representatives directly, that they did not instruct all representatives or the governor. Moreover, a large but undetermined percentage of towns failed to meet or vote, leaving their representatives without a mandate. [12]

The importance of the excise consultation is its demonstration of the law's vagueness. Here was one of the most dramatic consultations imaginable, called by the representative of the crown and accepted by the legislators, on just about the most divisive domestic issue of the eighteenth century. Yet it resolved nothing. The political animosity remained because the constitutional machinery of representation was not sufficiently manipulable, and the constitution itself not sufficiently democratic, to lift the issue above legislative politics. In the eighteenth century, the judiciary did not yet have a role to play and could not rule on the binding force of a consultation. Unanswered questions remained unanswered because they were not constitutionally answerable.

It could be objected that too much is being made of consultations as constitutional law. Better to see them for what they really were, devices to marshall public opinion either for a political cause or to resolve a dispute by reaching over the heads of the elected representatives. Perhaps so, but even to see them this way implies some sense of constitutional accountability. More immediately, the objection is not valid for the Massachusetts excise consultation. Because of the legal mechanics of consultation peculiar to New England, the appeal in that colony, even if seeking "public opinion," was not to some vague or politically manipulable expression of popular sentiment. The consultation was with a constituency that possessed a constitutional device for consulting. The town meeting could entertain the question, debate, and answer it.

The constitutional premises of the excise consultation were also less clear than they might have been in other jurisdictions because of a feature peculiar to Massachusetts law. The consultation was ordered with the towns, but the towns answered by utilizing a more formal and established constitutional technique, instructions. Thus, in Massachusetts, the question of the nature of instructions, considered in the next chapter, intruded on the issue of the constitutional force of consultation.

Sometimes the process was reversed: instructions initiated consultation. Boston once instructed its representatives "that any Bill relative to Bankrupts, that shall be brought into the House, be laid before the Town before it shall be passed into a Law." In other words, the instructions required that the representatives consult with the town in order to be instructed on how to vote. A few months later, when an indemnity bill was introduced, it was laid before the town, and the representatives were instructed to have it enacted.[13]

Outside New England, a consultation was less constitutionally structured. The procedures were less uniform and therefore the opinion consulted less precise and more subjective. The best example occurred in Pennsylvania as part of the campaign to alter the colony from a proprietary to a royal government. To strengthen their position, the anti-proprietary majority in the Assembly voted to "adjourn, in order to consult their Constituents, whether a humble Address should be drawn up, and transmitted to his Majesty, praying, that he would . . . take the People of this Province under his immediate Protection and Government." The governor was appointed by the proprietary family and represented its interests in the colony against the Assembly. The consultation, therefore, is best interpreted constitutionally as an attempt to add popular weight to the representational branch of government in its contest against the chief executive officer and the proprietary interest.[14]

Pennsylvania did not have the constitutional apparatus of town meetings through which consultation could be funneled. Instead, according to Joseph Galloway, leader of the anitproprietary party, "the People in many Places, held little Meetings with each other, the Result of which was, that they would manifest their Sentiments to their Representatives, by petitioning the Crown directly of themselves, and requesting the Assembly to transmit and support those Petitions." [15]

The consultation and its outcome have to be evaluated from two perspectives, the political and the constitutional. The political was largely an interpretation of fact and the constitutional largely of law. On the political side, the legal weakness of consultations became readily apparent, at least when they depended on *ad hoc* gatherings rather than constitutional assemblies such as town meetings. Without the supporting structure of official constitutional bodies, the interpretation of the evidence turned largely on the outcome favored by the interpreter. The proproprietary party, whose spokesman was John Dickinson, dismissed the petitions gathered by the other side as the work "of rash, and inconsiderable people," "many of whom could neither read nor write," who not only "did not understand" what they were doing but numbered not more than 3,500 out of a population of 300,000. The people wanting the change, by contrast, could just as persuasively argue that the signers of the petitions were "generally Men of the best Estates in the Province, and Men of Reputation." [16]

It is the other perspective, the constitutional, that is informative. One might expect that Dickinson, known to historians as a conservative lawyer, would have rested the opposition on law, denying the legality of consultation. That he instead conceded the constitutionality of consultation is a clear indication not only of the strength that the doctrine of accountability by popular approval enjoyed in the colonies but also of how far American constitutional thought had divided from British. In the mother country, most lawyers would have said that the consultation had no standing in law. Dickinson said that it could be valid but laid down a very heavy burden of proof. He wanted "our constituents more unanimous in their opinions," "to see a vast majority of them join with calm resolution in the measure, before I should think myself justifiable in voting for it, even if I approved of it." [17]

Dickinson's constitutional argument tells us much about the concept of representation among Americans in the age of the Revolution. He conceded the principle of responsibility and the duty of accountability. "[W]e are the servants of the people of *Pennsylvania*" was how he described provincial representatives. There is an implication that he would not have imposed a heavy burden of proof in most consultations. There were two facts, he said, making the charter controversy a special case. One was that changing the charter had not been an issue in the last election. "There was not the least probability at the time we were elected, that this matter could come under our consideration." The question had been introduced only after the session had begun, a fact that made the consultation the only evidence of the people's consent. Second was the fundamental nature of the issue submitted to consultation. There was none more basic in constitutional law. The antiproprietary party's reason for holding the consultation had been that changing the charter was so drastic a constitutional step that it needed popular consent. Dickinson thought it even more serious, so important it needed overwhelming consent. "We are not debating how much money we shall raise . . . nor on any thing of the same kind, that arises in the usual parliamentary course of business," he pointed out. "We are now to determine, WHETHER A STEP SHALL BE TAKEN, THAT MAY PRODUCE AN ENTIRE CHANGE OF OUR CONSTI-TUTION." As the people had elected the representatives, Dickinson's constitutional judgment was that on a question that might "endanger this constitution" the representatives "have *no right* to engage in it, without the *almost universal consent of the people,* exprest in the plainest manner." [18]

The Pennsylvania consultation need not be pursued further. It came down to an interpretation of facts, with the two sides finding facts that led to the result they wanted. For Galloway, the probative fact had been that there had been little organized opposition. "We have the Satisfaction to know that our Conduct is supported," he boasted, "and the Measure we are taking [petitioning the crown] approved of, by a very great Majority of the People, and all the independant Lovers of Liberty; not merely from the Petitions to his Majesty, now before the House, but by our mixing among them, during our Recess, and various other Means of consulting their Inclinations." By a majority of the people, he meant a majority of those who petitioned. Dickinson replied that the probative fact was that so few had petitioned. "Can petitions so industriously carried about, and after all the pains taken, signed only by about thirty five hundred persons, be look'd on as the *plainest expressions of the almost universal consent* of the many thousands that fill this Province," he asked. [19]

The significance of the Pennsylvania controversy is not the outcome but the constitutional law. John Dickinson provides striking evidence that before the Revolution American legal thought located sovereign power where it would be located after the Revolution, in the people. We know British legal thought was ambivalent on this point, but the better legal opinion would have held that Dickinson should have dismissed consultation as constitutionally irrelevant. It will not do, however, to imply that in the mother country consultation did not enjoy some niche of respectability. During the Wilkes election dispute, some members who favored Wilkes's expulsion moved that a new election not be held, giving the electors of Middlesex "Time to cool before the next Session." Lord Mulgrave would have used the period for consultation. To have postponed the Middlesex vote, he argued, would have provided members of the Commons

> Time to consult their Constituents during the Summer Recess, and to see how far the late Proceedings had alarmed the Fears or met with the Approbation of the People; whose Opinions are by no means to be slighted in Points that affect their Liberties. . . . If the former Proceedings were approved of, the Ministry would have returned strengthened by the Concurrence of the rest of the Kingdom against the single County of Middlesex. If, on the other hand, they were generally disapproved of, they would have found themselves at liberty by the Orders of the House to rescind their former Resolutions, and follow the Example of their Predecessors, by preferring the Affection to the Obedience of the People.

Mulgrave would have used consultation differently than the colonists. Whether in the Massachusetts excise fight or the Pennsylvania charter controversy, Americans wanted consultation to confer legitimacy on actions by obtaining the consent of the people: the sanction of popular endorsement. Mulgrave sought public opinion. Consultation would reveal what the people outside Middlesex thought of keeping John Wilkes out of Parliament, and once learning the answer members could vote the way they were told.[20]

E I G H T

Practice of Instructions

Consultation in Great Britain was a constitutional anomoly. It added a touch of democracy to the popular branch of an undemocratic government, making representative on a few great issues a system of "representation" that had evolved over the centuries to give government the people's constructive or constitutional "consent" to represent them, but only virtually, not actually. Consultation was also a constitutional transience. It had neither a constitutional past nor a constitutional future. It was an experiment with an ancient institution conducted before Anglo-American constitutionalism was ready to make the concept of representation *actually* representative. It could not be carried to full development because the area of constitutionalism it would have occupied was preempted by the stronger, more ancient, and far more useful accountability by instructions. Because of the constitutional practice of instructions, the technique of consultation, which had no past behind it, did not have the future before it.

It is easy to confuse constitutional techniques. Consultation, after all, could be described as instructions initiated by representatives rather than by the constituencies. And instructions, if one turned them upside down, were the constituencies initiating a consultation by letting the representatives know their unsolicited demands. Either way, the eighteenth-century constitution was seeking to break free of constructive or attenuated representation by developing a methodology for more popular participation by the represented. Owing to its comparatively inherent strengths, the practice of instructions shouldered aside consultation because it was the more democratic, the more effective, and what in the eighteenth century was called the "more constitutional" procedure.

There are two questions that will be answered separately. The first concerns the theory of instructions, what they were, and whether they were a constitutional method of popular influence on representatives either in Great Britain or in the colonies. Quite a different matter was the legal effect of instructions, whether they were merely advisory or were binding commands from the electors to those they had elected.

It might be thought that, because of George III's effective use of "influence" to control the House of Commons and the consequent deemphasis of political parties, instructions would have become less important rather than more in the 1760s. They previously had been used primarily as a tool of political opposition, most notably by the tories during their decades out of power under Walpole and Newcastle. Often the representatives drafted the instructions themselves as a means of framing issues embarrassing to the administration and of rallying support among the gentry and oligarchy of the countryside. That tradition continued after 1760, carried to a different, much more numerous section of the population by John Wilkes and the London radicals. The Wilkes phenomenon had the appearance of opening politics to greater numbers and of making representatives responsible to a wider constituency. Later, when the Yorkshire movement sought ways to publicize its demands for a more democratic, representative franchise, one effective technique it utilized was to frame the constitutional case for parliamentary reform in the guise of instructions from the people.[1]

Another cause for the increase of instructions may have been the Act of 1774, codifying customary practice by providing that members of the Commons did not have to reside in their constituencies. Realization that representatives were now more likely than ever to be strangers possibly caused some constituencies, especially commercial boroughs, to communicate by instructions. Edmund Burke, who would make instructions a major constitutional issue during the 1770s, was a true absentee, visiting the city he represented, Bristol, only twice after being elected.[2]

The most salient reason for the increase of instructing during the age of the American Revolution was constitutional controversy. Certainly this was true for the colonies, where the revolutionary crises spread the practice of instructions into all parts of the continent, making it one of the most effective constitutional tools the whigs had for influencing public opinion and publicizing the constitutional issues. In Great Britain, the constitutional crisis giving impetus to instructions was the growing influence of the king. Instructions not only informed the public of the constitutional issues, but they also served as a constitutional counterbalance to the crown by adding the appearance of popular weight to the representative branch.[3]

THEORY OF INSTRUCTIONS

A preliminary historical lesson needs to be stressed as it sometimes has been misstated. Instructions were not new to the age of the American Revolution or even to the eighteenth century. They had been known in the seventeenth century and earlier, blessed by the sanction of Lord Coke and given particular authority by the earl of Shaftesbury during the exclusion crisis. They had been a weapon of opposition in the middle years of the eighteenth century and sometimes a strategy for marshalling support for the whig governments. In 1733, the earl of Bath boasted that the "Right of *Petitioning* and *Instructing*" was "warranted by the Practice of all Ages," and, in 1769, Lord Mulgrave described the people as reaching "the Ears of their Representatives by the old Constitutional Method of Instructions."[4]

In the colonies, the practice of voting instructions commenced with the very beginning of New England. In 1641, the Massachusetts General Court asked the towns to instruct their representatives on two issues, one of which was the method of elections. Plymouth had a statute providing that town meetings should hear from their representatives what had been done in the legislature and vote "instructions for any other busines[s] they should have donne." Dover, New Hampshire, instructed its representative every year after 1658, and Boston did so almost annually after 1721. South of New England, aside from the colony of West Jersey, which had a clause in its organic laws authorizing instructions and implying that representatives were accountable for obeying them, there are few records of instructions until 1765 and the coming of the revolutionary crisis. The explanation is again due in part to the structure of town meetings. Colonies without town meetings lacked the constitutional apparatus to debate and vote instructions with the ease and authority that the New England electoral unit could. The same was true for the mother country. English counties seldom instructed their representatives. Corporations, especially London, with its organized liverymen or common council, were the source of most British instructions. When counties did instruct, it was often through "the high sheriff and the grand jury" or "the high sheriff, grand jurors, and gentlemen, assembled at the assizes." That was the same institution that the American colonies south of New England turned to when they began instructing their legislators about the Stamp Act and other parliamentary legislation. They did it through mass meetings most frequently, but grand jury presentments were also employed to give a color of constitutionality to what would otherwise have been pronouncements without formal legal sanction.[5]

The British had a less developed theory of instructions than did the Americans. One reason was that colonial instructions often contained a statement or preamble of constitutional justification. Much of the extant British theorizing, by contrast, was in pamphlets, especially in arguments why people should exercise the "right" to instruct. Instructions were said to be the people "offering their Opinions," people "determined to act the part of free-born Englishmen," by pointing out to their representatives what they believed was in the public interest. "These are Means which the Constitution of this Country has left in the Hands of every Man to express his Sense of public Affairs," a commentator on the Middlesex election dispute wrote in 1768, "and these are the most proper, nay, the only Means by which (in a well-regulated Government) the People should seek for a Redress of their Grievances." More important, another commentator argued, instructions compensated a bit for what was in some cases a defect in the constitution: "that the Powers vested in our Representatives are too independent of the People. The only Remedy to prevent the Abuse of these Powers which the People can apply, is, by their giving their Representatives Instructions how to behave in all Points of National Concern." Good and constitutional instructions, moreover, "would make the meanest, the most ignorant of the People Judges [of] how far their Members have acted consistently with the Interests of the People, which ought to be the Rule of all Government."[6]

There was a more developed philosophy explaining American instructional theory partly because the colonists—at least in New England—thought instructions more constitutional than did the British and much more binding on the representatives. Writing instructions for 1764, Samuel Adams told Boston's representatives that voters "delegated to you the power of acting in their publick Concerns in general as your own prudence shall direct you." He immediately added, however, "Always reserving to themselves the Constitutional Right of expressing their mind and giving you such Instruction upon particular Matters as they at any Time shall Judge proper." More than that, the representatives should welcome the effort. "The giving Instructions to Representatives in Affairs of public Concern," the voters of Portsmouth, New Hampshire, told their representatives, "Is a Privilege which must be highly valued by every true Patriot, as giving each Representative an Opportunity of knowing the Minds of his Constituents, to which he

ought to pay great Regard." It was not that they doubted the representatives' principles or integrity, "but we apprehend it will be a very pleas-
ing Reflection that the Resolution[s] you shall form, are bottomed on
the concurrent Sentiments of your Constituents."[7]

Education and propagation of ideas were other reasons for instructions, not only the education or persuasion of the representatives. This
purpose was why instructions became a major weapon in the colonial
whig defense against parliamentary rule. "It is a very common practice
for this town to instruct their representatives," Samuel Adams wrote in
a private letter referring to Boston, "which among other good purposes
serves to communicate their sentiments and spirit to the other towns,
and may be looked upon as fresh appeals to the world."[8]

There were questions raised from time to time about the legality of
instructions, not just their nature and whether representatives had to
read or obey them, but whether it was legal to draft them. No definitive
rulings were promulgated, but as a general proposition it might be said
that answers depended on which part of the British empire was instructing. In Ireland, instructions were common but could have been both
unconstitutional and illegal.[9] In England, they were legal but of doubt-
ful constitutionality. In the North American colonies and in Scotland,
they were both constitutional and legal.[10]

The argument that instructions in Great Britain were "not agreeable
to our Constitution" was not wholly persuasive. The contention was
based primarily on the fact that the constitution provided other methods, such as petition and consultation. Petitioning, after all, was the
better-known constitutional "and legal Way for the People to inform
their Representatives either of Grievances under which they suffered,
or of Benefits which they might expect." Petitioning and consultations
were also more constitutional than instructions as they did not "take
away the Freedom of the House of Commons," that is, its independence.
Baron Rivers protested that, "[i]f the opinions of all the electors in Great
Britain, even in their present pretended inadequate proportion, could,
by any magick, be let loose in the House of Commons, what confusion
would not ensue? and what end could be answered, either by the deliberations, or the conclusions of such assembly?"[11]

Rivers's objection could not have been raised in New England, where
the town meeting allowed instructors to speak with one voice. That was
the constitutional deficiency of British instructions. Except for borough
corporations and, to a limited extent, grand juries, it was often unclear

who was instructing. Petitions were ad hoc affairs, purporting to speak only for those signing them. Consultations were also different from instructions in this respect. Their effect depended on who was consulted, a choice generally at the discretion of the representative.

It is quite likely that many in the mother country who questioned the constitutionality of instructions did not doubt their legality. Assertions of the legality of instructions were as strong in old as in New England. Instructions were called "our indisputable Right" by London's Common Council, "the undoubted right of all constituents" by the freemen of Norwich, and "our undoubted right" by the mayor, jurats, and commonalty of Maidstone. There are too many similar statements from colonial New England to allow even a sampling. If anything, the right in the colonies was placed on firmer legal grounds than it was in Great Britain. Boston claimed that the right of instructing was "sacred and unalienable." The voters of Bellingham near the Rhode Island line put the right on the strongest legal premises. Instructing, they asserted, "has been a long Custom, and is now become Common Law." But the most convincing constitutional justification was formulated in instructions from Lancaster—whether the borough or the county is not clear—in the mother country. "It is, Gentlemen," Lancaster boasted, "a Happiness to this Country, that we have Representatives to whom we dare to talk at this rate, who know we have a Right to talk so, and will receive our Instructions with Pleasure." Put another way, instructions were a manifestation of liberty.[12]

There is no need to catalog all the issues raised by instructions. It is enough to note the earl of Bath's belief that instructions "may be, of singular Use to the Cause of *Liberty.*"[13] Of course there were mundane political problems mentioned in instructions, but that practice was rare. Instructions on both sides of the Atlantic almost always concerned serious questions of constitutional import.

In Great Britain, it is surprising how often the institutional independence of the House of Commons was the topic of instructions. What instructors most often sought were frequent elections, disqualification of members holding commissions or pensions from the crown, and that grievances be redressed before money was granted.[14] In Massachusetts, some concept of liberty was invariably on the minds of instructors. In a typical set of instructions, the voters of Worcester demanded that their representative vote to end chattel slavery and Latin grammar schools. The teaching of Latin probably would have nothing to do with liberty in most places. In colonial Massachusetts, there was a connection. Latin schools prevented people "from attaining such a Degree of English Learning as is necessary to retain the Freedom of any State."[15]

The vast majority of extant instructions relate to the constitutional controversy with the mother country. Every town in New England acted as if it not only had a right to interpret the constitution but also had a duty to proclaim what it thought. The instructions of even isolated, inland New England towns often had preambles filled with constitutional principles intended for more than propaganda. In an age of sparse settlements, vast distances, and slow communications, the votes of small, agrestic towns from Maine to Connecticut's southern line revealed a remarkably unified set of constitutional values. More than that, they told their representatives that their leadership was effective. On occasion, they might even instruct them how to vote. That certainly was the idea of the Massachusetts House of Representatives when it asked the towns of the rebelling colony their will on the most vital question of the age:

> *Resolved,* As the Opinion of this House, that the inhabitants of each town in this Colony, ought in full Meeting warned for that Purpose, to advise the Person or Persons who shall be chosen to Represent them in the next General Court, whether that if the honourable Congress should, for the Safety of the said Colonies, declare them Independent of the Kingdom of *Great-Britain,* they the said Inhabitants will solemnly engage with their Lives and Fortunes to Support the Congress in the Measure.

It was the most momentous decision of the century, and to meet it the Massachusetts representatives utilized two techniques of representative accountability. They consulted their constituents and asked them for instructions.[16]

FORCE OF INSTRUCTIONS

There was another distinction between instructions in the mother country and instructions in the colonies. In Great Britain, instructions were more likely to be the instrument of the opposition, used to compound an embarrassment suffered by the administration such as the 1733 excise crisis, the 1753 Jew Bill debacle, or the 1756 loss of Minorca. In North America, instructions were almost always the tool of the political majority, those wanting the Stamp Act repealed, the Townshend duties boycotted, or the Tea Act resisted. Different origins led to different expectations. Reed Browning has observed that "[t]o instruct was to bind," which, if true, was more true for the Americans than the British.[17] Certainly, there was a greater support for the concept of binding instructions in the colonies. Those who said instructions were not binding most likely belonged to a colonial political minority, especially to the imperialist party in the revolutionary controversy.[18]

It would be unwise to be guided by the instructions themselves. They speak a language of command not supported by constitutional law. "We require you," Devon instructions ordered. "[W]e do therefore insist and require you," York's common council told that city's representatives. "[W]e expected and do still expect that you will speak our Sense in every case when we shall expressly declare it, or when you can by other means discover it," the representatives of Orange County, North Carolina, were instructed. "This is our notion of the Duty of Representatives and the Rights of Electors." The trouble was that it might not be the notion of the representatives. In the colonies, they might agree that it was their duty to obey instructions. In the mother country, representatives most likely would have a different sense of duty.[19]

One difficulty lay with constitutional mechanics: who was authorized to instruct, and how could that authorization be certified? Unless instructions were voted by a legally warned town meeting or by the corporation of a British city, how would the representative know whether he was being instructed by the constituency or by a random group of perhaps eight or fifteen gentlemen? What were the rights of "the *noninstructing* part" of the constituency? Even should 99 percent of the electors instruct, if the rule was that the representative was bound to obey, would that rule destroy "the *Constitutional Right* which the remaining" 1 percent should enjoy in "the freedom" of his and their vote?[20]

It was typical of eighteenth-century constitutional law that, although such questions were frequently raised, there was no governmental agency empowered to answer them. It may be that few British representatives cared. If they disagreed with instructions, there were always grounds for disregarding them. The constitutional incapacity to answer these questions is not surprising; eighteenth-century British government was a riddle of customary practices defying adjective analysis. Yet it is important to understand that the law's imprecision probably had an effect on constitutional development. Had instructions both procedural competence and legal persuasiveness, eighteenth-century Britain might have experienced a greater degree of participatory democracy, at least on significant national issues. As it was, the most democratic part of the empire was New England, not alone for the wide franchise so often stressed by historians, but because the instrumentality of the town meeting provided instructions both a constitutional voice and the appearance of the force of law. The town meeting, after all, elected the representative. The town and its annual meeting was his constituency.

Outside New England, the force of instructions was left to constitutional theory and political practicalities. The stronger constitutional case by far was against their binding force.[21] The arguments that were made on both sides of the issue are worth summary discussion, for, although quite unsurprising, they were one of the very few occasions that eighteenth-century constitutional theorists had to consider the nature and function of representation.[22] What they said about the binding force of instructions depended largely on whether they thought the decisions of representatives were independent and autonomous or responsible and accountable.

People saying instructions were mandatory generally thought that representatives were the trustees or agents of the constituencies. They were intrigued by the illogic of "*servants* being greater than their masters." "If the members of the house of commons are not obliged to regard the instructions of their constituents," the *London Magazine* argued in the most comprehensive evaluation of the question, "the people of this country chuse a set of despots every seven years, and are as perfect slaves as the Turks, excepting the few months of a general election." The strongest British theory, very much in the minority, contended that the electors had the power "of directing every Thing which your Representatives, in a House of Commons, should actually do for the Prosperity of this People." The strongest American statement, written of course in New England, rationalized the force of instructions from the concept of consent as well as from the concept of representation. From the earliest period of settlement, a "Freeborn American" told the *Boston Gazette*, constituents had "a right on all occasions, when they think proper, to instruct them how they are to act; which instructions they are oblig'd to obey, tho' it should be against their own judgment; because by their appointment they are to represent their constituents, and act in their stead; otherwise it could properly never be said, the consent of the whole was obtained."[23]

If arguments for binding instructions seem more persuasive in this century of democratic premises, arguments that the representative was not bound to represent every whim or desire were more persuasive in the eighteenth century, and people making that contention certainly believed that they stated the strongest case. It was said that binding instructions deprived a legislature of its essence as a deliberative body, with debate in one arena and decision in another, the representative hearing or considering only one side; that under binding instructions the representative becomes a mere cipher, without judgment or, worse, without constitutional function; and that binding instructions carried democratic implications that could destroy the liberty of British balanced government.[24]

There is no need to dwell on the expected. The salient aspect of the case against binding instructions is that it was based almost entirely on arguments more obvious in the eighteenth century than today, arguments related to institutional perceptions of eighteenth-century British representation. For most of the opposition to instructions, binding or nonbinding, stemmed from constitutional values peculiar to the time: the "independency" of the representative, the autonomy of the legislature, the integrity of universal representation, and the balance of the balanced constitution.[25]

The simplest argument was that the representative was independent. It was the opposite of the concept of binding instructions. After all, if instructions were obligatory, the representative was not independent but was an "attorney," a "trustee," a "servant," or one of the other appellations of subordination considered earlier. It would mean that there was no "free *Inquiry*," no "Liberty of Judgment." The representative might be an agent, but he was not an independent agent if he were not as free of the people as he was of the crown. "I remember on my part, that to your independent voice, I owe my seat in parliament," Lord Percival told his constituency of Westminster; "on yours, you will not forget that I ought to be independent there."[26]

The objection most "constitutional" by eighteenth-century premises was the autonomy of the House. To bind a representative by instructions, a Walpolean pamphlet pointed out, was the same as "*transferring the Legislative Power from the Parliament to the People, and thus changing a happy well poised Constitution.*" To be dependent on the people, on democracy, would be as fatal to liberty as for the Commons to be dependent on the crown. It would even be worse, Attorney General John Willes claimed. The king, at least, could be expected to have the general interest at heart, "whereas the people of any county, city, or borough . . . may often be induced to give instructions directly contrary to the interest of their country."[27]

The most frequently stated case against binding instructions was the rule of universal representation. A member of Parliament, John Jebb

explained, "ought to consider himself as the Representative of the Kingdom at large; and therefore as not under any obligation to obey the
instructions of the County, or Borough which returns him." The objection to the representative being obliged "to obey the Instructions of the
particular District, or the Borough, which returns him" must not be misinterpreted as antidemocratic or a repudiation of the people's right to
consent. It was, rather, a matter of maintaining the institutional purity
of the balanced constitution, a purity that could be obtained not by increasing the democratic influence to counter the debalancing weight of
aristocracy or monarchy but by restoring the balance of the ancient constitution. "Were the undue influence of the Crown abolished, an equal
Representation established, and the duration of Parliaments reduced to
the ancient annual period," Jebb contended, "the compliance of the
Representative, with every reasonable wish of his constituents, would be
sufficiently secured."[28]

Two Cases

The legality of binding instructions was an easy question for British constitutional lawyers to resolve in the eighteenth century. It was a much
more difficult political matter for representatives. Some may have ignored instructions, but many others refusing to obey were very careful
to give no more offense than necessary.[29] "When I differ from your sentiments," Lord Percival told Westminster in reply to instructions, "I shall
do it with great reluctance, and then only when I am convinced, that
your *true interest* must exort it from me." Occasionally, fine distinctions
were drawn, members telling their constituents that they felt bound to
obey on matters affecting the local economy but that on national or constitutional questions they had to follow their own judgments. Lord Mulgrave cut the distinction along representational lines. "Though I may
think myself at liberty, in great national Measures, to follow my own
Judgment solely," he reasoned, "in Questions affecting the *substantial
Rights* or *Privileges of every individual Elector* or *Freeman* in *this Kingdom*, I
should think myself bound to obey implicitly the Instructions of those
who sent me."[30]

Mulgrave was writing about the Wilkes election contest and was saying
that on issues concerning freedom of elections his electors had their
interests so much involved that he had to obey their wishes. A representative who voted against the ministry on the Wilkes affair and lost his
seat was John Hope, member for Linlithgowshire. He had been elected
"for the honour of the family-interest in the county" through the influ-

ence of his uncle, the earl of Hopetoun, who also provided a substantial stipend. Hope not only believed that instructions should be obeyed but wanted to make them binding by statute. He received none about Wilkes, however, and learned that he had made a serious mistake when his father came to London to tell him that he ought "to have done nothing without" the "advice and approbation" of his political supporters. Hope wrote a cousin that he should have asked his patron for instructions and then obeyed them.

> [I]f my Lord your father should find, that in my conduct I am going contrary to his political principles, it certainly will be just that I should resign to somebody who, in conscience, can vote entirely with him. . . . I think myself responsible for my public conduct to the whole people of Great Britain, and that is what all the representatives of the Commons *ought to be;*—but in effect they *are not* so; for where property is, power will be also; and, it is but equitable, that your father should have his additional share in the legislature, as well as the other peers.

Hope was as good as his theory of accountability. Within a year he was out of Parliament and had lost his stipend.[31]

Edmund Burke's theory of accountability was quite the opposite of Hope's. He wanted representatives responsible to their constituents by being constitutionally independent of them. Burke was willing to serve the local constituency, representing its interests to the administration and guiding beneficial legislation through the House. "But *authoritative* instructions," he protested, "*mandates* issued, which the member is bound blindly and implicitly to obey, to vote, and to argue for, though contrary to the clearest conviction of his judgment and conscience,— these are things utterly unknown to the laws of this land, and which arise from a fundamental mistake of the whole order and tenor of our Constitution."[32]

In 1778, when Burke represented Bristol, Ireland sought the repeal of statutory restraints on its trade, which was depressed because of the American war. Burke supported Irish relief, and Bristol did not, nor did it favor bills for insolvent debtors and Catholic relief, which Burke also voted for. When the next election came, Burke went down to Bristol to explain his views on both the commercial rights of Ireland and the independence of representation. After a canvass of two days, he concluded that his candidacy was hopeless, and he declined the poll.

Two theories of representation came into conflict with Burke at Bristol: the representation of the constituencies and the independence of

universal representation. "When the Irish bills were agitated," a correspondent wrote of Burke to the *Gentleman's Magazine,* "he considered
first the interest of his native country, and conducted himself through
the whole of the matter more like a representative for Cork or Dublin,
than as a member for a trading city in England." That was the perspective of the accountable, instructable representative. Burke's perspective
was that of the autonomous, independent representative when he told
Bristol, "I did not obey your instructions: No. I conformed to the instructions of truth and nature, and maintained your interests against
your opinions, with a constancy that became me. . . . I am to look indeed
to your opinions; but to such opinions as you and I *must* have five years
hence. . . . I knew that you choose me . . . to be a pillar of the state, and
not a weathercock on the top of the edifice." [33]

There is no need in the twentieth century to agree with Edmund
Burke, but he does deserve to be understood if we are to appreciate the
concept of representation in the age of the American Revolution. "To
espouse without reserve the cause of Burke against Bristol," Sir Ernest
Barker admonished, "would be, in effect, to deny the cause of democracy." But Burke's case against instructions cannot be resolved by democratic values alone, although, as he was defending the independence
of the House of Commons, he was, in that strange, legalistic, eighteenth-
century way, defending the democratic voice in government. True, one
reason he could not obey the commands of the people was that their
judgment was not equal to the judgment of their betters. "To govern
according to the sense and agreeably to the interests of the people is a
great and glorious object of government," Burke contended. "[T]his object cannot be obtained but through the medium of popular election,
and popular election is a mighty evil." As he told the House of Commons, to obey instructions against their own judgment "we should basely
and scandalously betray, the people, who are not capable of this service
by nature, nor in any instance called to it by the constitution." [34]

The constitution's call was what shaped Burke's theory. He had, Linda
Colley recently remarked, a limited "perception of the extra-parliamen-
tary nation." [35] Maybe so, but that was precisely the constitutional point.
He was heeding the constitution rather than the people, for he was
aware that democracy was a force that might unbalance the constitution.

Burke's constitutional position had been anticipated by a 1740
pamphlet referring to "this anti-constitutional Practice of instructing." [36]
To increase the strength of democracy would endanger the true liberty
of the mixed constitution. The constituencies, after all, were not the

people. The people consented to government not directly but by constitutional representation, and representatives could be constitutional only if independent.

Members of the Commons who heard Charles James Fox knew that he spoke the sense of constitutional liberty when he reminded them that, "with respect to our duty as representatives of the people, it naturally follows, that we are by no means to act against our own judgment merely to gratify their ill humour or their caprice."[37] There were eighteenth-century men, especially in America, willing to run risks to constitutional liberty by making representation responsive to the electorate through binding instructions.[38] In Great Britain, instructions were an eighteenth-century constitutional potential that never took hold. Edmund Burke saw to it that the practice of instructing did not survive into the nineteenth century. The balanced constitution remained as a check on democracy as well as on the crown until constitutional rule was replaced by the arbitrary authority of a sovereign parliament. Only then did democracy become the dominant branch, but through universal manhood suffrage, not by the practice of binding instructions. In the United States, a different course was spun. The arbitrary will of democracy became the theoretical political objective, but its operation was tempered by the ancient English rule of law institutionalized in a supreme judiciary.

Corruption of Representation

A constitutional nightmare dominated eighteenth-century constitutional thought: the return of Cromwellian arbitrariness dressed in the trappings of the balanced constitution. The institutions and procedures of British limited government would remain in place to be honored by form but destroyed in substance. The balanced constitution would become an apparition, with the balancing weights removed, no longer able to check, restrain, or limit. British government would cease to be a *constitutional* government, except in appearance.

We might think that, with the new weights of consultations and instructions, the Wilkes movement, and the shift of the predominance of property from the aristocracy to the commonalty, the counterpoise unbalancing the tripartite constitution in the 1760s would be democracy in the House of Commons. Had eighteenth-century people thought of the future, they might have worried about a democratic Commons: the arbitrary, sovereign, unrestrained Commons that would emerge in the nineteenth century. The eighteenth-century British constitutional mind did think toward the future, but built on the past, postulating the hazards of today on dangers encountered yesterday. It was the crown that theorists worried about, not only because the crown had threatened liberty before, but because it was to check the crown that the constitution had been balanced. If the equilibrium came undone, constitutional experience warned that the weight would slide toward the king.

By the age of the American Revolution, constitutionalists no longer feared the king would use the army to close Parliament, abrogate the constitution, and govern by arbitrary decree. The rule of law was too powerful in Great Britain. The absolutism of France and Turkey could never cross the English Channel. Far more likely, as the bishop of Saint David's, Anthony Ellys, warned, the crown would slowly, perhaps imperceptibly, take "the liberties of the nation entirely in its power" without in the least altering "the outward circumstances of our constitution."[1]

Everyone who could read in the eighteenth century was familiar with some aspect of Ellys's warning; it had been repeated so many times. Perhaps the earl of Chesterfield's version was the best known. He had uttered it in the House of Lords in 1741, speaking against crown pensioners serving in Parliament. What he said was reprinted occasionally over the next decades, including appearances in British magazines in the year of the Declaration of Independence.

> Our constitution consists in the two houses of parliament being a *check upon the crown,* as well as upon *each other.* If that check should ever be removed; if the crown should by *corrupt* means, by *places, pensions,* and *bribes,* get the absolute direction of our two houses of parliament, our constitution will from that moment be destroyed. There would be no occasion for the crown to proceed any further, it would be ridiculous to lay aside the *forms of parliament,* for, under that shadow, our king would be more absolute, and govern more arbitrarily than he could do without it.

There was no mystery to the sequence of predictable events. The constitution would look the same yet be utterly different. Power would shift because the check of tripartite balance would yield to the arbitrariness of royal domination. There would be no revolution, no coup d'état, no wrenching dismemberment of the body politic. "[A]s Experience has long since convinc'd every one of the Impossibility of establishing arbitrary Power in its first Instances by Force, in this Country," the earl of Marchmont had written the year before Chesterfield spoke, "so has it suggested . . . the sole Method of introducing Slavery here, that is, by secret Influence and Corruption." [2]

The probative words were *influence* and *corruption.* Secrecy was no factor. Everything would be done in the open because everything would be by constitutional forms. But crown influence through corruption projected one of the most gravid definitions of representation in Great Britain during the age of the American Revolution, furnishing one more argument why colonial whigs could never be "represented" in the British Parliament, even if they had been permitted to elect directly an equal number of members of their own.

CORRUPTION

"From the time of Walpole to the American Revolution the House of Commons was at its worst as a freely chosen representation of the country," according to Edward Porritt. He was using *freely chosen* as those words were meant in twentieth-century Great Britain or in the eighteenth-century colonies. Porritt was also delineating the corruption of the electorate. It was but another facet of the representation definition separating eighteenth-century American constitutional ideals from eighteenth-century British political reality. Electors in the mother country made "a trade of voting," John Cartwright charged. Perhaps half the members of the House of Commons during the age of the American Revolution were like John Hope, owing, in one degree or another, their seats to patrons. "[A]lmost all the noblemen's sons in England, who are of a proper age, are members of the lower house," the *London Magazine* estimated, and "many commoners have obtained their seats there by the interest and countenance of some powerful nobleman."[3]

The conclusion is not just that the British definition of *election* was again different from the American. It is also that there was one more unbridgeable dichotomy between the two perceptions of "representation." Because of the way British elections were conducted—"intoxication, bribery, perjury"—Robert Robinson observed in 1782, "[c]andidates lose all reverence for the people, their constituents, and the people lose all that respect and reverence for representatives."[4]

Historical research may now teach us that corruption of elections was not as extensive as the opposition thought in the eighteenth century, but that is not the relevant point. What people then believed was what shaped the perception of representation, and that perception made virtual or constructive representation appear even less representative, especially to Americans looking back across the ocean. John Sawbridge spoke from that perspective in 1772 when he told the Commons that "men elected into this House, no longer consider themselves as representatives of the people, but as persons who have purchased a beneficial lease; which they are by all, and by any means to turn most to their own advantage."[5]

We need not dwell on electoral corruption. It was not a major ingredient of eighteenth-century influence, except in those cases in which franchises were in the hands of the treasury, the admiralty, or some other agency of the administration. The corruption that made representation even less representative than it otherwise would have been was a corruption characterized less by bribery than by pensions. The word, Edward Wynne explained, "is commonly used to denote pecuniary influence alone." Also called "influence," it was a financial relationship leading to loss of that cherished British trait of the true representative, independence. In its most theoretical sense, *influence* meant that the representative could not be autonomous. In its practical sense, it meant, in the words of David Hartley, that "Parliament becomes the representative of the Minister, and not of the people."[6]

Influence was a derogatory word if you were in the opposition. If you supported the administration, influence was the hinge on which the door of government swung. Of course the governor of Massachusetts was powerless "when he had not a single place in his gift," George Byng told the Commons. "Men look up to their superiors, and obey their directions according to the emoluments received from them; and when once there is no dependence in it, there will be no obedience." That idea was supposed to account for why, as "Cassius" explained, "we have in the nation only one set of men that pretend to the appearance of a party. These are those that adhere to the Court in every question." "If we ask who the friends of Government . . . are?" someone wrote in the *Political Register*, "the true answer is, all persons who, enjoying place or pension, are obliged to support whatever scheme is projected by the Crown, or proposed by the Ministry."[7]

Figures vary, but there is no need for precision. Rough estimates tell the story as dramatically as exact statistics. In a typical House of Commons during the age of the American Revolution, about half the members owed something to the crown: either their election, a sinecure, a pension, stipends, profits, honors, or a position of political power. These included perhaps as many as one hundred army and navy officers. The House of Lords was not significantly different. In the parliament of 1774, seventy peers held government offices, some of them new positions created or multiplied during the reign of George III.[8]

It is well to think of more than politics and power, of more than a shift of constitutional balance. There was also the despair of the "country" or the non- or anticourt party, the old established gentry, fearful that the weight of representation was slipping away as new money and new uses of money dissolved the familiar constitutional structure of counterpoised authority and submission. The gentry of Great Britain sensed the change not only because discernibly inferior men were supplanting the naturally superior but also because the representation that had been their constitutional security no longer was an assured check in the tripartite constitutional balance.[9]

American colonists may not have shared the social depression, but they understood the constitutional displacement. The military members of the House of Commons were "no more than *animated Puppets*, directed by the arbitrary Hand of our great *State Juggler,*" a New Yorker wrote, explaining why Parliament had jeopardized American rights by enacting the Stamp Act. And when Charles Turner warned Massachusetts legislators of "the known prevalence of bribery and venality in the land from which our Ancestors fled," he was not preaching morals but delineating one more reason why Parliament could not represent New Englanders.[10]

IMBALANCE OF CORRUPTION

"If, in Ages to come . . . all the Posts of Government should be given to Parliament-Men, or the Representatives of the People, what will become of our so much boasted liberty?" a New Yorker asked in 1732. By the year of the Declaration of Independence, there were people on both sides of the Atlantic who believed that the question had been answered. The Commons of Britain had become like the Commons of Ireland— "the *Representatives* of the *minister,* and the *Misrepresentatives* of the PEOPLE." A House of Commons under the control of the prime minister, the *London Magazine* lamented, was "the greatest danger to which our happy constitution now lies exposed."[11]

If the Commons could no longer perform its constitutional function as an independent check on arbitrary power, the constitutional question was whether Great Britain could still be said to have a "representative" government.[12] There were contrasting perspectives. Commentators less attuned to popular representation and more concerned with stable government thought influence necessary to preserve Parliament from chaos. Interestingly, both George III and Jeremy Bentham used the same word, *stagnation,* to describe the constitutionalism of corruption. Without influence, "the business of the state . . . would stagnate." There were two separate destabilizing forces that influence restrained, the private interest of factions and the potential flow of democracy. The parliamentary leader Henry Pelham warned that if the king did not utilize corruption "his government would be tore to pieces by a factious parliament, or he would be obliged to carry on without any parliament at all," and the American loyalist James Chalmers warned that, "without such controul in the Crown, our Constitution would immediately degenerate into Democracy." No one better summed up the constitutional theory of controlling representation "by the golden folder of corruption" than did "Julian" when he wrote of "melting down the democratic power of the constitution into the influence of the crown."[13]

Fear of anarchy was one constitutional perspective; fear of arbitrary power was the opposite. From the more popular perspective, royal corruption threatened *"legal* slavery" by "a *mercenary band"* executing "the will of *one* man." The constitutional forms remained unchanged, but the balance of the balanced constitution was undone. "For how can there be any *equilibrium,* when every weight is thrown into one scale," Joseph Priestley asked? "This influence," the duke of Richmond answered, "totally annihilate[s] every check which the constitution has framed to prevent the arbitrary will of the sovereign from becoming the sole power of the state." The role of representation was completely altered, "Junius" contended. The original balance had protected the representatives from the prerogative in order that they, in turn, could protect liberty and property. Now influence, not prerogativism, was to be feared, and constitutionalism had been set on its head. "Formerly it was the interest of the people, that the privileges of parliament should be left unlimited and undefined. At present it is not only their interest, but . . . necessary to the preservation of the constitution, that the privileges of parliament should be strictly ascertained, and confined within the narrowest bounds." Lord Chatham apparently agreed with Junius. He knew of one case in which influence had manipulated privilege to override freedom of representation. "Were the Commons not absolute slaves," he asserted, "they could never have rendered the very name of Parliament ridiculous by carrying on a constant war against Mr. Wilkes."[14]

The country or anticourt perspective contemplated a gloomy constitutional scene. "The forms of our free government have outlasted the ends for which they were instituted, and have become a mere mockery of the people for whose benefit they should operate," "Americus" lamented to John Wesley. Certainly that was the perspective that American whigs had of the mother country at the time that they rebelled. The British constitution had once been the boast of the people, Samuel Langdon, pastor of Portsmouth, New Hampshire, and president of Harvard College, preached a month after the battle of Lexington. "But in what does the British nation now glory?—In a mere shadow of its ancient political system, . . . in the many artifices to stretch the prerogatives of the crown beyond all constitutional bounds, and make the king an absolute monarch, while the people are deluded with a mere phantom of liberty." That was one of the themes of revolution: the constitution of representative government remained, but it was representative no more.[15]

CONSTITUTIONAL REACTION

The Americans had a case because the British had a case. The difference was that the British solution was less obvious than the American. For centuries, people in the mother country had feared the crown, not Parliament. Only in recent years had some of the apprehension shifted to the House of Commons because of Parliament's recent pretensions of sovereignty. James Burgh warned that it could be a mistake to think that the danger could come from a "representative" Parliament.

> For a parliament is not (as a king) *naturally* hostile to liberty. If ever a parliament comes to oppose, or injure the people, it must be in consequence of an *unnatural* influence acting in it. Therefore our modern male-contents seem to be in a wrong pursuit. To retrench the power of their *representatives*, would be lessening their *own* power. To break through the corrupt influence of the *court* over their representatives, would be making them truly their representatives. Take away court-influence, and the 558 [members of the Commons] will of course pursue the interest of their country, as any other set of gentlemen would do, because their *own* will be involved in it, when they have no places or pensions to indemnify them.[16]

Burgh's constitutional theory deserves scrutiny. It is the opposite of the American solution and is, in fact, the reform that the British will carry out in the nineteenth century. It did not curtail sovereignty; it made sovereignty representative. There is a paradox, however. The Americans would move away from the doctrine of legislative sovereignty and the British toward it, but to move toward it the British first tried to move back.

British constitutionalists in the age of the American Revolution proposed two reforms to curb royal influence: more frequent elections and the exclusion of placemen from the House of Commons. "I consider the many calamities which we at present labour under, as resulting from long Parliaments," Alderman Bull told the House; "under their sanction and influence corruption has been reduced to a system." He was against the Septennial Act, for Parliaments were believed less representative when elections were held every seven years rather than each year or at least every three. It was mainly a matter of accountability.[17] One way to state the argument for shorter parliaments was that they were more "representative."[18] What must be noted, however, is that many proponents of frequent elections, especially in the age of the American Revolution, favored annual or triennial elections to make the House of Commons more independent, not to make them what in the twentieth century would be called more representative. If there were annual elections, a New Yorker explained, "[t]he Ministry could not afford . . . to offer a Bribe high enough to corrupt their honesty, or to make it their Interest to sell and betray their Constituents; for as soon as they had engaged one Parliament in their Service, the speedy Expiration of it would make them liable to lose their Creatures." [19]

The second reform was to restrict membership in the representation. This, too, was occasionally put in terms of freeing representation. "Placemen and Pensioners sitting in your House can no ways be thought impartial Representatives of a free People" and therefore should be disqualified, the voters of Lichfield argued.[20] But, again, the more frequently stated benefit was institutional integrity. "As the Freedom and Independency of the respective Branches of the Legislature on each other is absolutely necessary for the Maintainance of those Rights and Liberties entrusted to them" was why the voters of the county of Aberdeen wanted a place bill enacted. The voters of Hereford wanted one so "that the Freedom and Independency of Parliaments may be better restor'd and preserv'd" and the voters of the county of Gloucester so "that our Electors and Representatives may be free and independent, our Choice frequent, and our Returns just." A number of statutes were enacted, forbidding placemen or pensioners, or certain classes of them, from meddling at elections or from serving as members of Parliament. They never operated to the satisfaction of their sponsors, for there were always categories not covered—military officers or "people who held lucrative contracts under the government"—and in an age of corruption they were too readily ignored or distinguished away by an administration needing influence more than it favored reform.[21]

It is not necessary to decide whether reformers demanding frequent elections and place acts were seeking to strengthen the constitutional concept of representation or the constitutional independence of the House of Commons. It can be agreed that to one degree or another they favored both ends. But what we should not overlook is that the constitutionalists and other people on both sides of the Atlantic who paid attention to the debate did not often think of the matter in terms of more representative representation. In the parlance of the eighteenth century, the process was more familiarly described as "the Restoration of the Constitution." [22] The concept of the ancient or timeless constitution may have been an ideal that was obliterated by the reality of ministerial government, but for constitutionalists it was the standard of constitutionality. A House of Commons that had lost the representational apparatus to restrain arbitary power was not functioning constitutionally. This sense of balanced constitutionalism gone awry was especially prevalent for those who viewed the revolutionary controversy from the perspective of American whigs.[23] What they saw had two components. One was, of course, that Parliament was not representative of the Americans, but that oddly was not the main complaint. More pressing was the corruption of the constitutional balance. Even if virtual representation, shared interests, shared burdens, equal assessments, and the other doctrines of constructive representation had been valid and had worked as they were supposed to in theory, Parliament could no longer protect the colonists because it was no longer representative of any interest except that of the administration. "The constitutional right of this country is, to be governed by three distinct powers; whereas now, by the prevalence of luxury, venality, and corruption, it centers intirely in one," a correspondent wrote the *London Magazine* in 1776. "This, the colonists are sensible of; and therefore they are willing to avoid its evil tendencies, by establishing a convention of their own." Constitutional government was not only government by rule of law. It was balanced government of restrained powers. In British constitutionalism, this meant the check of an institutional representative of some part of the commoners of the nation. For an eighteenth-century constitutionalist, such as Baron Rokeby, if the check and balance were removed, the government was no longer representative and no longer constitutional. "Did then the laws of nature, the constitution of our country, the charters of the colonies all unanimously conspire and concur after the strongest and the plainest manner in subjecting America to the taxation of a British Parliament; this would and could only be meant of a true Parliament, of a Parliament both in word and in deed, of a free Parliament, free from corruption and from pecuniary influence, as well as from force and from violence." Rokeby's constitutionalism had been good law once. It would not be good law by 1850, perhaps not by 1833. The question about which there was disagreement was whether it was law when he wrote it in 1776.[24]

Reformation of Consent

R epresentation may have been the first area of British constitutionalism to attract a serious reform movement. The doctrine that constitutional government required the consent of each citizen, but that
everyone did not have to be represented directly, was too glaring an
anomaly to have escaped questioning in an age that called itself enlight-
ened.[1] There had, of course, been earlier demands for reformation of
representation, but no major effort until the time of the American Revolution.[2] The American crisis and John Wilkes's Middlesex elections
provoked extensive debate about the definitions and shortcomings of
British representation. Then, too, there was the example set by the
newly independent American states. Forced to define the concept of
representation, they provided the British with models to think about.[3]
As the Society for Constitutional Information in 1783 told the merchants of "unrepresented towns," "[i]f representation be of no use to a
trading people, and if elections are nuisances, why have the industrious
citizens of Philadelphia, Boston, and all America, secured to themselves,
by their new constitution[s], an *equal representation* and *annual elections,*
as the very essence of that constitution which they inherit in common
with ourselves, and as that without which they knew they should not be
a free people?"[4]

Partly as a result of the American debate, certain changes occurred in
the way that people perceived representation, causing many Britons to
become dissatisfied with the old definitions of constructive consent and
vicarious representation. For one thing, the concept of virtual representation was discredited. By 1773, even the ministry ceased to justify
American legislation on the grounds of virtual representation, and, by
1776, the administration abandoned all efforts of colonial taxation
partly because the concept of virtual representation of the colonists by
Parliament had become untenable. Second, people began to rethink the
gravid concepts of slavery and liberty, and it became more fashionable
to argue that individuals "who have no Voice nor Vote in the electing of

Representatives, *do not enjoy* Liberty."[5] Third, questions were raised whether (in Blackstone's words) British representation was "complete," whether it was constitutionally sufficient that "every foot of land is represented," and even whether a legislature was "representative" if it represented property, not people. In fact, a few idealists not only wanted people represented but would have represented people who had no property. The less property one had, the Society for Constitutional Information claimed in an audacious argument, reversing traditional perceptions, the more one needed representation. "[T]he rich, in the defence of their liberty and property, have every advantage which wealth, knowledge, and the purchased services of others can afford them; while the poor, destitute of all these, have no security but in *the purity of legislation,* nor any means of self-defence, but in *retaining their share of the elective power.*"[6] Fourth, more and more commentators were saying that representatives should represent. "Representation may be considered as complete when it collects to a sufficient extent, and transmits with perfect fidelity, the real sentiments of the people," Robert Hall wrote in 1793. It was not a new argument, but as it gained more acceptance so did the related notions that a representative could not represent someone who had not voted for or deputed him and that a population was not represented if the electorate was a small part of the whole.[7]

EQUAL REPRESENTATION

There were several suggestions for reforms, from narrowing a too extensive franchise by raising the value of property qualifying an elector, to the most frequently favored reform, elimination of rotten boroughs. The proposal of interest to us was "equal representation." It took several guises but can be divided into two general categories: more equal representation of people and more equal representation of property.[8]

It is equal representation of people that was radical. The idea began to gain support with the coming of the American Revolution and was in some measure connected with the crisis. Some constitutional commentators claimed that equal representation was all that British constitutionalism needed to be restored to freedom.[9] "[A]n equal and adequate representation," John Jebb contended, was "a sufficient remedy for all our evils." The evil most reformers had in mind was the American war. We may not see a connection, but contemporaries did. One of the most extensive plans for reconciliation, published in 1775, included the proposal that to keep the colonies in the empire representation be made "equal over all Great-Britain, in proportion to the number of Inhabitants." Two years later, after the Declaration of Independence, Granville Sharp argued that reformation of representation would be "*a proof of sincerity*" reconciling the colonists, as it would demonstrate the intention by the British to govern themselves "according to the strictest rule of *legal* and *constitutional principles.*"[10] When the fighting was over and the British crown had lost America, the livery of London blamed representation.

> *Resolved,* That the unequal representation of the people, the corruption of parliament, and the perversion thereof from its original institution, have been *the principal causes* of the unjust war with America, of the consequent dismemberment of the British empire, and of every grievance of which we complain.[11]

All proposals for equal representation had so little chance for adoption that few detailed plans were drafted. Vaguely stated as either an equal representation of all property or an equal and universal representation of all males, they may have been intended to make the public familiar with the idea and have it debated.[12] We know equal representation was debated because it was widely condemned. It was dismissed as "absurd" since people were not equal, as "impractical" since equality could not give weight to influence, interest, or intelligence, and as dangerous to liberty. "If we are to be governed by a mob, farewel[l] to our religious and civil liberties forever," Francis Basset objected in a pamphlet attacking equal representation. "The first consequence of such a mad and wicked measure, would be a dislike of parliaments by all the men of sense and property in the kingdom," John Almon wrote. He knew that representational equality could not be successful in a society traditionally governed by interests rather than by numbers. "Parliaments being elected by a privilege, not founded upon, but distinct and separate from the interest of the country, gentlemen of property, could have no confidence in it; and many of them, it is more than probable, would desire to be relieved from the dangers of it."[13]

One fact should be emphasized, or we could easily be led astray by something said at the start of this chapter. British efforts for equal representation may have been influenced by but were not patterned on American law. Here and there, Americans could be quoted demanding equal representation, and, because Americans tended to associate consent with representation more than did the British, they had philosophical reasons to seek equality.[14] But universal manhood suffrage was nowhere the American norm. In fact, American law was cited in Great

Britain mainly by opponents of equal representation. The new American states all rejected it, Christopher Keld contended, proving that equal representation was incompatible with British constitutionalism. "There, where no doubt this matter has been fully considered, we find, by their constitutions . . . that some [property] qualification has been every where uniformly deemed necessary; and, considering the state of the two countries, a much greater qualification than what is required in this kingdom." Arthur Young thought that American law established the case for the representation of property rather than of equal people. "[P]roperty now has the power in this realm" rather than people, who, he assumed, would have the power with equal representation. "[I]n some governments of America, this is the case; but America has no indigent poor, or at least very few, arising from plenty of land; thus America is no example applicable to us." In other words, because Americans possessed more property, they could more safely risk equal representation.[15]

CONSTITUTIONALISM AND REFORM

American practice did not matter. Even had the states adopted equal representation whole and proved it safe, Great Britain was not ready for it. There are many explanations, but apprehension of democracy was not one. True, there were constitutional theorists doubting if people were capable of governing themselves and fearful of government responsive to popular will.[16] But no reformer proposed abolishing the House of Lords, and few advocates of equal representation were after democracy, at least not equal representation of numbers. Christopher Wyvill, founder of the most influential movement for parliamentary reform in the late eighteenth century, warned against unchecked democracy, and John Horne Tooke, one of the best known London radicals of the day and a member of every reform organization of the era, conceded that "extreme misery, extreme dependence, extreme ignorance, extreme selfishness . . . are just and proper causes of exclusion from a share in the government."[17]

Reformers sought equal representation because it would help ensure better or more "representative" government. They meant not government responsive to the people's wishes but government not contemptuous of the people's wishes. Sometimes they favored an equal representation that, by twentieth-century standards, not only seems less than democratic but not even equal. There were few more ardent advocates of parliamentary reform than Sir John Sinclair, yet for good eighteenth-century reasons he would not give equal representation to London and Middlesex. Proposing a plan for more equal representation in the House of Commons, Sinclair explained why London was entitled to more members as a matter of equality and why it should not receive its equal share. "But," he wrote, "such is the natural weight which the capital has in every country, and indeed such are the privileges and advantages which London has already received, even as it has been inadequately represented, that in prudence it ought not to claim such a number of representatives, as would probably excite the envy, suspicion, or jealously of the rest of the kingdom." [18]

Another incredible (yet characteristically eighteenth-century) factor was the inability of many reformers to escape from traditional patterns of thought, especially from the concept of the House of Commons as an institution of constitutional restraint rather than a legislature. This mind-set might have been a strength under other circumstances, but reform was less urgent for a House of Commons that guarded liberty by checking the crown than for a House of Commons that provided for liberty through representation of the people. [19]

Another aspect of eighteenth-century constitutional thought intruding on equal representation reform was the constitutional centrality of property. As often as not, equal representation was linked to the right of property. In a sense, this strategy—if strategy it was rather than habit—may have strengthened reform by tying equal representation to the strongest protection that traditional, conservative common law placed around the rights of British citizens, security of property. The point to be noticed, however, is that the reform was often put in terms of the right of property rather than the right of every male equally to consent directly or of the right to direct representation. [20] As a result, the emphasis of the reformer's debate was quite often on the familiar right of property rather than on new ideas about a more universal franchise, an equal representation, or democracy.

There were sincere reformers of suffrage who would have been satisfied if representation had been on equal portions of real property. Others sought to extend the right to vote to owners of all types of property, not just freehold, the "new" money equally with the old. Either way, applying eighteenth-century constitutional premises, they would have used property to obtain "equal" representation. The earl of Abingdon may have best formulated the idea of reformation of property representation when he wrote: "If therefore on the one Hand the Representation of the landed Interest is inadequate, that Representation must be made good in Proportion to the Quantity of Land that is occupied, and not in Proportion to the Number of its Occupiers: So on the other Hand, if the Representation of the monied or trading Interest be inadequate, this Representation must be made good in Proportion to the increased Quantum in both, and not in Proportion to the increased Number of monied Men and Traders."[21]

Astonishingly, many champions of "equal" representation continued to believe that electors had to be independent property owners. Their idea of equality was the equality of independent wealth. Wyvill could not recommend universal male suffrage for Ireland because Irish property was not widely distributed. The right to vote, he explained, could safely be vested only in men "who, from the possession of property to some small amount, may be thought likely to exercise their franchise freely, and for the public good." Perhaps equal representation reformers would have lowered the amount needed to be "independent," but we cannot be certain. Wyvill apparently believed that only in countries "where property is equally divided, or nearly so," could "the unlimitted right of suffrage . . . be established." One country met that standard. "In the American Republics, property is more equally divided, and the manners of the people are more simple, orderly, and incorrupt, than they are in these kingdoms." Yet, Wyvill noted, with surprising approval for an equal representation reformer, many states had property qualifications for voting. "In Massachusetts, and some other American States, the landed qualification exceeds that of any English Freeholders."[22]

Most remarkable of all, reformers championing universal manhood suffrage in its furthest extent justified the right to vote on the right to property. An example is the following striking argument made in the House of Commons in March 1776.

> The meanest mechanic, the poorest peasant and day labourer, has important rights respecting his personal liberty, that of his wife and children, his property, however inconsiderable, his wages, his earnings, the very price and value of each day's hard labour, which are in many trades and manufactures regulated by the power of parliament. Every law relative to marriage, . . . every contract or agreement with a rapacious or unjust master, is of importance to the manufacturer, the cottager, the servant, as well as to the rich subjects of the state.

The speaker was the London radical John Wilkes. It is said that the bill he was supporting was the most extensive proposal for equal represen-

tation ever drafted, a reform that would have abolished the rotten boroughs, eliminated the crown's influence in the Commons, and provided
for "a just and equal Representation of the People of England in Parliament." Of courses Wilkes had other arguments—historical, statistical,
theoretical, constitutional, and that owing to the existing laws of representation the American war "is carried on contrary to the sense of the
nation"—but we must be impressed that in arguing for equal representation of the poor he pleaded not for fairness, equality, liberty, or democracy but for the poor's right to share in the basic constitutional privilege of security of property.[23]

In fact, even reform aimed at the most notorious defect in parliamentary representation of that day, the "rotten borough," became entangled
in property rights. A Dublin magazine writer, for example, complained
that the rotten boroughs of Old Sarum, "where there is not a house,"
and "the pitiful town of *Newton*," on the Isle of Wright, "send in as many
members as the inestimable wealth of the City of *London*." He meant
"wealth," for his notion of reforming the rotten boroughs was to give
weight to property by measuring representation in terms of taxes paid.
There were 513 members of the House of Commons. "*Middlesex*, with
its towns, contributes of land-tax and subsidy together 265 parts of 513.
Therefore *Middlesex* ought to be represented by 265 Members. And
Cornwal[l] contributes of Land-tax and subsidy together 13 parts of 513.
Therefore *Cornwal[l]* ought to send 13 members."[24]

The rotten-borough issue delineates a final reason why eighteenth-
century constitutional thought made reform of representation difficult
if not unattainable: the reform movement encountered the immovable
force of British constitutionalism in the concept of the timeless, fixed,
perfect constitution that could not be tinkered with without placing liberty and the rule of law in jeopardy. Governor George Johnstone was
only one of many would-be reformers condemning rotten boroughs yet
doubting if anything could be done as they were private property beyond the constitutional authority of Parliament to abolish or alter. A
borough without voters, Johnstone admitted, was "a curious representation," but how could it be changed without destroying the rights of the
people who owned the boroughs? "I confess the basis of the constitution
depends on preserving their privileges entire, since no man can say how
far the reform would reach; and the whole art of Government consists
in preserving to every one his established rights."[25]

In this century, with Parliament sovereign and all government subject
to legislative experiment and ministerial whim, Johnstone's constitution

holds little meaning for Great Britain. In the eighteenth century, the notion of unalterable, changeless constitutional law was the ultimate barrier shielding liberty. The earl of Chatham called private boroughs "the rotten parts of the constitution." But he could not commit them to the surgery of legislative reform. "[T]hese Boroughs, corrupt as they are, must be considered as the natural infirmity of the constitution," he pleaded. "Like the infirmities of the body, we must bear them with patience, and submit to carry them about with us. The limb is mortified, but *amputation might be* DEATH." The security of liberty lay in constitutional continuity; it could end with constitutional experimentation. Every constitutional right depended on existing customs and institutions to a degree making any reform, no matter how meritorious in theory, constitutionally impossible.

> [T]he defects in our constitution . . . are not so much grown out of the lapse of time, but are owing to the original frame of that assembly [Parliament], which never had an idea of an equal representation as its object. To infuse, therefore, into it a principle so opposite to its institution, the whole mass must be melted down and new modelled. . . . [T]he inconveniences of such an attempt would be immediate and palpable; the *practical* advantages of it doubtful at least and problematical.[26]

Here was no idle theory. Some of the best, most imaginative writers on constitutional law in the eighteenth century could not contemplate the smallest reform. Unequal representation could well be a constitutional grievance, Edward Wynne conceded. "If it is a grievance, it is such a one as can not be redressed. . . . [T]he very attempt to do it would totally unhinge the Constitution." "I should rather look upon the expedient, in this case, not as an attempt to resettle, but to new-found the constitution," he explained, "by dispossessing every part of the Kingdom of Rights they have so long possessed of; and in their nature the most important of all others, because they are the foundation of their security and protection."[27]

It was for this reason, because the perceived risks of constitutional reform were so great, that Chatham felt it unsafe to do anything about representation except add a third member to the representation of each county. "The knights of the shires approach nearest to the constitutional representation of the country, because they represent the soil," he explained. "I would encrease that strength, because I think it is the only security we have against the profligacy of the times, the corruption of the people, and the ambition of the crown." Chatham was proposing the characteristic reform of the eighteenth century: change that changed nothing. And why not, for what would equal representation mean? Baron Basset asked. "The consequence would be, that the executive power, the peers, and the great commoners, would lose all their present proper interest, and would be forced to attempt to acquire power by the baneful means of bribery and corruption." Basset's work was entitled *Thoughts on Equal Representation*, but his main thought was locked into the existing constitution. Change might be introduced, but things would remain the same, for if the constitution survived it would revert to its former ways.[28]

ELEVEN

American Representation

If there is something familiar about colonial whig arguments concerning rights of representation, it is because those arguments were based on British constitutional principles. The following sentences sum up that constitutional case: "Our slavery is complete as long as we are subject to regulations made by a legislature, in the election of which we had not a voice, and over whose members we have not the least controul. If any thing could add to a slavery in its nature so perfect, it would be, that we are under the government of a power whose views may be distinct, and whose interests may be the opposite of ours." There, in those two sentences, are many of the constitutional issues as colonial whigs interpreted them—election, representation, shared interests, the slavery of arbitrary power. The lesson to be learned, however, is that these were not American words; they were written by an Irish writer defending the right of Irish Protestants to representation. They look familiar because they stated the same case that eighteenth-century American whigs consistently stated. It was the same case because it was the same constitution.[1]

The British solved the Irish constitutional dilemma by merging the three kingdoms into a single representation. They would solve the American constitutional dilemma for Canada and other parts of the old empire by abrogating the claim to tax and, in most matters, to legislate internally for the colonies. For Americans themselves, however, the British found no solution to the dilemma of how the colonists could be represented by "any body of men, with respect to whom they have no right of election, no power of controul."[2]

The answer that would convince us today—a minority view in the 1770s—was that the colonies were in a dependent status, that "wherever the British government and dominion can extend, *representation* can, and must extend." Stated as a constitutional rule, the principle was that no matter where subjects lived in the empire each citizen was "equally represented in the British Parliament." Put in nineteenth-century terms, the tripartite legislature was sovereign, and whatever (and wherever) it commanded was law.[3]

Americans answered the doctrine of absolute sovereignty with the constitutional theory that has been repeated over and over in this book: the institutional guardianship of the representative branch of the legislature. If Americans were subject to the sovereign power of a Parliament in which they were not represented actually, the Virginia convention instructed that colony's delegates to the Continental Congress, "[t]he End of Government would be defeated." This institutional imperative for constitutionality can perhaps best be summed up by quoting not from an official colonial whig pronouncement but from a restatement of the principle in a popular British periodical.

> [That] in every civil society, the only just foundation of government is the consent of those who are governed; and that in a free government (such as our own) the people, however they may divest themselves of the executive power, ought to retain a share in the legislative, and that their consent, or that of a majority of them, given personally or by their substitutes, should be necessary to the validity of any law. And this doctrine, it is true, is abundantly sufficient to justify the claim of the colonies to an exemption from the authority of parliament, so long as they are deprived of all participation in that authority.

Splitting legal hairs, the objection was less that Americans were not represented in Parliament than that Parliament, for them, was not a representative institution. To perform its constitutional role of restraint, Parliament had to be representative, and, if not representative, it was not constitutional.[4]

Constitutionalism was restraint when the government was balanced, and it was largely to maintain balance that English constitutionalism had developed the two-part principle that there could be no taxation without consent and that all grants of money had to originate in the representative branch of the legislature. "In the scale of this well-balanced Constitution," "Regulus" explained, "as revenue is a tax upon population, so representation is a check upon revenue, essentially necessary to poise the beam betwixt the two extremes of regal and democratic tyranny." The principle of taxation by consent, Daniel Dulany added, "results from the Nature of that mixed Government; for, without it, the Order of Democracy could not exist."[5]

The consent-to-tax doctrine was formulated not for restraining the power to tax but for restraining the power of government. To be an instrument of restraint, it needed to some degree the element of representation, that is, some representation of the commoners or the democratic part of the population in the institution that gave consent to taxation. A century and a half earlier, Massachusetts had made this point about English constitutionalism when telling the Long Parliament that, "[i]f the Parliament of England should impose laws upon us, having no burgesses in the House of Commons, nor capable of a summons by reason of the vast distance, we should lose the liberties and freedom of English indeed."[6] Consent and representation were what, in British constitutional theory, gave constitutional legitimacy to the institution that restrained arbitrary power, and without constitutional legitimacy there could be no sovereignty. What colonial whigs were saying was not that a sovereign power lacked authority to promulgate law by command but that the British sovereign could not promulgate American law because the British sovereign—Parliament—was not sovereign for them as it lacked the constitutional balance in relation to them that made it sovereign in British constitutionalism.

The constitutional conclusion can be easily missed. "Vindex Patriae" was wrong to think that the American notion "that no man is represented in parliament but persons who vote in elections" meant that Americans were saying that the Navagation Act was invalid, that Great Britain could not legislate control of colonial trade with the world, or that the colonies were independent.[7] Americans did not say that only electors were represented in Parliament or that Parliament was not supreme in many matters. What they said was that their part of the British population was not represented in Parliament and that they did not share with those parts of the population that were represented the constitutional institutions that made British government legitimate by preventing it from being arbitrary.

BURDENS AND INTERESTS

Sovereignty is our issue because sovereignty is the doctrine that in the nineteenth century would take over constitutional theory and definitively settle all those questions. It was not, of course, the issue in 1776 except for a minority of British leaders of the school of Lord Mansfield. For the majority of constitutional commentators, who said that the colonies were bound by parliamentary legislation, the reason was not parliamentary sovereignty but that Americans were in law represented in the House of Commons. As they were represented, they, in law, consented, and through consent they were bound.

There is no need to repeat the explanation of attenuated or constructive consent by law, or what Capel Lofft called "[o]ur corrupt, defective, nominal representation." Applied to the Americans, the doctrine of constructive representation in Parliament had at least three exclusive forms. One was the general constitutional rule that the colonists were in fact and law represented in the House of Commons to the same constitutional extent that British nonelectors were represented. The favored explanation was virtual representation. A related though different argument was that Parliament could legislate but that, as the Americans were not actually represented, Parliament had to act cautiously and—eventually—would have to grant representation to the colonies. A third was that Parliament could legislate by right of virtual representation but could not tax without actual representation. Lord Chatham espoused the last theory. Under his constitutionally eccentric law, Americans were subject to parliamentary supremacy but not parliamentary taxation. "To be taxed without being represented," Chatham expounded, "is contrary to the maxims of law and the first principles of the constitution."[8]

The first, or general, constitutional rule was summarized on the tax question by a pamphleteer claiming that, "by the constitution, representation is not necessary to taxation; and that, if it was, the Americans are represented." That is, there was no distinction between legislation and taxation, but even if there were it would not matter—not because of sovereignty but because the colonists were represented.[9]

The constitutional defense that Americans were not represented in Parliament was more complicated than the constitutional argument that they were not subject to Parliament's sovereignty. From the beginning to the end of the revolutionary controversy concerning representation, the colonial whig constitutional case was both consistent and stated as two distinct propositions. The first proposition, phrased by the Stamp Act Congress was "[t]hat the People of these Colonies are not, and from their local Circumstances cannot be, Represented in the House of Commons in *Great-Britain*."[10] The corollary proposition was "[t]hat the only lawful representatives of the freemen of this colony are the persons they elect to serve as members of the General Assembly thereof."[11] The Continental Congress joined the two propositions:

> That the foundation of English liberty and of all free government, is a right of the people to participate in their legislative council: and as the English colonists are not represented, and from their local and other circumstances cannot properly be represented in the British parliament, they are entitled to a free

and exclusive power of legislation in their several provincial Legislatures, where their right to representation can alone be preserved, in all cases of taxation and internal polity, subject only to the negative of their sovereign.[12]

The issue posed by the revolutionary controversy was not the constitutionality of virtual representation in either Great Britain or the colonies but whether it could constitutionally and legally be extended to a part of the empire in which the protection and security of shared interests, shared burdens, and equal assessments might not operate to the same degree of exactitude as in the electoral part. If one accepted the argument, as American whigs did, that virtual representation was constitutional in Great Britain because of the safeguards of shared interests, shared burdens, and equal assessments, the constitutional question became whether these safeguards provided similar constitutional security to colonial rights.

A partial answer has been discussed earlier, and this chapter is not designed to repeat it. The present point rather is that American whigs and their British supporters determined constitutional security by British constitutional principles. Stated positively by David Hartley, the member of Parliament who would negotiate the Treaty of Paris for London, the question was whether it was "contrary to the principles of the British constitution, to tax unrepresented colonies in a British parliament, who are to save the money of their constituents and of themselves, in proportion as they tax those who are unrepresented." The discussion can be limited to taxation as it amply illustrates the constitutional issue. "The Commons of Great Britain," Virginia's Council and House of Burgesses pointed out, shared the burdens of British taxation because the members could "impose no Tax on the People there without burthening themselves in some Proportion." For Americans, it was different. Parliament's authority to tax them would not be subject to "those constitutional checks, to prevent an abuse of that dangerous power, which is in truth the essence of the British Constitution."[13]

Application of the British constitutional doctrine of shared interests led to the same conclusions: by British constitutional principles, the American colonists were not virtually represented in the British Parliament. As Governor George Johnstone explained, "because the interest of every particular member remains as a pledge, that no individual can be overburthened: when this security is removed, there is no longer any safety for those to whom the fact does not apply." For Americans, this security was removed. In fact, Edward Bancroft argued, "[e]very Restraint . . . which affords Security to the unrepresented Inhabitants of *Great Britain,* is either removed or converted into a *Stimulus* to Oppression; and every Temptation which Interest (the most universal and prevalent of all Passions) can suggest, must operate against them." In British constitutional terms, therefore, for both taxation and legislation, Americans were being asked, a "Freeholder" of Worcester contended, "to yield up our lives, and property, to be solely at the arbitrary will of a parliament, which is under no restraint, in our favor either of interest or affection; but whose interest and affection are against us." Such a blatant constitutional deviation was not only unconstitutional. It was so contrary to constitutional norms of liberty that it was anticonstitutional, for it was slavery by constitutional forms.[14]

To colonial whigs and their British supporters, the failure of security destroyed the doctrine of virtual representation because that doctrine rested on sharing burdens and interests.[15] "[T]he *Americans,*" they contended, "do not say that they are imperfectly represented, but that they are not represented at all" in Parliament.[16] The reason was British constitutional law. "I do not claim a *better* constitution, than my mother country," a Boston pamphleteer wrote. "I claim *as good* a constitution."[17] That constitution would not be as good if he were "represented" without sharing the interests of the electors of the representatives and without the representatives sharing the burdens that they imposed on him.[18]

LOCAL KNOWLEDGE

The dynamics of the imperial dispute led American whigs to formulate a reemphasis of localism in representation that they would eventually incorporate into their constitutional law. It was the local necessity, the local advantage, the benefit of local representatives, that is, of representatives who were residents of the electing district and who knew the electors, their circumstances, needs, and desires. Josiah Quincy, Jr., was not alone in thinking the element of localism essential for legitimate or constitutional government. "Regular government is necessary to the preservation of private property, and personal security," he wrote. "What regular government can America enjoy with a legislative a thousand leagues distant, unacquainted with her exigencies, militant in interest, and unfeeling of her calamities?"[19]

It was a matter of British constitutionalism, but British constitutionalism meant more than established government. It meant government by the rule of law and, for the Americans at least, rule by consent through representation. British imperialists agreed, as long as consent was not limited to direct consent of every citizen and representation did not require "actual" representation. But notions were changing, and, by 1776 and the Declaration of Independence, if not by 1766 and the repeal of the Stamp Act, imperialists could not postulate the constitutionality of vicarious or attenuated representation with the same confidence that it could have been expounded a half or even a quarter century before. In 1785, in his best-selling text, *Principles of Philosophy*, William Paley defined law and constitution as they would be defined in the nineteenth century, as commands at the whim of Parliament. Even so, he described representation as localism joined with local knowledge. "Every district of the empire enjoys the privilege of chusing representatives, informed of the interest and circumstances and desires of their constituents, and entitled by their situation to communicate that information to the national council," he wrote. Americans, although by then out of the empire, could have complained that again representation was defined as a right they had not possessed. They also could have complained of what Paley said next. "The meanest subject has some one whom he can call upon to bring forward his complaints and requests to public attention." Americans might have answered that if that was one of the constitutional elements of representation it was an aspect that they had not enjoyed.[20]

"Pray by what members" were Americans even virtually represented? Connecticut's *New London Gazette* had asked at the time of the Stamp Act crisis. "Is it those chosen by the city of London or any other city, Shire or Borough? For we know not to whom to apply as our representatives." The question was more than rhetoric or a claim that representation should be actual rather than virtual. A point of constitutional law was raised by asking, as Daniel Dulany asked, "But who are the representatives of the colonies?" It was a point of constitutional law to the extent that a British subject had a right to have a representative introduce reasonable private bills on traditional matters. Who introduced private bills for Americans, and to whom could Americans "send their instructions when desirous to obtain the repeal of a law striking at the root and foundation of every civil right should such an one take place?" Dulany wondered. "Instructions to all the members who compose the House of Commons would not be proper. To them the application must be by petition."[21]

At the beginning of the revolutionary controversy, Sir William Meredith told the House of Commons that the colonists, "as not being represented," had "a peculiar right" to petition. If so, it was an unenforceable right. Not only could Americans not instruct, but they often could not petition. Sometimes no member could be found to introduce a petition, even one from a colonial assembly. More often, the houses of Parliament refused to receive petitions that raised arguments of objectionable constitutional law, as, for example, one from the New York Assembly because it "expressed a doubt of the right of the legislature of Great Britain to tax the colonies." Thus, on the very issue in controversy between the colonies and the mother country, Americans were denied one of the constitutional purposes of representation—the representation of the grievances of the locality.[22]

A related constitutional complaint was that American arguments were often not heard in Parliament. The theory that Americans were represented by friends who spoke on their behalf and for their rights was more often articulated than proven. Even after 1765, there were several occasions when the House of Commons considered duties on colonial trade without listening to any speaker for colonial interests—or, if someone spoke, American views could be misstated.[23] More important, Parliament demonstrated that colonial rights could be overlooked simply because there were no representatives watching out for them. That event occurred when the crown, by its sole authority, promulgated taxes on the islands ceded by France following the Seven Years' War. Prerogative taxes would have outraged Parliament had they been imposed on Great Britain instead of on a part of the realm not *actually* represented by the House of Commons. There was a lesson for American whigs, Quebec's attorney general warned, when the Commons failed to defend its most cherished privilege.

> This omission of the British parliament to take any notice of so dangerous an act of royal prerogative, merely, (as it should seem,) because it happened out of the narrow limits of their own island, seems to justify, in some degree, the desire of the Americans to be exempt from its authority. For, if the parliament is disposed to exert its authority only for the purpose of laying taxes on them, when desired by the officers of the Crown to do so, and not for the purpose of procuring taxes to be taken off, when illegally laid upon them by the single authority of the Crown, the Americans will have a right to say that the members of the British parliament have not that fellow-feeling for the condition of their American fellow-subjects which is necessary to induce them to take proper care of their interests, and to qualify them to be the constitutional guardians of their liberties.[24]

The argument was that Parliament was incapable of considering American interests and protecting American rights, just as it was insensitive to the interests and rights of the underclasses of British society that were virtually, not actually, represented in the House of Commons.[25]

We cannot say that a new ingredient was being added to the definition of constitutional representation. The independent member of the House of Commons, representing the constitution rather than the electoral district and expressing the grievances of the nation rather than promoting local legislation, was still the constitutional criterion. What was changing once Parliament began to legislate for the colonies was the perception of constitutional independence. The dynamics of imperial posturing demonstrated what truly independent representation could mean to separate geographic regions that had neither actual representation nor representation by shared interests, shared burdens, and equal assessments. As a Philadelphia pamphleteer argued in 1768, "No absolute Monarch is more independent of his People, than [the] British Commons are of our Favours and Frowns."[26] It was to make their favors and frowns "constitutional" and to protect themselves from royal arbitrariness that the English and Scots had developed representation. For the British, representation in Parliament protected at least some of the people. Representation in Parliament could fail to protect any Americans—a reason why, for them, it was not constitutional representation.

Dilemmas of Consent

The American Revolution controversy caught the British constitution in the predicaments of its own inconsistencies. From one direction came the ancient law of restrained, limited, balanced government protected and guaranteed by the twin privileges belonging to every citizen, the right to consent and the right to representation. In the other direction lay the law of the future, of the supreme, arbitrary legislature that represented the "one single undivided state" that was the British empire and that, as sovereign, constructively consented to government on behalf of every commoner in the empire. "The British legislature is the great representative of this *one* state; and is, indeed, politically speaking, the state itself," a writer on the topic of representation claimed in 1770. He was speaking both from the past, calling the three branches of Parliament "representative," and to the future, saying that the legislature rather than the constitution was the "state."[1]

There was no inconsistency. All constitutional commentators in the last quarter of the eighteenth century had to reconcile two constitutions—the remnants of the ancient constitution and the constitution of sovereign command. "[I]t is the undoubted birth-right of every Briton, that no law can pass, without his free consent, through his representative," Richard Phelps, undersecretary to Lord Hillsborough, wrote. "But this must be a representative in a British Parliament, not a deputy in an American assembly." The premises were traditional British constitutional law: "undoubted right" to "free consent" and a "representative." By the old prescriptive, precedential, customary constitution, these words might mean direct consent and actual representation of some people and constructive consent and virtual representation of others. Those others gave "consent" and had "representation" through the constitutional mechanisms of shared burdens, shared interests, and equal assessments. For the Americans, these mechanisms were missing. For them, Phelps's constitutional formula was a sleight of hand. He used the words and values of the old constitution of restraint and customary right to bind them by the new constitution of parliamentary supremacy and sovereign command.[2]

Perhaps more than any other participants in the revolutionary debates, Joseph Galloway tried to reconcile the tug and pull of the two constitutions. An uncompromising loyalist, he worked for British military victory and—supposed—for the triumph of the constitution of arbitrary command. We cannot be certain of the last point, however, for, troubled by the memorabilia of the old constitution of customary right, Galloway was never able to accept the newer meaning of sovereign power. When addressing the first Continental Congress, Galloway both defended parliamentary supremacy and backed away from parliamentary sovereignty. There was something about unchecked arbitrary power that stuck in the throat of an eighteenth-century common lawyer, an eighteenth-century British constitutionalist, an eighteenth-century American. Thoughts about liberty, balance, representation, and constitutionalism led Galloway "to confess" that, even though Americans could not deny the "supreme authority" of Great Britain,

> the exercise of that authority is not perfectly constitutional in respect to the Colonies. We know that the whole landed interest of Britain is represented in that body, while neither the land nor the people of America hold the least participation in the legislative authority of the State. Representation, or a participation in the supreme councils of the State, is the great principle upon which the freedom of the British Government is established and secured. I also acknowledge, that that territory whose people have no enjoyment of this privilege, are subject to an authority unrestrained and absolute; and if the liberty of the subject were not essentially concerned in it, I should reject a distinction so odious between members of the same state, so long as it shall be continued.

What Galloway wanted was American representation. The constitutional complaint against the tea tax or any parliamentary taxation was the "want of constitutional principle in the authority that passed it," that is, want of consent through some degree of actual representation.[3]

One lesson of this book has been that to understand the eighteenth-century constitution we must first understand what words meant in the eighteenth century. It is too easily forgotten that Americans generally employed words and phrases much as they were used in Great Britain.

J. R. Pole has complained that "[t]he concept of consent was central to the case made by the Declaration of Independence against the British, but only in Massachusetts and New Hampshire was the concept put to the test of a formal ratification by the people of their state constitution."[4] Although the question whether consent was central to the Declaration's case could be debated, the relevant question is whether consent was meant in the way Pole assumes. The Declaration said that "Governments are instituted among Men, deriving their just powers from the consent of the governed." Among the governed to whom the Declaration referred were slave men and all women. The word *consent* may have meant something different in Philadelphia in 1776 than it did in London, but it had not lost that attenuative or constructive quality that made it operative as a constitutional fact-fiction. Although it is difficult to associate the Declaration with constitutionalism, it seems fair to say that the Declaration's "consent of the governed" was a constitutional manner of speaking.

The constitutions of the two states that Pole said put the concept of consent "to the test" are evidence that Americans in the 1780s thought that consent could be as much vicarious as direct. The New Hampshire Constitution is not as clear as we might like, and we must imply its meaning of consent partly from the fact that only males of majority were permitted to give direct consent by voting and only Protestant males of majority could consent by serving as representatives. "[N]o part of a man's property shall be taken from him, or applied to public uses, without his own consent, or that of the representative body of the people. Nor are the inhabitants of this state controllable by any other laws than those to which they or their representative body have given their consent." The Massachusetts Constitution was more clear. It did not mention direct consent and required consent only by *constitutional* representation. "In fine, the people of this Commonwealth are not controullable by any other laws, than those to which their constitutional representative body have given their consent."[5]

It does not do to say that the eighteenth century was careless with words, that an anonymous writer in 1793 knew he was writing fiction when he said that the British constitution had a "full and free representation of the people," or that a future bishop of London was untruthful in 1764 when boasting "that the people of this nation do enjoy, as fully as in the nature of things they are capable of enjoying, and as far as they have the will and virtue to enjoy it, the great advantage of being governed by laws of their own framing, or to which they give their free consent."[6] We must allow for constitutional language. Two hundred years later, Great Britain and the United States both say that they have representative government. So also do the Federal Republic of Germany and the German Democratic Republic. The Union of the Soviet Socialist Republics has a representative government, as do the Republic of China and the People's Republic of China. All these nations also claim that they are democracies, and we understand what they mean. If democracy is equated with rule by the represented majority, an eighteenth-century common lawyer would say that by eighteenth-century standards Great Britain is today more democratic than the United States, for the degree of rule by the majority is greater in the former mother country. For the same reason, a twentieth-century American civil libertarian, equating "democracy" with rule of law free of the arbitrary caprice of the political majority and promulgated by lawyer-judges, would say that Great Britain was less democratic and the United States more. The eighteenth-century common lawyer would reply that the rule of law alone is not a sufficient test for saying that the United States is more "democratic" in the eighteenth-century sense than is Great Britain. Rather, what is crucial is that the United States retains more of a balanced government, guaranteeing the people greater "liberty" to the degree it is balanced and is not majoritarian.

Changes of the legal theory of representation have not been chronicled in the previous chapters because they are not readily measured. They are more matters of perception than of legislation. It was during the age of the American Revolution that public galleries were built in colonial assemblies and that the houses of Parliament ceased prosecuting publishers of their debates. Although the argument was made that "the People have a Right to know," there was no moment in time when the right became law. What occurred was a slow evolution of attitudes changing the meaning of *representation*. The galleries might serve to intimidate the unpopular side from speaking boldly, but open proceedings and publication of debates also had the effect of spurring new attitudes about responsibility to the electorate. The debate whether instructions were binding was an episode involving the defeat of a method of accountability, not of the principle itself. Perhaps this process redefining the concept of representation was part of the rise of democracy, but it also owed much to the growth of political publication and greater recognition of press freedom.[7]

The process of change and redefinition was long, and the finer details may be imperceptible. The alteration was from the early eighteenth-century concept that representation was the institutionalization of one third of the tripartite constitutional balance to the nineteenth-century notion that the person who was elected representative was supposed to represent a constituency. Another symptom of the change manifested during the age of the American Revolution was a rising sense of dissatisfaction with the "representativeness" of the House of Commons. True, the complaint was part of the politics of the day, but it was so tied to the projection of a constitutional ideal that those complaining about the unrepresentativeness of the Commons could not escape making a legal argument about the nature of representation. It was a combination of first the Wilkes election controversy and then the American Revolution that gave a political faction in Great Britain the opportunity to dramatize the argument that the representative branch of the balanced triangle should represent the people. "[T]here is a time, when it is morally demonstrable that men cease to be representatives," the mayor, aldermen, and livery of London complained to George III. "That time is now arrived. The present House of Commons do not represent the people." To say that the members of the Commons were "the representatives of old deserted walls and empty ruinous houses" rather than the people was to raise a point more readily appreciated after the Middlesex elections than before.[8]

After the Revolutionary War started, there were a surprising number of adherents to the imperial side who thought representation the cause of the conflict. Joseph Galloway hoped that representation could also become the solution—a solution with a jurisprudential twist.

> If the British state therefore means to retain the colonies in a due obedience on her government, it will be wisdom in her to restore to her American subjects, the enjoyment of the right of assenting to, and dissenting from, such bills as shall be proposed to regulate their conduct. Laws thus made will ever be obeyed; because of their assent, they become their own acts.—It will place them in the same condition with their brethren in Britain, and remove all cause of complaint.

Galloway's theory is difficult to place historically. It is possible that he was saying nothing new, yet he may have suggested an additional element—perhaps only for the Americans—to the familiar constitutional concept of consent. He went beyond the traditional British argument that consent was necessary to bestow legitimacy on governmental command and to fix the obligation to obey on the individual citizen. Galloway was contending that, along with the constitutional obligation of obedience created by constructive consent, there was an extralegal obligation generated by actual consent. Laws made by actual consent will be obeyed because the people, having in fact consented, obey what they sense is their own act. Whether it was a moral or a legal obligation probably did not matter. What was significant is that the concept was based on the most fundamental of English and British constitutional principles. Galloway was divided between his sense of legal duty and his sense of constitutional right, and there is no more conclusive evidence of the hold that the concept of consent had on the eighteenth-century legal mind than that there were constitutionalists like Galloway who could not tear themselves from it even while acknowledging that the command requiring their allegiance was Parliament's sovereign promulgation.[9]

Galloway wrote in 1775, and he may have been speaking from experience. He had been a delegate to the first Continental Congress and to adhere to the sovereignty of Parliament had to repudiate the authority of Congress, a step he and other loyalists took on incontestable legal grounds. Not only did they dismiss Congress as a rump without sanction of the superior legislature, but, with irony, they repeated the arguments about consent and representation that American whigs had for ten years been using against Parliament's claim of supremacy. It was the same constitutional case, only more persuasive in law and constitutional precedent. Yet it did not persuade enough Americans. Congress commanded more obedience than did Parliament, and one reason seems to be that people thought the congressmen their representatives and accepted Congress's resolutions as mandates to which they had consented. Jack N. Rakove refers to "the astonishing power" of Congress, a power reflected in the hapless comments of royal officials. The authority of the Continental Congress was so widely accepted in all colonies, New Hampshire's governor lamented, "that it was impossible to prevent this Province from joining therein, and accepting the measures recommended, which are received implicitly. So great is the present delusion, that most people receive them as matters of obedience, not of considerate examination, whereon they may exercise their own judgment." We cannot be certain what the governor had in mind, but most likely he was describing a constitutional trait that eighteenth-century Britons thought both constitutional and characteristically American. Sir William Beckford had discussed that trait two decades earlier when telling the House of Commons:

> [I]n most of our colonies in America, it is ordained by their own laws, that in time of war, or imminent danger of being invaded, the martial law shall be in force, and that the commander in chief, in a general council of war, shall establish such laws and articles of war as shall be thought necessary: such laws the people always submit to without murmuring, because they know the law-makers, and have a confidence in them, that they will not consent to any law but what is necessary for the good of the service; but we cannot expect the same submission to military laws advised by persons they never knew.[10]

We cannot measure the depths of belief, but we should be impressed that British officials thought that, American respect for government depended on consent. Whenever the British military established control over a substantial part of a rebelling colony, there was talk of restoring representation. Two reasons were generally expressed. One was the British constitution: martial rule was alien to English common law. The other was American obedience: the people would not respect and probably would not obey a government to which they did not consent.

The American concept of consent as understood by a British imperialist can be gleaned by considering James Simpson. Formerly royal attorney general of South Carolina, he was sent back to that colony as intendant of police in the wake of reoccupation by the imperial army. At first, Simpson thought the countryside would rise up in support. After a year, and discovering that the loyalists "are not so numerous as I expected," he reported that many Americans of influence believed that the whig cause "ought never to be relinquished but by the general Consent of America."

Simpson was a laywer and seems to have been writing as one. American conditions, he concluded, required "the restoration of a legal government," by which he meant representation, for, "unless that government so far accords with the sentiments and even the prepossessions of the people as to afford them just reason to be contented, they will no longer submit to it than it is beyond their power to resist." What persuaded Simpson to this conclusion was not indigenous American constitutionalism; it was the ancient constitution of the English common law.

It would be endless to attempt to point out the advantages that must accrue from a respectable representation of the people cooperating with the executive power, or how effectually it would at once overthrow the remnant of the rebel authority. It may be more to the purpose to say that every day's experience brings additional conviction that it is only from the wisdom and authority of those Assemblies that the establishment of the public tranquility and a due subordination to the laws can be hoped for. The example of the mother country might be quoted if it was necessary in support of a theory which from apparent facts is too notorious to be doubted, for I believe that from the Conquest until the present moment it hath been always judged expedient after any advantage which hath been gained in our civil wars or other dangerous commotions to summon a Parliament as speedily as possible, and from the uniformity of the practice the necessity of it may be inferred as the only cure to eradicate the disorder.[11]

Great Britain had to accord Americans rule by representation, or Americans would not again acknowledge British rule. But it had to be government by local colonial representation.[12] It was no longer possible for American whigs to put their constitutional trust in British legislators. John Cartwright was behind the times when arguing in 1778 that "the *independency of parliament*," restored and guaranteed, was "the only lasting security for the confidence of America after the wished-for reconciliation may take place."[13]

It was too late. Although the Americans and the British had trudged through history down the same constitutional path, they had begun to think different constitutional thoughts. The new contrast of constitutional emphasis was outlined by two dissenting clergymen, one British preaching in 1780, the other American preaching in 1778, the same year that Cartwright wrote. At the university town of Cambridge, the Baptist minister Robert Robinson stated the highest British constitutional value: the old constitutional rule. In the liberated town of Boston, addressing the representatives of a new commonwealth, Phillips Payson reflected on the highest American constitutional value: the new constitutional criterion. The Briton: "A good civil government protects each individual in the absolute enjoyment and disposal of his *property.* Property is the ground of power, and power will always follow property. A people, who would enjoy freedom, can never be too cautious in disposing of their property. While they hold it themselves, they hold the golden sceptre of government: when they transfer it to their rulers, and alienate it from themselves, they exchange that sceptre of gold for a rod of iron." The American: "[A] free and righteous government originates from the people, and is under their direction and control; and therefore a free, popular model of government—of the republican kind—may be judged the most friendly to the rights and liberties of the people, and the most conducive to the public welfare." [14]

The Anglo-American constitution had arrived at a parting of the nations. For the British, the purpose of constitutionalism remained security of property. They would continue to find security in institutions such as representation even if those institutions were more form than substance, until the forms were so twisted and altered that representation would emerge not only as the dominant force in the constitution but as the constitution itself. In the United States, the purpose of representation was changing from liberty through security of property to liberty by orienting the public welfare in tune with freedom. Even so, representation would remain locked into the constitutional balance, not just a check on other authority but itself checked from following the British model and from becoming the sovereign authority. Yet within constitutional continuity there was political change. With representation released from its ancient role of constitutional guardian against arbitrary power, Americans reshaped the image of the representative and new modeled the politics of representation. The constitutional objective would no longer be to elect independent representatives—morally superior men of relative wealth and local social position. Elections would become mechanisms of affecting public policy and, legislation would become the primary function of the representative. Americans would vote for candidates because of popularity and political programs, expecting them to win votes by discussing issues in open forum. [15]

Yet the final irony remains. Great Britain in the age of the American Revolution had been ruled by a haughty, small, arrogant aristocracy, an aristocracy against which the colonists rebelled. The Americans rebelled in part because for them the British constitution was no longer representative, and within less than a century that same constitution made Great Britain, by any definition, the more representative of the two nations, with law the command of the majority political party, metamorphosed by the process of election into the surrogate of the sovereign people. America, by contrast, had been the most democratic, egalitarian society of the eighteenth century, and yet, in the same hundred years, it became the final home of restrained English constitutionalism. For it is in the United States that the eighteenth-century concept of the rule of law retains its constitutional sway as a check on the caprice of the people, and the balanced constitution has been permanently encased in a remodeled constitutional superstructure premised on an ancient constitutional barrier.

ACKNOWLEDGMENTS

The research for this study was supported by a number of sources. Leave from teaching duties at New York University School of Law was provided by the Filomen D'Agostino Greenberg and Max E. Greenberg Faculty Research Fund at the School of Law and by Norman Redlich, dean of the School of Law. Time spent at the Huntington Library in San Marino, California, was supported by a Huntington Library–National Endowment for the Humanities Fellowship. The weeks spent at the Bodleian Library of Oxford University were made possible—and enjoyable—by Professor Paul Langford and the fellows of Lincoln College. The pleasure of being at the Huntington Library was made more productive by the generous and very professional staff directed by Virginia Renner. The completed manuscript received its imprimatur from America's premier band of legal history scholars: William E. Nelson, Norman Cantor, Lawrence Fleischer, Michael Les Benedict, Barbara Kern, and the student members of the New York University School of Law Colloquium in Legal History. They made their most telling contribution by persuading me that the title was not too long. Other indispensable contributions were made by Katharine Jansen, who did the cite and substance checking for New York and Princeton, Elise Histed, who did the same for Cambridge and London, Susan Naulty, who thought about the jacket, and Martin Ridge, who chased away the Huntington's coyotes. As with the other books in this Revolution-era series, the index was prepared by Carol B. Pearson of Alhambra, California, and the Huntington Library. A final debt is owed to Eleanor Searle, who called my attention to the fact that it was Franklin Pierce, not Lord North, who remarked that "Taxation without representation may be tyranny, but taxation by representation is government for flagellants."

N O T E S

The sources cited are generally combined in groups. Often when the references are readily identified in the text, two or more sources are joined in a single note. In some notes, additional authorities are cited when they support the point made in the text. In addition, other supporting sources are cited, generally by the qualification "see also" or "also see." These authorities may not make the same argument as the primary sources, but they make closely related arguments that support and enforce some aspects of the primary arguments. The purpose is to provide scholars with as much evidence as possible. With that in mind, a special effort has been made to cite authorities such as assize sermons and grand-jury charges that are often unknown or overlooked by historians who are not legal or constitutional specialists.

PREFACE

1. "Letters," 25 *William and Mary Quarterly* 330–39 (1968).

2. Pocock, "Classical Deference."

3. Anon., *Reflexions on Representation,* at 38.

4. Bailyn, *Pamphlets,* at 98.

5. *Authority of Rights,* at 5, 11–15, 67–68.

6. It may be objected that it is unrealistic to refer to an American theory of representation when representation in the colonies differed from colony to colony—from the universal manhood representation of a New England town meeting to the disenfranchisement of the entire Carolina backcountry. That objection, however, relates to the legal mechanics of representation and concerns differences comparable to those between English boroughs determining the eligibility of electors. Constitutional theory was more uniform, a fact that may have been reflected in Article I, Section 2, of the United States Constitution. It provided: "The House of Representatives shall be composed of Members chosen every second Year by the People of the several States, and the Electors in each State shall have the Qualifications requisite for Electors of the most numerous Branch of the State Legislature." It is unlikely that the framers of the Constitution would have entrusted the qualifications for electors to state law if there had not been a relatively uniform constitutional theory of representation inherited from colonial law.

7. Surprisingly little historical work has been done on the origins of representative government in the colonies. The best we have is an interesting collec-

tion of documents, unfortunately accompanied by an undistinguished, narrative discussion. Kammen, *Deputyes & Libertyes*.

8. The public-interest analogy was suggested by Daniel A. Farber of the University of Minnesota Law School.

9. Sharp, *Legal Means*, at 32, 14n; [Almon,] *Free Parliaments*, at 37.

10. Cartwright, *Appeal on Constitution*, at 17, 16, 17; [Galloway,] *Historical Reflections*, at 78.

11. Rossiter, *Six Characters*, at 191 (quoting Bland).

12. *London Journal* (no. 696), 28 October 1732, at 1, col. 2.

13. Carroll, "First Citizen," at 127; 2 Burgh, *Political Disquisitions*, at 60 (quoting Chesterfield).

14. Wilson, *Considerations*, at 727.

CHAPTER ONE

1. [Cartwright,] *Take Your Choice*, at 40; greatest people: Anon., *Evidence of Common and Statute Laws*, at 13; best government: [Stevens,] *Discourse on Constitution*, at 40; wisest system: "British American," Williamsburg, 30 June 1774, 1 *American Archives*, at 498; Massachusetts writer: Rusticus, *Good of Community*, at 33; [Meredith,] *Question Stated*, at 11–12 (quoting Blackstone). See also Anon., *Letter to Robert Morris*, at 32; Cooke, *Election Sermon*, at 160; Allen, *American Crisis*, at 48; [Ramsay,] *Historical Essay*, at 6; [Rivers,] *Letters*, at 51; Browning, *Court Whigs*, at 180 (quoting the 1734 pamphlet *An Address to the Freeholders of Great Britain, in Favor of our Constitution*).

2. Other nations: Eliot, *Give Cesar his Due*, at 33; Barnard, *Election Sermon*, at 35; theorist: "Observations on the Freedom of Elections," 4 *Political Register* (1769), at 224–25. See also Anon., *Rights Asserted*, at 12–13; Bolingbroke, *Political Writings*, at 30; Principles and Resolutions of the Constitutional Society at Cambridge, 1783, in Wyvill, *Defence of Price*, at 99; "Book Review," 46 *Gentleman's Magazine* (1776), at 127. For the significance of "security," see *Concept of Liberty*, at 68–73.

3. [Fitch et al.,] *Reasons Why*, at 3 (on behalf of the Connecticut Assembly); *Essex Result*, at 14; Fairfax Resolves, 18 July 1774, 1 *Revolutionary Virginia*, at 127. See also Continental Congress Resolves, 14 October 1774, *Extracts from the Votes and Proceedings*, at 4; South Carolina Resolves, 6 July 1774, Greenberg, "Representation," at 723; Taunton Resolves, 21 May 1770, *Boston Gazette*, 4 June 1770, at 4, col. 2; Boston Resolves, 13 September 1768, *Boston Chronicle*, 19 September 1768, at 361, col. 3; Letter from Virginia Committee to Agent, 28 July 1764, 12 "Proceedings Committee of Correspondence," at 10; Virginia Petition to King, 18 December 1764, Morgan, *Prologue*, at 14; Richard Bland (1766), reprinted in 1 *Revolutionary Virginia*, at 39; [Downer,] *Discourse in Providence*, at 6; Joseph Warren (1772), *Massacre Orations*, at 19–20; [Hicks,] *Nature of Parliamentary Power*, at 4.

4. Radicals: Resolutions of the Constitutional Society at Cambridge, 1783, in Wyvill, *Defence of Price*, at 98; Carysfort, *Thoughts on Constitution*, at 4; Speech of 21 March 1776, 1 *Speeches of John Wilkes in Parliament*, at 88; 1 Burgh, *Political Disquisitions*, at 3; Bonwick, *English Radicals*, at 20; political catechisms: Arbuth-

not, *Freeholder's Catechism*, at 22; *Guide to Rights*, at 2; Anon., *British Liberties*, at xx; Bolingbroke's catechism in 43 *London Magazine* (1774), at 478, and *Gazette and Post-Boy*, 27 February 1775, at 2, col. 1. For the doctrine expounded in Bolingbroke's newspapers, see *Craftsman* (no. 56), 29 July 1727, at 72, and (no. 470), 5 July 1735, at 36.

5. Lowth, *Durham Assize Sermon*, at 10; Watson, *Assize Sermon*, at 2; Head, *Carlisle Assize Sermon*, at 7–8; Gallaway, *Sermon at St. Mary's*, at 18; Lediard, *Charge to Westminster Jury*, at 7; Mountagu, *Wiltshire Grand Jury Charge*, at 18–19; Sykes, *Winchester Rebellion Sermon*, at 13. See also equivalent American occasions: Jonathan Mayhew, Election Sermon (1754), reprinted in *They Preached Liberty*, at 69; Judge Drayton's Address to South Carolina Grand Jury (1774), 44 *London Magazine* (1775), at 126. Contrary, see Anon., *Justice to a Judge*, at 9.

6. Ashby v. White, *Salkeld Reports*, (K.B.), at 21; Letter to the Editor [from Governor Stephen Hopkins], *Providence Gazette* (Postscript), 8 April 1765, at 1, col. 3.

7. [Whately,] *Regulations*, at 104; Anon., *Arguments in Support of Supremacy*, at 31–32; [Macpherson,] *Rights of Great Britain*, at 4.

8. Plowden, *Friendly and Constitutional*, at 27, 20.

9. Eliot, *Give Cesar his Due*, at 33; "British American," Williamsburg, 30 June 1774, 1 *American Archives*, at 495; Speech of Mr. Wilkes, Commons Debates, 21 March 1776, *Society for Constitutional Information*, at 12; Anon., *Evidence of Common and Statute Laws*, at 27–32; Whitaker, *Manchester*, at 171–72; [Squire,] *Ballance of Power*, at 34; Kramnick, *Bolingbroke's Circle*, at 179 (quoting *Craftsman*, 5 July 1735). See also Letter from C. Wyvill to Belfast Committee, 1783, *Collection of Irish Letters*, at 25–26; Clarke, *Representation and Consent*, at 247. For origins of consent in Roman, canon, and civil law, see Tierney, *Religion, Law, and Growth*, at 39–42.

10. Anon., *Evidence of Common and Statute Laws*, at 2–4 (discussing 25 Hen. 8, cap. 21); Carlyle, *Political Liberty*, at 20 (discussing 1 *Statutes of the Realm*, at 189); Quincy, *Observations with Thoughts*, at 450n; Anon., *Three Letters*, at 13; Keir, *Constitutional History*, at 7–8, 100.

11. Smith: Pollock, "Sovereignty in English Law," at 244; Thorne, "Introduction," at 31; Pole, *Representation*, at 4–5; Saint German: *St. German's Doctor and Student*, Selden Society, vol. 91 (London, 1974), at 279; Hooker: Hooker, *Laws of Ecclesiastical Polity*, bk. 1, chap. 10, secs. 4, 8; Locke, *Two Treatises*, bk. 2, sec. 134 (quoting Hooker in a note); Anon., *To Tax Themselves*, at 74; "Answer to Wesley," 5 *Hibernian Magazine* (1775), at 784; 2 Hoadly, *Works*, at 251; Eccleshall, *Order and Reason*, at 139–41; Shirley, *Richard Hooker*, at 99; Carlyle, *Political Liberty*, at 53.

12. [Care,] *English Liberties First Edition*, at 3 (quoting Fortescue); 1 [Oldfield,] *History of the Boroughs*, at 126 (quoting Fortescue); Skeel, "Influence of Fortescue," at 81. Fortescue wrote *De Laudibus Legum Angliae*. See also Egerton, *Discourse*, at 108; von Mehren, "Legislation in Tudor England," at 752; Haskins, "Rule of Law," at 532.

13. Tanner, *Constitutional Conflicts*, at 118 (quoting Edmund Ludlow). See also Remonstrance for bill of tonnage and poundage, 25 June 1628, 4 *Commons*

Debates 1628, at 470; Case of Proclamations (1610), 2 *State Trials,* at 725 (quoting Sir Edward Coke); [Mantell,] *Short Treatise of the Lawes,* at 7, 10; Ball, *Power of Kings,* at 132; Anon., *Priviledges of Parliament,* at 41–42; Speech of Henry Ireton, 29 October 1647, "Putney Debates," at 72; Judson, *Crisis,* at 309–10, 418–19.

14. Bill of Attainder against Strafford, 11 May 1641, 1 Rushworth, *Historical Collections: Third Part,* at 263; Pym, *Speech of summing up,* at 18; Manning, "Levellers," at 145, 152, 156; Eccleshall, *Order and Reason,* at 168–69 (quoting Richard Overton). Consent was central to the Putney Debates. Speech of Colonel Thomas Rainborough, 29 October 1647, "Putney Debates," at 53; Robbins, "Republicanism," at 45.

15. *A True Copy,* at 30–31. See, similarly, the grievance against Oliver Cromwell, "In Levying Taxes upon the People without consent in *Parliament," Remonstrance of the Cities* (1659), at 2. But see Cragg, *Freedom and Authority,* at 86–87.

16. *His Majesties Declaration,* at 1; Speech to Lincoln, 15 July 1642, Charles I, *Several Speeches,* at 30.

17. *A True Copy,* at 48.

18. Chancellor: Somers, *Security of Englishmen's Lives,* at 8; Anon., *Judgment of Whole Kingdoms,* at 20, 21, 26–27 (popularly attributed to Somers); Sharp, *Declaration of Natural Right,* at 3–4 (quoting Somers); chief baron: Atkyns, *Enquiry into Power,* at 6, 7–8, 19, 20. See also Sydney, *Discourses Concerning Government,* at 4; Petyt, *Antient Right,* at 39–50; [Tyrrell,] *Brief Enquiry,* at 11; Trenchard, Letter of 6 January 1721, "Cato's Letters," at 116; Gordon, Letter of 14 October 1721, 2 *Cato's Letters,* at 112; [Barrington,] *Revolution Principles,* at 9–16; Schwoerer, "Bill of Rights," at 231–32; Browning, *Court Whigs,* at 82. At the impeachment trial of the high tory Henry Sacheverell, the Glorious Revolution was explained in terms of consent. Speech of Sir Joseph Jekyll, 28 February 1709/10, *Trial of Sacheverell,* at 49 (see also Speech of Lechmere, at 23). For extreme statements of consent, see Sherlock, *Present Majesties Government,* at 6–7; Anon., *Confutation of Sherlock,* at 2–3, 9–10. For rejection of the doctrine, see Hobbes, *De Cive,* at 156–57; [Brydall,] *New-Years-Gift,* at 21.

19. Allen, *In English Ways,* at 205, 210–13; Williamson, "Imperial Policy," at 218–19 (Barbados); Wood, *Creation,* at 183–84; Boucher, *Causes and Conquences,* at 533n; Baldwin, *New England Clergy,* at 26–27 (quoting Thomas Hooker, 1638).

20. [Rawson,] *Revolution in New England,* at 6; Breen, *Good Ruler,* at 157 (also 143, 144); Barnes, *Dominion of New England,* at 90, 118–19. See also Logan, *Antidote,* at 4; Wiltse, *Jeffersonian Tradition,* at 27.

21. Frink, *Election Sermon,* at 80n; [Hurd,] *Moral and Political Dialogues,* at 310–11.

22. Kramnick, "Augustan Reply," at 581; Ludlow: Gooch, *English Democratic Ideas,* at 210; Handlin and Handlin, "James Burgh," at 47; Rossiter, *Political Thought,* at 164 (quoting Wilson). However, *salus populi suprema lex* had long been an English political value. [Johnson,] *Defence of Magna Charta,* at lxii (quoting Sir William Temple).

23. Filmer, *Observations upon Aristotle,* at 225; 2 Hume, *Essays,* at 298; [Anderson,] *Free Thoughts,* at 16, col. 1; Anon., *Defence of English History,* at 66; [Ramsay,] *Origin and Nature,* at 19–48; Campbell, *Duty of Allegiance,* at 21; *New and*

Impartial Letters, at 122; Tucker, *Four Letters to Shelburne*, at 55; Fletcher, *Vindication of Wesley*, at 37–38.

24. Consent was also thought necessary for the right to property (and the right to consent was itself a property right, "the inherent Birth-right of *Englishmen*"). Shelton, *Charge to Suffolk Grand Jury*, at 21; 1 Rutherforth, *Natural Law*, at 47; Address of Virginia's Council and Burgesses to King, 18 December 1764, *Boston Post-Boy*, 25 March 1765, at 1, col. 1; Northcote, *Observations on Rights*, at 10; Haskins, "Rule of Law," at 532.

25. Wooddeson, *Jurisprudence*, at 32, 33; God's ordinance: [Downer,] *Discourse in Providence*, at 6; [Livingston,] *The Other Side*, at 16; Fletcher, *Vindication of Wesley*, at 42; Bainbrigg, *Seasonable Reflections*, at 12; observable nature: Harris, *Eighteenth-Century England*, at 143; Boston Resolves, 13 September 1768, *Boston News-Letter*, 15 September 1768, at 2, col. 1; Tucker, *Election Sermon*, at 13–14; *They Preached Liberty*, at 151 (quoting Jason Haven, *Election Sermon* [1769]); Patten, *Discourse at Hallifax*, at 7, 10; Tucker, *Treatise*, at 97–98; Northcote, *Observations on Rights*, at 10; "Rational Principles of Government," 45 *London Magazine* (1776), at 355; Anon., *Letter to Cooper*, at 15–16; Anon., *Liberty in Two Parts*, at 54; 2 Hume, *Essays*, at 289–90; Jackson, *Grounds of Government*, at 6; Locke, *Two Treatises*, bk. 2, secs. 22, 99, 119. See also Cartwright, *Letter to Abingdon*, at 7; Mayhew, *Election Sermon*, at 6; Anon., *Rights Asserted*, at 12; Anon., *Whigs and Jacobites*, at 15–16; Hooker, *Laws of Ecclesiastical Polity*, bk. 1, chap. 10, sec. 4; Tierney, *Religion, Law, and Growth*, at 34. Contrary, see Warrington, *Grand Jury Charge*, at 20.

26. Wilson, *Considerations*, at 723.

27. Anon., *Considerations on National Independence*, at 57–58, 64, 72.

28. [Nedham,] *Excellencie of Free State*, at 90; Shelton, *Charge to Suffolk Grand Jury*, at 7. See also Towers, *Vindication of Locke*, at 52; Anon., *Appeal to Reason and Justice*, at 83; Anon., *Inquiry into the Nature*, at 19; Anon., *British Liberties*, at lxix; Candidus, *Two Letters*, at 9–10; [Brooke,] *Liberty and Common Sense: Letter II*, at 14; [Williams,] *Essential Rights*, at 4; Trenchard, Letter of 6 January 1721, 2 *Cato's Letters*, at 226; Johnson, *Argument Proving*, at 58; Toohey, *Liberty and Empire*, at 68 (quoting James Burgh); Baldwin, *New England Clergy*, at 27 (quoting Roger Williams); Schwoerer, "Bill of Rights," at 230–31.

29. Rous, *Thoughts on Government*, at 22–23; Adams, "Novanglus," at 241; Baldwin, *New England Clergy*, at 178 (quoting D. S. Rowland, *Thanksgiving Sermon* (Providence, R.I., 1766)); Speech of Hans Stanley, Commons Debates, 2 May 1774, 1 *American Archives*, at 85; Trenchard, Letter of 22 September 1722, "Cato's Letters," at 229; Locke, *Two Treatises*, bk. 2, sec. 112; Kenyon, *Revolution Principles*, at 61; Tierney, *Religion, Law, and Growth*, at 35.

30. Proclamation of Massachusetts General Court, 23 January 1776, *Remembrancer of 1776: Part II*, at 53; Boorstin, *Mysterious Science of Law*, at 156 (quoting Blackstone); New London Resolves, 10 December 1765, *Boston Post-Boy*, 16 December 1765, at 3, col. 2; Welsteed, *Dignity and Duty*, at 11–12; Shelton, *Charge to Suffolk Grand Jury*, at 13–14. See also Burlamaqui, *Politic Law*, at 97; 2 Rutherforth, *Natural Law*, at 215; Rous, *Thoughts on Government*, at 22, 23, 47; Trenchard, Letter of 8 June 1723, 4 *Cato's Letters*, at 231; 2 Hoadly, *Works*, at 259–60; Browning, *Court Whigs*, at 82; Toohey, *Liberty and Empire*, at 60 (quoting Richard

Hooker). Contrary, see Filmer, *Observations upon Aristotle,* at 225; 2 Hume, *Essays,* at 293; Anon., *Confutation of Sherlocke,* at 5; Anon., *Divine Rights,* at 59 (quoting Fortescue).

31. Trenchard, Letter of 21 January 1720, 1 *Cato's Letters,* at 86, 87; [Nedham,] *Excellencie of Free State,* at 2.

32. Parent and obligation: 3 Wynne, *Eunomus,* at 123; Message from House to Governor Francis Bernard, 13 June 1769, *Gazette and Post-Boy,* 19 June 1769, at 1, col. 2; Speech of Sir Joseph Jekyll, 28 February 1709/10, *Trial of Sacheverell,* at 48. See also Jamaica Petition to King, 45 *Gentleman's Magazine* (1775), at 617n; Massachusetts Resolves, 29 June 1769, *Boston Post-Boy,* 3 July 1769, at 1, col. 1; [Lee,] *Speech Intended,* at 60 (citing Coke); Adams, "Novanglus," at 201; *American Gazette,* at 49; [Bancroft,] *Remarks,* at 88–89; [Knox,] *Controversy,* at 68–69; Rossiter, *Political Thought,* at 158–59 (quoting *Boston Gazette,* 18 November 1765); Johnson, *Notes on Pastoral,* at 30; Petyt, *Lex Parliamentaria,* at 19; Manning, "Puritanism and Democracy," at 144–45 (quoting Thomas Cartwright and Jeremiah Burroughes).

33. Petyt, *Jus Parliamentarium,* at "Preface"; Yale, "Hobbes and Hale," at 140 (discussing Chief Justice Matthew Hale); Address of Richard Henderson to Transylvania House of Delegates, 23 May 1775, 9 *North Carolina Colonial Records,* at 1269; Tyrrell, *Politica,* at 218; Locke, *Two Treatises,* bk. 2, sec. 134; [Claridge,] *Defence of Government,* at 2 (quoting Hooker). See also Resolves of 12 September 1768, 16 *Boston Town Records,* at 261; Cartwright, *People's Barrier,* at 21; [Brecknock,] *Droit le Roy,* at 34; [Sheridan,] *Review of Three Questions,* at 31; Toohey, *Liberty and Empire,* at 54; Carlyle, *Political Liberty,* at 54. Contrary, see Tucker, *Four Letters to Shelburne,* at 19–20, 47. In the thirteenth century, Bracton said: ". . . whatever has been rightly decided and approved with the counsel and consent of the magnates and the general agreement of the *res publica,* the authority of the king or prince having first been added thereto, has the force of law." 2 Bracton, *Laws and Customs,* at 19.

34. Shelton, *Suffolk Grand Jury Charge,* at 12. See also Shelton, *Charge to Suffolk Grand Jury,* at 14; Sir John Gonson, Charge to Westminster Grand Jury, 9 October 1728, Gonson, *Charges,* at 103; A.B., "To the Editor," 43 *London Magazine* (1774), at 479; Gray, *Right of the Legislature,* at 29–30.

35. Abingdon, *Thoughts on Burke's Letter,* at xlvii (agreeing with Blackstone). See also De Lolme, *Constitution: New Edition,* at 310 (agreeing with Lord Lyttelton); [Marchmont,] *Serious Exhortation,* at 26; Johnson, *Remarks on Sherlock,* at 6–7; [Stillingfleet,] *Discourse,* at 7, 18–19; Pole, *Legislative Power,* at 9 (quoting Philip Hunton). Contrary, see Lawson, *Politica Sacra,* at 66–67.

36. Anon., *Divine Rights,* at 46; Anon., *Animadversions on Discourse,* at 38–39; Atkyns, *Enquiry into Power,* at 19.

37. Chrimes, "Introduction," at xx; Kern, *Kingship,* at 73–74, 186.

38. Wood, *Creation,* at 362 (Massachusetts General Court); Speech of William Pierrepont, 6 July 1641, in 4 *Somers' Tracts,* at 306. See also Kenyon, *Revolution Principles,* at 61; Tierney, *Religion, Law, and Growth,* at 80. Contrary, see Filmer, *Necessity of Absolute Power,* at 320.

39. *British Lightening* (1643), in 5 *Somers' Tracts,* at 19; [Rivers,] *Letters,* at 76; [Defoe,] *A Speech Without Doors,* at 11. See also Turner, *Election Sermon,* at 16;

Hamilton, *Duty of Obedience to Laws*, at 15; Anon., *British Liberties*, at xx; [Somers,] *Brief History*, at 17; Kenyon, *Revolution Principles*, at 7–8; 1 Macaulay, *History of England*, at 38; Allen, *English Political Thought*, at 343.

40. Ownership: Sir John Gonson, Charge to Westminster Grand Jury, 24 April 1728, Gonson, *Charges*, at 7–8; accountable: *They Preached Liberty*, at 61 (reprinting Cooke, *Election Sermon*); Molesworth, *Principles of a Real Whig*, at 6; security: [Bland], *Colonel Dismounted*, at 21; Petyt, *Jus Parliamentarium*, at vii-viii.

41. Price, *Two Tracts: Tract One*, at 100n; *Reliquiae Sacrae Carolinae*, at 32 (quoting Charles I); Dobbs, *Letter to North*, at 9. See also James Iredell (1774), 1 *Papers of Iredell*, at 256; James Duane (1774), 1 *Letters of Delegates to Congress*, at 52; Tucker, *Treatise*, at 85, 98; Anon., *Letter on Parliamentary Representation*, at 34; *American Gazette*, at 45; [Rokeby,] *Further Examination*, at 189; Anon., *Reflections on Wilkes*, at 8–9. For a discussion of the meaning of slavery, see *Concept of Liberty*, at 38–54.

42. The literature is too vast to be discussed here. The basic argument was whether it was enough for liberty to be governed by the rule of law or whether the laws had to be enacted by free consent of the governed, arbitrary or not. See, e.g., *Essex Result*, at 14, 27; Price, *Two Tracts: Tract One*, at 7, 19–20; Anon., *Prospect of the Consequences*, at 14; [Keld,] *Polity of England*, at 278–79, 284, 484–85; Priestley, *First Principles* (1768), at 12–13; Anon., *Reflections on Wilkes*, at 9–10; [Brooke,] *Liberty and Common Sense: Letter II*, at 9–10; Anon., *Whigs and Jacobites*, at 15–16. For contrary, see John Wesley, "Some Observations on Liberty," reprinted in Peach, *Richard Price*, at 247; [Anderson,] *Free Thoughts*, at 19, col. 1; Anon., *Case of Great Britain*, at 6; Anon., *Experience preferable*, at 18–19; Anon., *Defence of English History*, at 66–67. For discussion, see *Concept of Liberty*, at 74–83.

43. *Boston Evening-Post*, 2 October 1769, at 2, col. 2.

44. Anon., *Civil Liberty Asserted*, at 31–32; Anon., *Letter to the Essay Author*, at 14–15. See also Price, *Two Tracts: Tract Two*, at 10; Guttridge, *English Whiggism*, at 12.

45. For barristers on the Anglo-Saxons, see St. Amand, *Historical Essay*, at 197; [Ibbetson,] *National Assemblies*, at 3–4.

CHAPTER TWO

1. Pole, *Legislative Power*, at 29; Lutz, *Popular Consent and Control*, at 43.

2. [Knox,] *Letter to a Member*, at 18.

3. Shirley, *Richard Hooker*, at 102 (quoting Hooker); [Jones,] *Constitutional Criterion*, at 10; "Regulus," *Defence of the Resolutions*, at 33. Contrary, see Wesley, *Calm Address*, at 5–7; [Young,] *Political Essays*, at 35; Filmer, *Observations upon Aristotle*, at 225–26.

4. Sherlock, *Present Majesties Government*, at 11; [Barrington,] *Revolution Principles*, at 10–11. Contrary, see Wesley, *Calm Address*, at 7–8. For answer, see "Answer to Wesley," 5 *Hibernian Magazine* (1775), at 787. Another theory implied consent from people serving on juries. [Ramsay,] *Historical Essay*, at 165; Browning *Court Whigs*, at 162 (quoting Lord Chancellor Hardwick. See also Anon., *Taxation, Tyranny*, at 33.

5. Lofft, *Observations on Wesley's Address*, at 37; Paley, *Principles of Philosophy*,

at 415; common-law writers: Wooddeson, *Jurisprudence*, at 69; 2 Rutherforth, *Natural Law*, at 2, 216; [Hale,] *History*, at 77–78; Locke: Locke, *Two Treatises*, bk. 2, secs. 117, 118; Pitkin, "Obligation and Consent," at 995 (quoting Locke); Gough, *Locke's Political Philosophy*, at 55–56; Pole, *Representation*, at 23, 343–44; [Blacklock,] *Remarks on Liberty*, at 52. See also [Cary,] *Answer to Molyneux*, at 65–68; [Evans,] *Letter to John Wesley*, at 7–8; [Anderson,] *Free Thoughts*, at 17, col. 2; Wills, *Inventing America*, at 82–83. Contrary, see Bentham, *Comment on Commentaries*, at 221. Another theory implied consent when laws were good laws, in the interest of all the people. [Jones,] *Constitutional Criterion*, at 11.

6. Pitkin, "Obligation and Consent," at 993.

7. Wooddeson, *Jurisprudence*, at 35–36. See also ibid., at 36, 47–48, 74–75.

8. 2 Rutherforth, *Natural Law*, at 292.

9. Bentham, *Comment on Commentaries*, at 332.

10. Traditional common law: Hale, "Reflections," at 507; Case of Tanistry, Davis, *Reports*, at 37; ancient constitution: Kern, *Kingship*, at 73–74. See also [Baillie,] *Appendix to a Letter*, at 51 (a Scots lawyer writing of English consent); Anon., *Letter to the Essay Author*, at 2–3; Petyt, *Lex Parliamentaria*, at 20–21; Yale, "Hobbes and Hale," at 140; Clarke, *Representation and Consent*, at 249. But see [Downley,] *Sentiments*, at 2; Jezierski, "Parliament or People," at 99–100 (discussing Wilson and Blackstone). There was also consent by implication of law. "[T]o an Act of Parliament every Man in judgment of Law is [a] Party, as being present by his Representative." [Wood,] *Institute of the Laws*, at 9. From this rule followed the doctrine that no one was ignorant of statute law. Anon., *Triumphs of Justice*, at 32.

11. Wooddeson, *Jurisprudence*, at 79; 2 Rutherforth, *Natural Law*, at 223; *Essex Result*, at 28–29; West, *Election Sermon*, at 19; Anon., *Constitutional Advocate*, at 41; Hamilton, *Farmer*, at 92; "To the Printer," 11 *Political Register* (1772), at 229; *Boston News-Letter*, 6 March 1766, at 2, col. 1; Anon., *Reflexions on Representation*, at 10–11; Lowth, *Durham Assize Sermon*, at 10–11; Anon., *Political Disquisitions*, at 50–51; Petyt, *Lex Parliamentaria*, at 20, 108; [Steuart,] *Jus Populi*, at 333; Speech of William Pierrepont to Lords, Sir Robert Berkley Impeachment, 6 July 1641, 1 Rushworth, *Historical Collections: Third Part*, at 326.

12. Theory: [Knox,] *Controversy*, at 67; 1 [Oldfield,] *History of the Boroughs*, at 9; taxation: 2 Burgh, *Political Disquisitions*, at 306–7; Anon., *Letter to Mansfield*, at 17; Garth, "Letter," at 69 (quoting Commons speech of William Pitt); Anon., *Three Letters*, at 16–17; colonies: *Authority to Tax*, at 19–20, 150–53. For an elaborate theory that the Lords were as much the representatives of the people as were the Commons, see [Knox,] *Present State*, at 90–91. The American theory was that the Lords were "the fixed and hereditary guardians of *British* Liberty." Petition of the Virginia Council and Burgesses to House of Lords, 14 April 1768, 11 *Journal of Burgesses*, at 166; Petition of Pennsylvania House of Representatives to House of Lords, 22 September 1768, 7 *Pennsylvania Archives*, at 6274.

13. Thus it was consistent for George Grenville to say that "no man can be tax'd without his own Consent or the Consent of those whom Society has empower'd to act for the whole" and yet think that representation was "irrelevant." Langford, "Old Whigs," at 109.

14. Goodricke, *Observations*, at 8; Anon., *Arguments in Support of Supremacy*, at 31–32, 30–31. See also 55 *Monthly Review* (1776), at 240 (criticizing Goodricke); Anon., *Civil Liberty Asserted*, at 16; "Regulus," *Defence of the Resolutions*, at 31; 1 Burgh, *Political Disquisitions*, at 25; [Cartwright,] *Take Your Choice*, at 29; Anon., *Remarks on the New Essay*, at 8; Pole, *Representation*, at 4–5, 388, 462–63; Courtney, *Montesquieu and Burke*, at 56.

15. Price, *Two Tracts: Tract Two*, at 36. In the eighteenth century, the doctrine of the delegated right to consent was thought part of the ancient constitution. Lofft, *Observations on Publication*, at 13; Anon., *Representative of London*, at 6.

16. By the eighteenth century, the judicial functions of representation were no longer important in Great Britain and limited to appellate jurisdiction in the colonies. May, *Parliamentary Practice*, at 6–7.

17. [Robinson,] *Political Catechism*, at 59; "Observations on Elections," 4 *Political Register* (1769), at 226. See also De Lolme, *Constitution: New Edition*, at 309; "Regulus," *Defence of the Resolutions*, at 81; [Ibbetson,] *National Assemblies*, at 29; Anon., "Second Part," at 224. During debates on the American constitutional controversy, an opposite purpose was stated for the House of Lords. It served as a check on "that Democratic Interest" of representation. Speeches of Lord Sandwich and Lord Suffolk, Lords Debates, 11 March 1766, "Stamp Acts Debates," at 580, 582.

18. [Meredith,] *Question Stated*, at 12; inquisitors: Speech of Sir William Yonge, Commons Debates, 23 January 1745, 13 *Parliamentary History*, at 1078; watchmen: Tucker, *Election Sermon*, at 22; Bolingbroke, *Political Writings*, at 29–30 (see also 41); Bolingbroke, *Craftsman*, at 60; *Craftsman* (no. 151), 24 May 1729, at 3. See also Price, *Two Tracts: Tract One*, at 11–12; Price, *Two Tracts: Tract Two*, at 35; 44 *Gentleman's Magazine* (1774), at 204; Anon., *Abuse of Standing Parliaments*, at 18; Anon., *Danger of Incapacities*, at 36; Anon., *Representative of London*, at 6.

19. Speech of Watkins Williams Wynn, Commons Debates, 13 March 1734, 9 *Parliamentary History*, at 430 (see also 459); Speech of the King, 4 December 1741, 5 *Proceedings and Debates*, at 111; Speech of Thomas Carew, Commons Debates, 23 January 1745, 13 *Parliamentary History*, at 1059 (see also 1058). See also Devon Instructions, 7 October 1756, *Voice of People*, at 25–26; [Bolingbroke,] *Dissertation*, at 128; Instructions from Chester Grand Jury, 5 September 1740, and Flint Instructions, 23 October 1740, 1 *Britain's Memorial*, at 33–34, 41; Anon., *Representative of London*, at 6; Petyt, *Antient Right*, at "Preface" 40.

20. For the constitutional theory that there could be no conflict between the House of Commons and the people because "the House of Commons for the time being, and the people was the same," see Report of Commons debate, 42 *Gentleman's Magazine* (1772), at 99.

21. Anon., *To Freeholders of Pennsylvania*, at 1–2; Anon., *Observations on Assembly*, at 3–4. See also Williams, *Election Sermon*, at 23; Bellamy, *Sermon*, at 34–35; Frink, *Election Sermon*, at 92; Mayhew, *Election Sermon*, at 44; Anon., *O Liberty*, at 2; Chandler, *Representation in Virginia*, at 13.

22. *Thoughts on the Present Discontents* (1770), reprinted in 2 *Burke Writings*, at 292. For some British commentators who mentioned statute making, see 38 *Scots Magazine* (1776), at 227 (reprinting *London Chronicle*); Cartwright, *Legisla-*

tive Rights, at 27; [Ferguson,] *Remarks on Dr. Price,* at 13; Speech of Charles James Fox, Commons Debates, 25 March 1771, 1 Fox, *Speeches,* at 10; "Grand Jury Charge," Warrington, *Works,* at 647; Cook, *King Charls His Case,* at 7.

23. For a detailed analysis of the differences between British and American legislation, see Bailyn, *Origins of Politics,* at 101–4.

24. Rusticus, *Good of Community,* at 12–13. See also *Maryland Gazette,* 20 January 1748, at 3, col. 2. For the best summary of the constitutional theory of representation, see 1 Blackstone, *Commentaries,* at 9. To contrast British theory with American, compare Williams, *Parliamentary Reformation,* at 5, to Resolutions of Caroline County, Virginia, 14 July 1774, 1 *American Archives,* at 539–40.

CHAPTER THREE

1. Rous, *Thoughts on Government,* at 7–8; Young, *Example of France,* at 232 (see also 106). See also [Anderson,] *Free Thoughts,* at 15–16.

2. [Basset,] *Equal Representation,* at 2 (see also 13); Speech of Lord Camden, Lords Debates, February 1766, 16 *Parliamentary History,* at 179; Pulteney, *Plan of Reunion,* at 40; Sharp, *Legal Means,* at 74; Abingdon, *Dedication,* at lxxxn, lxxvn. See also 3 *Works of Burke,* at 299.

3. Anon., *Letter to English,* at 6–7; [Lind,] *Thirteenth Parliament,* at 355–56; Anon., *Representative of London,* at 31.

4. Anon., *Civil Liberty Asserted,* at 20–21; 3 *Works of Burke,* at 298. But see also Batley, *Letter to Wyvill,* at 6–7. Consider also another explanation that belongs to the eighteenth century and has no constitutional force today. Fundamental laws, it was noted, were called *lex terrae.* "Not the law of the land-holders, but the law of the *land* itself. . . . It is a solecism in language to say, that the people represent the people. . . . But this nonsense does not occur when we say, the people represent the land." Anon., *Constitution,* at 59.

5. Robinson, *Christian Submission,* at 15; Dalrymple, *Feudal Property,* at 344. See also [Powis,] *Dialogue on Parliament,* at 19; [Squire,] *Ballance of Power,* at 42; Trenchard, Letter of 7 July 1722, 3 *Cato's Letters,* at 151; [Neville,] *Plato Redivivus,* at 35.

6. *Daily Gazetteer* (no. 30), 2 August 1735, at 1, col. 2. See also Glanville, *Reports,* at iv–v; [Basset,] *Equal Representation,* at 3–5, 13; [Squire,] *Ballance of Power,* at vi; Pocock, *Ancient Constitution,* at 138–43; Kramnick, "Introduction to Writings," at xxii.

7. Anon., *Essay on Constitutional Liberty,* at 23n. See also 3 *Works of Burke,* at 299; [Keld,] *Polity of England,* at 389; Browning, *Court Whigs,* at 120; O'Gorman, "After Namier," at 120. Ironically, the weight of property even provided an argument for universal suffrage. "It has been a maxim, that Dominion should follow Property. The greatest property of a country is the people—the mass of the people, whom Dominion should follow." Williams, *Parliamentary Reformation,* at 9.

8. Langford, *Excise Crisis,* at 162 (quoting 1733 progovernment pamphlet). Ireton defended the same concept in the seventeenth century. Carlyle, *Political Liberty,* at 188–89.

9. Anon., *Letter to English,* at 8; [Ramsay,] *Letters on Present Disturbances,* at

29; Anon., *Constitution*, at 97–98. See also Speech of Lord Chatham, House of Lords, 20 January 1775, Chatham, *Genuine Abstracts*, at 9–10; Pocock, "Mobility of Property," at 145; Hutson, "Country, Court, and Constitution," at 358; Moore, "Comment," at 167.

10. Chatham, *Speech of 20 January*, at 8–9; [Robinson,] *Political Catechism*, at 80. An effective argument for the Quebec Act was that, because of the nature of trade and the amount of property in the colony, the people there were not ready for representation. Anon., *Thoughts on Quebec Act*, at 12–13. For perhaps the best discussion of the destructive force of lawyers on landed independence, see Charge II (1765), *Worcester Charges*, at 14–15. See also *Craftsman* (no. 488), 8 November 1735, at 175; Pocock, "Mobility of Property," at 147, 155; Moore, "Comment," at 168. Contrary, see Williams, *Parliamentary Reformation*, at 7–8; [Bolingbroke,] *Dissertation*, at 235.

11. 30 *London Magazine* (1761), at 13; 10 *Gentleman's Magazine* (1740), at 450 (reprinting the *Craftsman*); Anon., *Civil Liberty Asserted*, at 19; Young, *Example of France*, at 83. See also [Keld,] *Polity of England*, at 242–45; [Rivers,] *Letters*, at 268–69; Anon., *Address to Free*, at 8; Gibbons, *Ideas of Representation*, at 15; Worcestershire Grand Jury Charge, 1765, *Worcester Charges*, at 10; "To Electors," 30 *London Magazine* (1761), at 117; Pocock, *Politics*, at 91. But see Speech of Watkins Williams Wynn, Commons Debates, 13 March 1734, 9 *Parliamentary History*, at 431 (saying the representatives should have "large properties in the country . . . who by living in the country are perfectly acquainted with the circumstances of the people").

12. Molesworth, *Principles of a Real Whig*, at 13; Batley, *Letter to Wyvill*, at 3. See also Speech of Sir Philip Jennings Clerke, Commons Debates, 13 April 1778, 19 *Parliamentary History*, at 1090; 17 *Gentleman's Magazine* (1747), at 368 (reprinting *Westminster Journal*, 8 August 1747); Kenyon, *Revolution Principles*, at 206 (quoting Robert Walpole).

13. Paley, *Principles of Philosophy*, at 489; [Powis,] *Dialogue on Parliament*, at 16. See also 10 *Gentleman's Magazine* (1740), at 450 (reprinting the *Craftsman*); [Grange,] *Late Excise*, at 13.

14. 9 Anne, cap. 5; Wooddeson, *Laws of England*, at 46; [Ramsay,] *Historical Essay*, at 126 (see also 131, 138); Instructions of 24 June 1773, *Addresses and Petitions of Common Council*, at 42–43; Instructions of Gloucester, 24 September 1740, 1 *Britain's Memorial*, at 37. See also Speech of Sir Robert Walpole, Commons Debates, 29 January 1740, 11 *Parliamentary History*, at 367; Speech of Sir John Barnard, Commons Debates, 13 March 1734, 9 *Parliamentary History*, at 448–49; [Almon,] *Free Parliaments*, at 25–26; 30 *London Magazine* (1761), at 9; 17 *Gentleman's Magazine* (1747), at 366–67 (reprinting *Westminster Journal*, 8 August 1747); 10 *Gentleman's Magazine* (1740), at 450; 11 *Craftsman* (no. 375), 8 September 1733, at 149; Pocock, *Politics*, at 92–93.

15. Young, *Example of France*, at 84.

16. [Wheelock,] *Reflections*, at 11, 12; sycophants: Anon., *Letter to Freemen of New York*, at 11; independent of governors: Anon., *To Freeholders of Pennsylvania*, at 1; Broadside from John Cruger et al., "To the Freeholders . . . of New York," 9 January 1764 (Huntington Library rare book no. 108949); study: Moss, *Con-*

necticut Election Sermon, at 27–28. At least one preacher believed that the qualifications for representatives were the same in New as in old England. Cotton, *Election Sermon,* at 26–30.

17. Anon., *To Freeholders of New York* (1768a), at 4; Turner, *Election Sermon,* at 11–12; Mayhew, *Election Sermon,* at 27; Rusticus, *Good of Community,* at 5–6; Anon., *Letter to Freeholders* (1749), at 6, 7; "Americanus," *Letter to Freeholders,* at 2, 5. For a British constitutionalist saying, "Knowledge of the State of the Country is a necessary Qualification," see Arbuthnot, *Freeholder's Catechism,* at 21.

18. White, *Connecticut Election Sermon,* at 25; Perry, *Connecticut Election Sermon,* at 18; Tucker, *Election Sermon,* at 44; Dickinson, *Connecticut Election Sermon,* at 54; Woodbridge, *Connecticut Election Sermon,* at 43; *South-Carolina Gazette,* 5 October 1765, at 3, col. 1.

19. Probity: Anon., *Letter to Freemen of New York,* at 11; "steady Conduct" and "Estates": Anon., *Letter to Freeholders* (1742), at 5. Another Massachusetts election pamphleteer urged the voters to elect men "who govern themselves by natural Principles, and fixed Rules laid down in the Constitution, and not by unaccountable Humours, or Arbitrary Will which is liable to the greatest Levity and Inconstancy." Anon., *Letter to Freeholders* (1749), at 7–8. See also Galloway, *Speech in Answer,* at xxi; Checkley, *Election Sermon,* at 31–32; Moss, *Connecticut Election Sermon,* at 37. A New York campaign against and for the election of lawyers also revealed American attitudes about representation in unusually sharp details. Anon., *Observations on Assembly,* at 6; Anon., *To Freeholders of New York* (1768c), at 1, col. 2; Anon., *To Freeholders of New York* (1768a), at 4; Anon., *To Freeholders of New York* (1768b), at 1, col. 3; Champagne, "New York Elections," at 65.

20. 1 Blackstone, *Commentaries,* at 165; Blackstone, *Tracts,* at 203–4. But see the former or timeless "theory of the British constitution" regarding representation, which was "to give every man, as near as possible, an influence in the publick deliberations proportioned to his interest in them." Anon., *Reflexions on Representation,* at 4.

21. Williamson, *American Suffrage,* at 3; Speech of Henry Ireton, 29 October 1647, "Putney Debates," at 63; [Keld,] *Polity of England,* at 244.

22. Petty quoted in Pole, *Legislative Power,* at 17 (see also 18–19); Pocock, "Mobility of Property," at 141; Anon., *Political Disquisitions,* at 57 (see also 52–53); [Keld,] *Polity of England,* at 244. See also Gordon, Letter of 3 March 1721, 2 *Cato's Letters,* at 321–22; Pocock, "English Ideologies," at 555, 560–66. Contrary, see Batley, *Letter to Wyvill,* at 19–20; "Declaration of Rights," Cartwright, *People's Barrier,* at 21; Carlyle, *Political Liberty,* at 191–92 (quoting Cartwright).

23. Anon., *Application of Political Rules,* at 66; Clark, *British Opinion,* at 218.

24. Copyholders: Carysfort, *Letter to Huntingdonshire,* at 6; Anon., *Reflexions on Representation,* at 10; new property: Anon., *Political Disquisitions,* at 55–59; Anon., *Reflexions on Representation,* at 6, 12n; Lofft, *Observations on Publication,* at 21. For a discussion of the statutes that helped freeze legal theory, see Pole, *Representation,* at 412–13; Witmer, *Property Qualifications,* at 45, 78, 80–81.

25. For a reevaluation of the British franchise that convincingly shows that political participation (including public opinion) was more widespread than has been thought, see O'Gorman, "After Namier," at 116–17.

26. Letter to Thomas Jefferson, 10 August 1776, 1 *Letters and Papers of Pen-*

dleton, at 198; Letter from John Adams to James Sullivan, 26 May 1776, 4 *Letters of Delegates to Congress,* at 73; Iredell, "To Inhabitants of Great Britain" (September 1774), 1 *Papers of Iredell,* at 257. See also [Thomas Mason,] "British American," 30 June 1774, 1 *Revolutionary Virginia,* at 174; Jensen, *Revolution Within,* at 74 (quoting *Boston Gazette,* 22 February 1768); Wood, *Creation,* at 168; Pole, *Legislative Power,* at 72. Contrary, see Lloyd, *Legislative Power,* at 3.

27. Hamilton, *Farmer,* at 106–7. See also Anon., *Letter to English,* at 7.

CHAPTER FOUR

1. Cato in *Connecticut Gazette,* reprinted in *Boston Post-Boy,* 9 September 1765, at 1, col. 2; Instructions of Braintree, 24 September 1765, *Boston News-Letter,* 10 October 1765, at 2, col. 3; Camden's Speech on Declaratory Act, 44 *Gentleman's Magazine* (1774), at 117; Camden, "Speech on American Taxation," at 120.

2. "L[ord] C[amden's] Speech on the declaratory bill," 29 *Scots Magazine* (1767), at 527; London Letter, *Boston News-Letter,* 8 May 1766, at 2, col. 3 (quoting Grenville); Blackstone: Gipson, "Debate on Repeal," at 17; Speech of Sir Charles Yorke, Commons Debates, 3 February 1766, Ryder, "Parliamentary Diaries," at 266; writer: [Gray,] *Right of the Legislature,* at 26. See also Anon., *Reflexions on Representation;* Anon., *Inquiry into the Nature,* at 28–29, 67.

3. [Whitelocke,] *Concerning Impositions,* at 19; Speech of Thomas Walpole, Commons Debates, 1 December 1776, 46 *Gentleman's Magazine* (1776), at 152. See also 38 *Scots Magazine* (1776), at 27n; 5 *Hibernian Magazine* (1775), at 164, 784; Rossiter, *Political Thought,* at 159 (quoting *Salem Gazette,* 19 August 1774); 39 *London Magazine* (1770), at 417; Anon., *Constitutional Advocate,* at 8; Anon., *To Tax Themselves,* at 92.

4. Pole, *Representation,* at 443 (attributing the doctrine to Burke); Paley, *Principles of Philosophy,* at 472. For a statement of the doctrine before Burke's birth, see [Barrington,] *Revolution Principles,* at 49–50.

5. [Meredith,] *Question Stated,* at 14; Jefferson's Notes of Proceedings, 12 July–1 August 1776, 4 *Letters of Delegates to Congress,* at 443 (quoting Adams); Somerville, *Observations on the Constitution,* at 36; [Lind,] *Thirteenth Parliament,* at 83–84; Pulteney, *Effects from East India Bill,* at 30; [Howard,] *Defence of the Letter,* at 19–20. See also New York Resolves, 18 December 1765, Morgan, *Prologue,* at 61–62; Anon., *Answer to Sheridan,* at 16; Anon., *Essay on Constitutional Liberty,* at 29n, 56; Adams, *Thoughts,* reprinted in 6 *Revolutionary Virginia,* at 409–10; Anon., *Observations of Consequence,* at 24, 33; Price, *Two Tracts: Tract Two,* at 42–43; [Serle,] *Americans against Liberty,* at 19.

6. Pulteney, *Plan of Reunion,* at 43. See also Rous, *Thoughts on Government,* at 39; 38 *Scots Magazine* (1776), at 227 (reprinting *London Chronicle*); Kammen, *Empire and Interest,* at 113 (discussing and quoting Burke). Contrary, see Anon., *British Liberties,* at xxv.

7. [Heath,] *Case of Devon to Excise,* at 1–3; [Ramsay,] *Historical Essay,* at 131; Clark, *British Opinion,* at 134–35; Brewer, *Party Ideology,* at 212.

8. 4 *Hibernian Magazine* (1774), at 207; Letter from Lord North to Buckinghamshire, 18 August 1778, Porritt, *Unreformed House,* at 278–79. See also Kramnick, "Republican Revisionism," at 640 (quoting James Burgh); Brewer,

"English Radicalism," at 355 (quoting Edward Bancroft); Sutherland, "City of London," at 67; Clark, *British Opinion*, at 129. Contrary, see Gibbons, *Ideas of Representation*, at 10.

9. [Maseres,] *Considerations on Admitting Representatives*, at 7–8; Anon., *Honor of Parliament*, at 29. See also Pulteney, *Plan of Reunion*, at 28–29.

10. Sugar Acts: Anon., *Considerations Upon the Act*, at 20, 22–24; Anon., *Reasons Against*, at 3–4; Speech of Richard Hussey, Commons Debates, 3 February 1766, 2 *Proceedings and Debates*, at 142; Wilson, "Parliamentary Authority," 17 August 1774, reprinted in *Commemoration Ceremony*, at 57–58. See also Anon., *Observations of Consequence*, at 25, 30; [Pulteney,] *Reflections on Domestic Policy*, at 66; Clark, *British Opinion*, at 132, 134, 162.

11. Anon., *O Liberty*, at 2; Spottsylvania Resolves, 24 June 1774, 1 *American Archives*, at 448; [Hawley,] 30 March 1775, 2 *American Archives*, at 247; Paley, *Principles of Philosophy*, at 473. See also [Keld,] *Polity of England*, at 219; [Knox,] *Controversy*, at 83–84 (quoting Locke). For a significant American affirmation of the doctrine, see Fish, *Connecticut Election Sermon*, at 41–42.

12. [Bancroft,] *Remarks*, at 95; De Lolme, *Constitution: New Edition*, at 283; Dobbs, *Letter to North*, at 8. See also Pulteney, *Plan of Reunion*, at 38–40; [Ferguson,] *Remarks on Dr. Price*, at 13; [Meredith,] *Question Stated*, at 12.

13. Whole empire: Pulteney, *Plan of Reunion*, at 43; Priestley, *First Principles* (1771), at 22. See also Speech of Thomas Pownall, Commons Debates, 15 May 1767, 2 *Proceedings and Debates*, at 485; New York Petition to Commons, 18 October 1764, Morgan, *Prologue*, at 10; Johnstone, "Speech of November, 1775," at 86; [Rokeby,] *Further Examination*, at 190; Christie and Labaree, *Empire*, at 47 (quoting Sir William Meredith). In Massachusetts, it was argued that because of shared burdens the members of the General Court should not have enacted the 1754 excise tax, yet they enacted and reenacted it. Anon., *Observations on Excise Bill*, at 11.

14. Speech of John Wilmot, Commons Debates, 24 February 1778, 19 *Parliamentary History*, at 789.

15. Anon., *To Committee of London Merchants*, at 20–21; [Scott,] *Remarks on the Patriot*, at 30–31; Pole, *Representation*, at 339.

16. Speech of George Grenville, Commons Debates, 6 February 1765, Ryder, "Parliamentary Diaries," at 254; Speech of Lord Mansfield, Lords Debates, 3 February 1766, Holliday, *Life of Mansfield*, at 247; 38 *Gentleman's Magazine* (1768), at 293, reprinted in *Boston Chronicle*, 26 September 1768, at 368, col. 1. For the best discussion of the doctrine, see 30 *Scots Magazine* (1768), at 284–85. See also [Blacklock,] *Remarks on Liberty*, at 40–41, 53; Fletcher, *Vindication of Welsey*, at 26; [Ramsay,] *Historical Essay*, at 193–94; *Boston Evening-Post*, 26 September 1768, at 2, col. 2. For criticism, see Cartwright, *Appeal on Constitution*, at 20; Cartwright, *Postscript*, at 5; Jones, *Speech to Middlesex*, at 16–17; Price, *Two Tracts: Tract One*, at 41, 100.

17. King: Anon., *American Resistance Indefensible*, at 20; agents: Anon., *To Committee of London Merchants*, at 20; American born: [Lind,] *Englishman's Answer*, at 6 (similarly, see Shebbeare, *Essay on National Society*, at 94); commercial ties: Anon., *Honor of Parliament*, at 38 (similarly, see Anon., *Free and Candid Remarks*,

at 13; Lecky quoted in Hosmer, *Adams*, at 76–77); "advocates": [Maseres,] *Considerations on Admitting Representatives*, at 7.

18. *Annual Register 1766*, at [43]; Pownall, *Administration*, at 148; Extract of a Letter from a Member of Parliament to his Friend in America, 7 June 1765, *Boston Evening-Post*, 12 August 1765, at 3, col. 1; Extract of a letter from a gentleman in London to his friend in Charles-Town, 8 February 1765, *South-Carolina Gazette*, 20 April 1765, at 3, col. 2 (also printed in *Boston News-Letter*, 9 May 1765, at 3, col. 1); "John Ploughshare," *London Chronicle*, 20 February 1766, reprinted in Morgan, *Prologue*, at 102.

19. Hawkins, *Life of Johnson*, at 502; *New York Gazette*, 6 June 1765, quoted in *Boston Evening-Post*, 24 June 1765, at 1, col. 2; Soame Jenyns quoted in 1 Bailyn, *Pamphlets*, at 601; Anon., *Rights of Parliament*, at 14n; Speech of Lord Mansfield, Lords Debates, 10 February 1766, "Lords Debate on Declaratory Act," at 118; [Dulany,] *Considerations on the Propriety*, at 6; McCulloh, *General Thoughts*, at 2; Anon., *Common Sense Conferences*, at 43; *South-Carolina Gazette* (Supplement), 20 July 1765, at 1, col. 1; Speech of George Grenville, 1 *Anecdotes of Pitt*, at 331.

20. [Pownall,] *Considerations*, at 5–6; Thomas Whately reprinted in *Boston News-Letter* (Supplement), 11 April 1765, at 1, col. 3; Morgan, *Prologue*, at 21; 1 Bailyn, *Pamphlets*, at 94; *Boston Evening-Post*, 24 June 1765, at 1, col. 2; [Young,] *Political Essays*, at 34; [Gray,] *Right of the Legislature*, at 28; Anon., *Speech Never Intended*, at 12.

21. Anon., *Answer to Pitt's Speech*, at 13; Thomas Whately reprinted in *Boston News-Letter* (Supplement), 11 April 1765, at 1, col. 3; Morgan, *Prologue*, at 21. Paradoxically, although property was represented, it was not accorded weight on the basis of equal proportion. Middlesex County "paid one-sixth part of the land-tax, and a full third of all other taxes, yet it had not more than a fifty-fifth part of the representation." Speech of Charles James Fox, Commons Debates, 7 May 1782, 2 Fox, *Speeches*, at 68–69.

22. Anon., *Defence of English History*, at 65–66; Anon., *Civil Liberty Asserted*, at 78–79. See also Paley, *Principles of Philosophy*, at 485–86; Letter from C. Wyvill to John Campbell, 1783, *Collection of Irish Letters*, at 47–48; [Almon,] *Free Parliaments*, at 35 (quoting Thomas Pitt); [Robinson,] *Political Catechism*, at 57–58; Day, *Two Speeches*, at 13; Cartwright, *Letters to Deputies*, at 3; 4 *Hibernian Magazine* (1774), at 205; Anon., *Representative of London*, at 30; Keir, *Constitutional History*, at 323; Maccoby, *English Radicalism*, at 85; Derry, *Fox*, at 19.

23. "No cause": 31 *Scots Magazine* (1769), at 147; great cities: [Ramsay,] *Historical Essay*, at 193; same footing: Anon., *Speech Never Intended*, at 12. See also [Goodricke,] *Observations*, at 52; [Gray,] *Right of the Legislature*, at 12; Anon., *Answer to Pitt's Speech*, at 14–15.

24. *Boston News-Letter*, 8 May 1766, at 1, cols. 1–2; 1 *Anecdotes of Pitt*, at 334; Anon., *Celebrated Speech*, at 13; Morgan, *Prologue*, at 139.

25. [Scott,] *Remarks on the Patriot*, at 31; Leeds et al.: Anon., *To Tax Themselves*, at 78; Massachusetts House: Letter from James Otis, Thomas Cushing, Samuel Adams, and Thomas Gray [Committee of the House] to Dennys de Berdt, 20 December 1765, 1 Adams, *Writings*, at 66 (similarly, see Anon., *Dia-*

logue on the Constitution, at 38); protection: Pulteney, *Thoughts on Present State*, at 22; Price, "Civil Liberty," 6 *Hibernian Magazine* (1776), at 183.

26. [Dulany,] *Considerations on the Propriety*, at 7; [Erskine,] *Reflections on the Rise*, at 15–16. See also [Canning,] *Letter to Hillsborough*, at 29–30; "Answer to Wesley," 5 *Hibernian Magazine* (1775), at 787.

27. [Ramsay,] *Historical Essay*, at 194. People making this argument did not think the costs high as they viewed the matter from the upper reaches of the economic ladder: "[W]hat is the property required to make them voters for the County; about fifty times less than qualifies them to shoot a partridge." It was from that perspective a "pittance." Anon., *Dialogue on the Constitution*, at 38.

28. [Evans,] *Letter to John Wesley*, at 12–13.

29. Anon., *Power and Grandeur*, at 12.

30. [Dickinson,] *New Essay*, at 47n.

31. [Dulany,] *Considerations on the Propriety*, at 10.

32. "Answer to Wesley," 5 *Hibernian Magazine* (1775), at 788.

33. Proprietors of funds: [Dickinson,] *New Essay*, at 47n; copyholders etc.: Pownall, *Administration*, at 135–36; quotation: Evans, *Reply to Fletcher*, at 37. A similar distinction could be drawn between the Irish and the Americans. *Annual Register 1765*, at [35].

34. Instructions from the House of Representatives to Richard Jackson, 22 September 1764, 7 *Pennsylvania Archives*, at 5644.

35. Otis, *Vindication*, at 567; *Public Advertiser*, 11 January 1770, reprinted in *Franklin's Letters to the Press*, at 173 (see also argument at 174; *Public Advertiser*, 8 January 1770, ibid., at 171); competent judge: Anon., *Case of Great Britain*, at 4; Letter from Samuel Adams to the Reverend G.W., 11 November 1765, 1 Adams, *Writings*, at 31.

36. Anon., *Observations of Consequence*, at 23–24; "Letter to Langrishe" (1792), 4 *Works of Burke*, at 293. See also Anon., *Honor of Parliament*, at 37–38 (applying virtual representation by interests to the colonists); 38 *Gentleman's Magazine* (1768), at 270; [Keld,] *Polity of England*, at 371–72; Gibbons, *Ideas of Representation*, at 29; Kammen, *Empire and Interest*, at 122–23; Derry, *Fox*, at 19.

37. General interest: Trenchard, Letter of 18 August 1722, 3 *Cato's Letters*, at 200 (see also [Lind,] *Letters to Price*, at 120–21; Wood, *Creation*, at 174); interest of representatives: Anon., *Essay on Constitutional Liberty*, at 56 (see also Trenchard, Letter of 6 January 1721, 2 *Cato's Letters*, at 232–33; Anon., *Prospect of the Consequences*, at 11–13; Gerard, *Liberty Cloke of Maliciousness*, at 9–10; [Ramsay,] *Historical Essay*, at 194); women: A Letter from a Plain Yeoman, *Providence Gazette*, 11 May 1765, Morgan, *Prologue*, at 76 (see also Anon., *Celebrated Speech*, at 13; [Bancroft,] *Remarks*, at 95–98; Anon., *Dialogue on the Constitution*, at 38; Anon., *Constitutional Answer to Wesley*, at 5–6; [Rokeby,] *Further Examination*, at 190; "D.Y.," 38 *Gentleman's Magazine* (1768), at 270, reprinted in *Boston Evening-Post*, 15 November 1768, at 1, col. 1).

38. Capital spring: Fletcher, *American Patriotism*, at 27; security: Gerard, *Liberty Cloke of Maliciousness*, at 11; community of interests: 1 [Maseres,] *Canadian Freeholder*, at 164–67; benefit: [Tod,] *Good Humour*, at 23.

39. Intercourse: Anon., *To Tax Themselves*, at 79; Speech of Hans Stanley,

Commons Debates, 1766, "Stamp Act Debates," at 566. See also Anon., *Honor of Parliament*, at 29; Anon., *Argument in Defence*, at 78–79.

40. Speech of Governor George Johnstone, Commons Debates, 6 February 1775, 45 *Gentleman's Magazine* (1775), at 160. For a refutation of the argument of shared interests between British and American trading towns, see 2 Anon., *History of North and South America*, at 258–59.

41. *Gentleman's Magazine*, January 1768, reprinted in *Franklin's Letters to the Press*, at 111–12 (also reprinted in 29 *Scots Magazine* (1767), at 692); "D.Y.," 38 *Gentleman's Magazine* (1768), at 270.

42. Anon., *To Tax Themselves*, at 79–80 (similarly, see Quincy, *Observations with Thoughts*, at 397; 2 Burgh, *Political Disquisitions*, at 308); Anon., *Argument in Defence*, at 81; Anon., *To Tax Themselves*, at 82–83; [Lind,] *Thirteenth Parliament*, at xiin. See also Anon., *Tyranny Unmasked*, at 40.

43. *Gazette and Post-Boy*, 18 July 1774, at 2, col. 1. See also Estwick, *Letter to Tucker*, at 78.

44. Resolutions of the Westmoreland Association, 27 February 1766, 1 *Revolutionary Virginia*, at 23–24. See also Petition from Virginia General Assembly to House of Lords, 16 April 1768, 1 *Revolutionary Virginia*, at 58.

45. Pulteney, *Thoughts on Present State*, at 18 (the rule was termed "fundamental law" in 39 *London Magazine* (1770), at 418).

46. [Knox,] *Extra Official Papers*, at 2 of app.; Anon., *Case of Great Britain*, at 4.

47. Memorial of the Council and Burgesses of Virginia to House of Lords, 18 December 1764, 1 *Revolutionary Virginia*, at 12.

48. Anon., *Constitutional Answer to Wesley*, at 11; [Priestley,] *Address to Dissenters*, at 18 (similarly, see Pulteney, *Thoughts on Present State*, at 19–20; [Serle,] *Americans against Liberty*, at 18, 24–25).

49. Dulany quoted in Becker, *Declaration*, at 88.

50. British nonelectors were said to be "secured" by "an effectual Barrier against Oppression." [Bancroft,] *Remarks*, at 95. This barrier or "constitutional security" assured the British that "they never can be oppressed but by themselves." 53 *Monthly Review* (1775), at 441. An American loyalist warned that "this security" might not be "so effectual" because the "rich are never taxed so much in proportion to their estates as the poor," yet he argued that Americans would be "secure" under parliamentary rule because members of Parliament "cannot hurt us without hurting themselves." [Seabury,] *View of the Controversy*, at 18. The nonsense to which the platitude of "security" could lead was demonstrated by the following claim: "I think the Americans have a real security in parliament, which is, that you can do nothing that does not affect Great Britain equally with America." Speech of Constantine Phipps, Commons Debates, 19 April 1774, 4 *Proceedings and Debates*, at 235. See also "General View of the British Constitution," 38 *Scots Magazine* (1776), at 228.

51. Speech of Sir William Meredith, 6 February 1765, Ryder, "Parliamentary Diaries," at 259. See also [Knox,] *Claim of the Colonies*, at 25; Anon., *Case of Great Britain*, at 4.

52. Instructions of the Town of Salem, 21 October 1765, *Boston Evening-Post*

(Supplement), 28 October 1765, at 1, col. 3. Similarly, see Estwick, *Letter to Tucker*, at 81; Pulteney, *Thoughts on Present State*, at 23; Petition from New York General Assembly to House of Lords, 18 October 1764, *New York Journal of Votes*, at 774; Petition from Pennsylvania House of Representatives to House of Commons, 22 September 1768, 7 *Pennsylvania Archives*, at 6277; Message from Virginia House of Burgesses to Massachusetts House of Representatives, 9 May 1765, *American Gazette*, at 20.

CHAPTER FIVE

1. Anon., *Reflections on the Contest*, at 8; Pole, *Representation*, at 391, 52 (see also 54); Massachusetts: "Americanus," *Letter to Freeholders*, at 6; Connecticut: Eliot, *Give Cesar his Due*, at 37; Trumbull, *Discourse at New Haven*, at 27; Hobart, *Civil Government*, at 37. See also Welsteed, *Dignity and Duty*, at 33–34 (Massachusetts election sermon); Williams, *Election Sermon*, at 24; Barker, "Natural Law," at 29, n. 1; Kenyon, "Ideological Origins," at 8.

2. Instructions of 24 May 1764, 16 *Boston Town Records*, at 120; Fish, *Connecticut Election Sermon*, at 49–50; Instructions of Oxford, 1 December 1756, and Bristol, December 1756, *Voice of People*, at xi, xii.

3. Instructions of Devon, 7 October 1756, *Voice of People*, at 25; defend: [Wheelock,] *Reflections*, at 21; 1 Burgh, *Political Disquisitions*, at 363. For a series of instructions against placemen, all stressing independence of Parliament, see 1 *Britain's Memorial*, at 2–62. See also "On Parliamentary Corruption," 1 *Hibernian Magazine* (1771), at 187.

4. Speech of Sir John St. Aubyn, Commons Debates, 13 March 1734, 9 *Parliamentary History*, at 403; Kemp, "Parliamentary Sovereignty," at 13, col. 2. In the colonies, of course, "the Freedom of the House" was also valued. Frink, *Election Sermon*, at 92.

5. The best discussion is Greene, *Quest*. See also Pole, "American Whig," at 230.

6. 2 Burgh, *Political Disquisitions*, at 197 (paraphrasing Mulgrave; for the recorded quotation, see 5 *Parliamentary History*, at 748).

7. Moore, *Taxing Colonies*, at 41. For Britain, see also Canning, *Letter to Hillsborough*, at 30; Anon., *Review of Constitution*, at 28–29; for America: Bailyn, *Pamphlets*, at 92–93, 97.

8. [Adams,] *Thoughts*, at 9. See also "Notes of Proceedings" (1776), 1 *Papers of Jefferson*, at 326–27 (reporting ideas of James Wilson at the Continental Congress); *Essex Result*, at 29–30. For British views moving closer to American theory, see Meeting of 30 May 1783, *Society for Constitutional Information*, at 7.

9. Brewer, "English Radicalism," at 341; sense of nation: Anon., *Considerations on the Addresses*, at 10.

10. Speech of Edmund Burke, Commons Debates, 7 February 1766, 2 *Burke Writings*, at 52. See also Anon., *New System of Policy*, at 60.

11. Chapman, *Burke*, at 317, n. 67; *Thoughts on Discontents* (1770), reprinted in 2 *Burke Writings*, at 292.

12. [Rivers,] *Letters*, at 286, 76; distinct interest: [Keld,] *Polity of England*, at 218; [Downley,] *Sentiments*, at 3; Salem: *Boston Evening-Post*, 15 August 1768, at 2, col. 2. See also 38 *Scots Magazine* (1776), at 226 (reprinting *London Chronicle*);

Speech of Sir William Yonge, Commons Debates, 13 March 1734, 9 *Parliamentary History*, at 450; Pole, *Legislative Power*, at 70–71; Kramnick, *Bolingbroke's Circle*, at 124–26.

13. [Bolingbroke,] *Dissertation*, at 209; Letter from William Knox to George Grenville, 9 August 1768, 4 Grenville, *Papers*, at 336–37; Young, *Example of France*, at 90–91; Lofft, *Observations on Publication*, at 18, 2. See also 43 *London Magazine* (1774), at 537; Anon., *Liberty in Two Parts*, at 77–78; Anon., *Second Letter to Member*, at 16–18. For American arguments, see [Galloway,] *True and Impartial State*, at 26–28; Boyer, "Borrowed Rhetoric," at 348.

14. [Forester,] *Answer to the Question Stated*, at 4; not "Creatures": Anon., *Second Letter to Member*, at 17; Speech of Charles James Fox, Commons Debates, 25 March 1771, 1 Fox, *Speeches*, at 14, 11, 14 (see also 12–13). See also Derry, *Fox*, at 34, 43.

15. Letter from Jared Ingersoll to Governor Thomas Finch, 11 February 1765, "Ingersoll Correspondence," at 307. See also Speech of Attorney General John Willes, Commons Debates, 13 March 1734, 9 *Parliamentary History*, at 435; Young, *Example of France*, at 89–90; Tucker, *Treatise*, at 39; Bailyn, *Pamphlets*, at 91–92; Thomson, *Constitutional History*, at 245; Kramnick, "Idea of Representation," at 84–85; Kramnick, *Bolingbroke's Circle*, at 126; Brewer, *Party Ideology*, at 236. Contrary, see Anon., *Abuse of Standing Parliaments*, at 12.

16. "Arguments . . . to prove Duty of Representatives," 4 *Hibernian Magazine* (1774), at 700; [Ramsay,] *Historical Essay*, at 128.

17. Address of Wilkes to Middlesex, 4 February 1769, Wilkes, *English Liberty*, at 291. See also Towers, *Letter to Wesley*, at 24–25.

18. See, e.g., Speech of 22 February 1775, 1 *Speeches of John Wilkes in Parliament*, at 43; Remonstrance of London to King, March 1773, 2 *Correspondence George III*, at 463–64; Remonstrance to King, 15 December 1770, *Addresses and Petitions of Common Council*, at 25; Address of Wilkes to Middlesex, 23 March 1769, 4 *Political Register* (1769), at 241; [Downley,] *Sentiments*, at 1; Anon., *Fair Trial*, at 221, 225; [Meredith,] *Question Stated*, at 11–12, 72; Anon., *Reflections on Wilkes*, at 11; Anon., *Cautionary Address*, at 1; Anon., *North-Country Poll*, at 20.

19. Witmer, *Property Qualifications*, at 92; [Towers,] *Letter to Samuel Johnson*, at 40–41; [Carysfort,] *Serious Address*, at 22; Gibbons, *Ideas of Representation*, at 28.

20. Address of Wilkes to Middlesex, 23 March 1769, Wilkes, *English Liberty*, at 310. In the colonies, the issue of the right of election generally concerned the executive rather than legislators barring an elected representative from his seat. See, e.g., Christopher Gadsden, "To the Gentlemen Electors," 5 February 1763, Gadsden, *Writings*, at 20–31.

21. Glanville, *Reports*, at ix; not exist: [Dyson,] *Case of Middlesex*, at 41; Reprimand of 10 February 1768, 30 *Scots Magazine* (1768), at 88; "brought into a contest": [Downley,] *Sentiments*, at 51; Speech of George Onslow, Commons Debates, 25 January 1770, 16 *Parliamentary History*, at 791. Supporters of Wilkes also argued the "independency of parliaments" as grounds for seating him. Anon., *Serious Reflections*, at 24–25. See also Speech of Robert Henley-Ongley, Commons Debates, 25 January 1770, 16 *Parliamentary History*, at 789; [Macfarlane,] *George Third*, at 303–5; North, *Argument in Soames Case*, at 23.

22. Petition of Lord Mayor et al. to King, 17 March 1770, Anon., *History of Lord North*, at 12; Address of Wilkes to Middlesex, 23 March 1769, Wilkes, *English Liberty*, at 311. See also Letter from John Wilkes to Speaker Sir Fletcher Norton, 20 April 1773, 35 *Scots Magazine* (1773), at 249; [Grenville,] *Speech on Wilkes*, at 53; [Towers,] *Observations on Liberty*, at 8–9; [Towers,] *Letter to Wesley*, at 24; Anon., *Serious Reflections*, at 20; [Macfarlane,] *George Third*, at 304, 307–9.

23. [Dyson,] *Case of Middlesex*, at 42. See also [Wheelock,] *Reflections*, at 21–22. There was another question that belongs in a history of the meaning of law rather than representation in the eighteenth century: whether the resolution of the Commons made law and therefore exceeded the Commons' jurisdiction.

24. [Downley,] *Sentiments*, at 4 (this pamphlet has been attributed to Dowdeswell); [Macfarlane,] *George Third*, at 365. See also Speech of John Wilkes, Commons Debates, 29 April 1777, 19 *Parliamentary History*, at 197; Speech of Edmund Burke, Commons Debates, 15 April 1769, 2 *Burke Writings*, at 229; Middlesex Petition, 9 April 1770, 2 *Town and Country Magazine* (1770), at 220; Letter of 10 February 1770, Hope, *Letters*, at 69–70; [Macfarlane,] *Second Ten Years*, at xi; Price, *Two Tracts: Tract Two*, at 49.

25. Speech of Willam De Grey, Commons Debates, 25 January 1770, 16 *Parliamentary History*, at 796; Anon., *First Letter to Grafton*, at 36. See also Anon., *Serious Considerations*, at 6, 21–22; Anon., *Some Few Observations*, at 41; [Macfarlane,] *George Third*, at 300–302; [Dyson,] *Case of Middlesex*, at 12–13.

CHAPTER SIX

1. Anon., *Second Letter to Member*, at 17. See also Speech of Robert Henley-Ongley, Commons Debates, 25 January 1770, 16 *Parliamentary History*, at 788; [Forester,] *Answer to the Question Stated*, at 5; *London Journal* (no. 726), 26 May 1733, at 1, col. 2; Kramnick, "Idea of Representation," at 85–86.

2. Speech of Charles James Fox, Commons Debates, 25 March 1771, 1 Fox, *Speeches*, at 11.

3. Speech of Thomas Townshend, Commons Debates, 25 January 1770, 16 *Parliamentary History*, at 789; [Carysfort,] *Serious Address*, at 29–30; [Williams,] *Letters on Liberty*, at 77–78. See also Carysfort, *Letter to Huntingdonshire*, at 11–12; Abingdon, "English Constitution," 9 *Town and Country Magazine* (1777), at 454: [Rokeby,] *Further Examination*, at 100; [Keld,] *Polity of England*, at 485; Fowle, *Total Eclipse*, at 10n; Locke, *Two Treatises*, at pt. 2, secs. 221–22; Lawson, *Politica Sacra*, at 162–63.

4. [Mulgrave,] *Letter from a Member*, at 77–78.

5. Ibid.; Howard, *Election Sermon*, at 364–65; [Joseph Hawley,] 9 March 1775, 2 *American Archives*, at 97; Anon., *Letter to the Essay Author*, at 14–15; Shute, *Election Sermon*, at 25; 1 Burgh, *Political Disquisitions*, at 108–205; *Voice of People*, at i-ii; [Fowle,] *Appendix to Eclipse*, at 1; [Bolingbroke,] *Dissertation*, at 128–29, 209; [Steuart,] *Jus Populi*, at 334.

6. Day, *Two Speeches*, at 15; Anon., *Evidence of Common and Statute Laws*, at 51–52; Anon., *Critical Review of Liberties*, at 14. Contrary, see Anon., *Letter Concerning Home and Abroad*, at 2–3.

7. Advocates: [Bollan,] *Freedom of Speech*, at 148; stewards and plenipotentiaries: Speech of Sir George Yonge, Commons Debates, 25 January 1770, 16

Parliamentary History, at 793; Anon., *Abuse of Standing Parliaments,* at 19; servants: Speech of Sir William Yonge, Commons Debates, 23 January 1745, 13 *Parliamentary History,* at 1078; Dickinson, *Letter to Merchants,* at 444; proxies: Cartwright, *People's Barrier,* at 20; *London Journal* (no. 740), 1 September 1733, at 1, col. 2; Brewer, "English Radicalism," at 351. But see Declaration of Rights (1782), *Society for Constitutional Information,* at 37 (see also 7).

8. Bound: [Meredith,] *Question Stated,* at 13–14 (see also 63); Speech of Henry Pelham, Commons Debates, 29 January 1740, 11 *Parliamentary History,* at 346; [Downley,] *Sentiments,* at 53; not autonomous: [Bath,] *Review of Excise,* at 44. See also Instructions of County of Lincoln, 12 October 1756, *Voice of People,* at 27–28; Hamilton, *Farmer,* at 92; Burke, *Thoughts on the Present Discontents* (1770), 2 *Burke Writings,* at 292; [Brooke,] *Liberty and Common Sense,* at 5; [Bolingbroke,] *Dissertation,* at 38; 11 *Craftsman* (no. 375), 8 September 1733, at 146; Anon., *Representative of London,* at 8.

9. [Downley,] *Sentiments,* at 52; *Craftsman* (no. 56), 29 July 1727, at 72; [Atkyns,] *Treatise of Jurisdiction,* at 8.

10. Missing, *Letter to Mansfield on Instructions,* at 18; Anon., *Letter to the Essay Author,* at 16–17; 3 *Hibernian Magazine* (1773), at 67.

11. Speech of Sir William Yonge, Commons Debates, 23 January 1745, 13 *Parliamentary History,* at 1078; Anon., *Liberty in Two Parts,* at 77; "*may be abused*": [Downley,] *Sentiments,* at 52. See also Anon., *Letter Concerning Home and Abroad,* at 2–3.

12. Pulteney, *Plan of Reunion,* at 86n; Anon., *Some Reasons,* at 7–8; McAdam, *Johnson and Law,* at 106 (quoting Samuel Johnson); Anon., *Honor of Parliament,* at 28; Young, *Example of France,* at 89 (quoting Blackstone); Lofft, *Observations on Publication,* at 15 (quoting Sir Edward Coke); Kramnick, *Bolingbroke's Circle,* at 173.

13. Style: Letter from George Grenville to William Knox, 16 August 1768, *Grenville Letterbooks;* Anon., *Letter to a Member,* at 26–27; voted on all: [Rivers,] *Letters,* at 282; Anon., *Letter to the Essay Author,* at 15–16; general good: [Basset,] *Equal Representation,* at 21.

14. Guardians: [Wheelock,] *Reflections,* at "Preface"; maxim: Petyt, *Lex Parliamentaria,* at 7.

15. Anon., *Honor of Parliament,* at 28.

16. Reform: Anon., *Letter to De Brett,* at 21; virtual representation: Anon., *Letter to People of Great Britain,* at 7, 9–10; Lofft, *Observations on Publication,* at 16; [Blacklock,] *Remarks on Liberty,* at 66. But see the same argument conclude that Britons only, not Americans, were represented. 1 Adams, *Writings,* at 271–72 (reprinting *Boston Gazette,* 19 December 1768); "Regulus," *Defence of the Resolutions,* at 32.

17. Answer: [Macfarlane,] *George Third,* at 238; [Howard,] *Defence of the Letter,* at 13. See also Anon., *Supremacy of Legislature,* at 34–35; Anon., *Letter to a Member,* at 27; Anon., *Letter to People of Great Britain,* at 7; *Boston Chronicle,* 26 September 1768, at 368, col. 1.

18. [Otis,] *Vindication,* at 567, 565.

19. [Rivers,] *Letters,* at 288, 257, xxxvn; Speech of Sir William Yonge, Commons Debates, 23 January 1745, 13 *Parliamentary History,* at 1078.

20. Speech of Thomas Carew, Commons Debates, 23 January 1745, 13 *Parliamentary History*, at 1058; Speech of Watkins William Wynn, Commons Debates, 13 March 1734, 9 ibid., at 430.

21. Cartwright, *Legislative Rights*, at 91; Bailyn, *Pamphlets*, at 96 (quoting Zubly); Anon., *New System of Policy*, at 53; Speeches of William Bromley, Sir John St. Aubyn, and Walter Plumer, Commons Debates, 13 March 1734, 9 *Parliamentary History*, at 399–400, 400, 438. See also Declaration of Rights (1782), *Society for Constitutional Information*, at 38; [Gray,] *Right of the Legislature*, at 27–28.

22. [Forester,] *Answer to the Question Stated*, at 4.

23. Remonstrance of the Council and Burgesses to the House of Commons, 18 December 1764, 10 *Journal of Burgesses*, at 303; Resolves of the House of Burgesses, 30 May 1765, ibid., at 360; Morgan, *Prologue*, at 48. For similar claims by colonial legislative bodies, see Petition of Massachusetts Council and Representatives to House of Commons, 3 November 1764, *Speeches*, at 22–23; Resolves of New York General Assembly, 18 December 1765, Morgan, *Prologue*, at 61–62; Letter from House of Burgesses to Pennsylvania Assembly, 9 May 1768, 7 *Pennsylvania Archives*, at 6189; New Jersey Resolves, 30 November 1765, Morgan, *Prologue*, at 60; Petition from Stamp Act Congress to House of Commons, Morgan, *Prologue*, at 68; Petition from Council and Burgesses to House of Commons, 14 April 1768, 11 *Journal of Burgesses*, at 170; Instructions of House of Representatives to Richard Jackson, 20 October 1764, 7 *Pennsylvania Archives*, at 5679; Letter from a House Committee of James Otis, Thomas Cushing, Samuel Adams, and Thomas Gray to Dennys De Berdt, 20 December 1765, 1 Adams, *Writings*, at 67–68.

24. Fairflax Resolves, 18 July 1774, 1 *American Archives*, at 598; [Mauduit,] *Northern Colonies*, at 22.

25. *Boston Evening-Post*, 24 June 1765, at 4, col. 3 (reprinting *New York Gazette*, 6 June 1765). See also Instructions of 24 May 1764, 16 *Boston Town Records*, at 120; Monitor, March 1775, 2 *American Archives*, at 6; Address of Commons House to Governor, 16 November 1769, 15 *Georgia House Journal*, at 47–48. The need that representatives have local knowledge was cited as a reason to reform British representation. 30 *London Magazine* (1761), at 15–16.

CHAPTER SEVEN

1. *London Journal* (no. 726), 26 May 1733, at 1, col. 2, (no. 740), 1 September 1733, at 1, col. 2, and (no. 727), 2 June 1733, at 1, col. 2. The word *accountable* was used to dismiss precedents from the reign of Edward III when members of Parliament said that they would consult electors about new taxes. "They consulted them, not as Persons to whom they were *strictly and properly accountable*, but as Persons whose *Interest and Welfare* they were under the highest Obligations to regard." Ibid. (no. 755), 15 December 1733, at 1, col. 1.

2. [Towers,] *Letter to Samuel Johnson*, at 22; Sharp, *Legal Means*, at 40; Day, *Two Speeches*, at 15.

3. Bonomi, *Factious People*, at 10, 10, n. 13. For instances of New York whig sensitivity to public opinion, see *Gazette and Post-Boy*, 1 August 1774, at 1, col. 2.

4. Message from Massachusetts House to Governor William Burnet, 9 Au-

gust 1728 and 30 August 1728, *Collection on Salaries,* at 47, 54; House Resolution of 7 September 1728, ibid., at 65.

5. Message from Massachusetts House to Governor William Burnet, 30 August 1728, ibid., at 55.

6. Know "Minds": Minutes of 7 September 1728, ibid., at 64; drafted account: Message from Massachusetts House to Governor William Burnet, 20 September 1728, ibid., at 75.

7. Message from Governor William Burnet to the House, 24 September 1728, ibid., at 79–80.

8. Anon., *Review,* at 2; Anon., *Eclipse,* at 2; Schutz, *Shirley,* at 177; Speech of Governor William Shirley to House, 17 June 1754, *Massachusetts Representatives Journal* (1754), at 47. See also Mayhew, *Election Sermon,* at 45–46; Rusticus, *Good of Community,* at 7; Anon., *Voice of People* (Boston), at 2; Colegrove, "Town Mandates," at 434.

9. Motion of 18 June 1754, *Boston News-Letter,* 20 June 1754, at 1, col. 2; Resolution of 18 June 1754 and Motion of 22 October 1754, *Massachusetts Representatives Journal* (1754), at 48, 60. See also Anon., *Observations on Excise Bill,* at 2; Anon., *Plea for Poor,* at 14.

10. Anon., *Review,* at 2–3; Anon., *Relapse,* at 3.

11. Anon., *Eclipse,* at 5.

12. Anon., *Observations on Excise Bill,* at 8; Colegrove "Town Mandates," at 435; Boyer, "Borrowed Rhetoric," at 350.

13. Meetings of 6 May 1766 and 1 December 1766, 16 *Boston Town Records,* at 180, 194.

14. Galloway, *Speech in Answer,* at xix.

15. Ibid., at xix–xx.

16. "Preface" to Dickinson, *Speech Delivered,* at iv; Galloway, *Speech in Answer,* at xxi.

17. Dickinson, *Speech Delivered,* at 24.

18. Ibid., at 24, 24–25, 25–26.

19. Galloway, *Speech in Answer,* at 35 (see also xxn, 2–3); Dickinson, *Speech Delivered,* at 26.

20. [Mulgrave,] *Letter from a Member,* at 12–14. A variation, associated with the "radicals" and John Wilkes, was not to consult after election but to obtain "pledges" of certain conduct prior to election, engagements by candidates seeking support. See Resolves of London Livery, 11 March 1773, 35 *Scots Magazine* (1773), at 160–61; Letter from Benjamin Franklin to Joseph Galloway, 12 October 1774, 1 Valentine, *Lord North,* at 336; Free, *Speech of John Free,* at 12–14; Sutherland, "City of London," at 71–72; Sutherland, "Burke and Members," at 1018–21; Clark, *British Opinion,* at 219.

CHAPTER EIGHT

1. Tories: Colley, *Defiance of Oligarchy,* at 167; Wilkes: Sutherland, "Burke and Members," at 1007–10; Yorkshire movement: Butterfield, *George III and People,* at 345.

2. Barker, *Essays,* at 194–95.

3. Influence of crown: Guttridge, *English Whiggism*, at 38; Clark, *British Opinion*, at 219.

4. Seventeenth century: Speech of Alderman William Beckford to London Livery, 10 February 1769, *Cambridge Magazine*, at 78; Anon., *Letter to the Common Council*, at 5–6; Thomson, *Constitutional History*, at 117, n. 1; Jones, *Country and Court*, at 213; Porritt, *Unreformed House*, at 263; Kramnick, *Bolingbroke's Circle*, at 172–73; eighteenth century: Colley, *Defiance of Oligarchy*, at 167; Kramnick, "Idea of Representation," at 90; [Bath,] *Review of Excise*, at 48 (see also 45–46); [Mulgrave,] *Letter from a Member*, at 81. For a brief history of the legal theory of instructions in Great Britain that concludes that there was not much precedent for the more "radical" of the positions to be discussed in this chapter, see Kelly, "Constituents' Instructions," at 170–78.

5. New England: Bailyn, *Pamphlets*, at 93; Colegrove, "Town Mandates," at 414–16, 422–23; Pencak, *War, Politics, and Revolution*, at 70; Anon., *Letter to Freeholders* (1742), at 8; West Jersey: Dargo, *Roots*, at 142. For British counties instructing via the grand jury, see *Voice of People*, at 9–10. For a contrary analysis, see Pole, *Representation*, at 72, 73, n.1.

6. Offering opinion: [Bath,] *Review of Excise*, at 42; act part and point out: Instructions of Bristol, December 1756, and of Lincolnshire, 12 October 1756, *Voice of People*, at xi, 27; 1768: Anon., *Reflections on Wilkes*, at 15; only remedy: Anon., *Conduct of Livery-Men*, at 28, 29. See also [Short,] *Rights*, at 18; Missing, *Letter to Mansfield on Instructions*, at 6; [Priestley,] *Present State of Liberty*, at 22; Brown, *Estimate of Manners*, at 75–76; Anon., *Seasonable Expostulations*, at 5; Colley, *Defiance of Oligarchy*, at 167; Browning, *Court Whigs*, at 27–28.

7. Hosmer, *Adams*, at 50–51; Portsmouth Instructions, 23 December 1765, *Boston Evening-Post*, 6 January 1766, at 2, col. 3. See also Lemisch, "New York Petitions," at 316, n. 9.

8. Letter from Samuel Adams to Arthur Lee, 6 May 1773, 3 Adams, *Writings*, at 38. Adams stated the same purpose publicly. *Journal of the Times*, 29 May 1769, at 103, col. 2.

9. For an example of Irish instructions, see *Gazette and Post-Boy*, 21 February 1774, at 2, col. 2. Later in the century, they could have led to prosecution. See *In a Defiant Stance*, at 128–30.

10. It is said that Scottish representatives were bound by instructions. Kelly, "Constituents' Instructions," at 178–79.

11. Anon., *Second Letter to Member*, at 20, 21–22, 25–26, 32–33, 30; [Rivers,] *Letters*, at 278–79. See also [Jebb,] *Address to Freeholders*, at 6, 10–11; Anon., *Letter to the Common Council*, at 5; 1 Burgh, *Political Disquisitions*, at 181; [Bath,] *Review of Excise*, at 47; Dickinson, *Liberty and Property*, at 102.

12. Instructions of 24 June 1773, *Addresses and Petitions of Common Council*, at 43; Porritt, *Unreformed House*, at 268–69 (quoting Norwich Instructions, 1768); Instructions of Maidstone, 21 September 1756, *Voice of People*, at 26; Instructions of 26 May 1766, 16 *Boston Town Records*, at 182; Proceedings of Bellingham, 19 May 1773, *Boston Evening-Post*, 18 October 1773, at 1, col. 1; Lancaster Instructions, 23 August 1740, 1 *Britain's Memorial*, at 31. See also Missing, *Letter to Mansfield on Instructions*, at 7, 17–18; Bailyn, *Pamphlets*, at 96–97. It was

understood in Massachusetts that Governor Hutchinson denied the right to instruct. Compare Address of Hutchinson, 6 January 1773, *Briefs of Revolution,* at 17, to Lynn Resolves, 19 May 1773, Brown, *Revolutionary Politics,* at 103–4. The town of Salem made one of the most detailed defenses. Pronouncement of 7 June 1773, Phillips, *Salem,* at 315. In both countries, instructing was said to be a duty as well as a right. *Boston Gazette,* 27 April 1767, at 1, col. 3; Lichfield Instructions, 12 November 1756, *Voice of People,* at 50.

13. [Bath,] *Review of Excise,* at 43.

14. Instructions of Nottingham, 1756, *Voice of People,* at 47; Denhigh Instructions, 24 December 1741, 2 *Britain's Memorial,* at 6; London's Instructions, [ca. 1681], and Bedford Instructions, 14 February 1680/81, Anon., *Right to Petition,* at 17, 19–20.

15. Worcester Instructions, May 1767, *Boston Gazette,* 1 June 1767, at 2, col. 2.

16. Massachusetts Resolutions, 10 May 1776, Colegrove, "Town Mandates," at 425.

17. Browning, *Court Whigs,* at 187. See also Pole, *Representation,* at 403; Wood, *Creation,* at 189–90; Bailyn, *Pamphlets,* at 96.

18. For example, Thomas Hutchinson, who commenced the debates of 1773 in part to counter instructions. Address of Hutchinson, 6 January 1773, *Briefs of Revolution,* at 17; Message from Hutchinson to House, 16 March 1770, *Boston Evening-Post,* 19 March 1770, at 2, col. 1; Tucker and Hendrickson, *Fall,* at 301 (quoting Hutchinson to John Pownall, 7 January 1773); Pole, *Representation,* at 72 (quoting Hutchinson to William Bollan, 22 November 1766); Brown, *Middle-Class Democracy,* at 220. In Virginia, the binding force of instructions was denied by people in the majority. Dargo, *Roots,* at 142–43. See also Anon., *Answer to Foolish Reason.*

19. Devon Instructions, 7 October 1756, *Voice of People,* at 25; Instructions of York Common Council, 6 October 1740, 1 *Britain's Memorial,* at 55; Orange County Instructions, 1773, 9 *North Carolina Colonial Records,* at 699–700.

20. Anon., *Æolus,* at 164–67; Anon., *Scandalous Paper.* See also 38 *Scots Magazine* (1776), at 230; Anon., *Some Few Observations,* at 29–30, 32–33; Pole, *Gift,* at 97.

21. It is worth noting in this regard that opinion on both sides of the Atlantic thought that the rule that representatives did not have to obey was the innovation, that the rule in ancient times had been that instructions were binding. 43 *London Magazine* (1774), at 537; Kramnick, "Idea of Representation," at 88–89 (quoting Lord Egmont); Dulany, *Considerations,* at 608; Kramnick, *Bolingbroke's Circle,* at 176.

22. For a summary of arguments in 1784, following the end of the American Revolution, see Kelly, "Constituents' Instructions," at 170.

23. 43 *London Magazine* (1774), at 540, 537; British statement: Anon., *Cautionary Address,* at 1–2; American: *Boston Gazette,* 27 April 1767, at 1, col. 1. See also [Towers,] *Letter to Samuel Johnson,* at 22; [Marat,] *Chains of Slavery,* at 202–3; Price, *Two Tracts: Tract Two,* at 7; Anon., *Considerations on the Addresses,* at 9–10. For what may be the most comprehensive British argument, see "Arguments and

Authorities to prove the Duty of Representatives to obey the Instructions of their Constituents," 4 *Hibernian Magazine* (1774), at 696–700. For American values, see Wood, *Creation*, at 190.

24. Deliberative: Anon., *Rise and Fall of Excise*, at 28; [Wheelock,] *Reflections*, at "Preface"; Sutherland, "Burke and Members," at 1005 (quoting Burke); cipher: 2 *Works of Burke*, at 95–96; democratic: Browning, *Court Whigs*, at 187. For American (Virginian) arguments against binding instructions, see Pole, *Representation*, at 162.

25. "An obligation upon the members [of Parliament] to follow the instructions of their constituents, would give too much power into the hands of the lower classes of people of this nation . . . or, at least, it would encourage and foment such a democratical spirit in them, as would by degrees, weaken and destroy the essential balance of power in our constitution." *Annual Register 1765*, at 301–2.

26. Anon., *Rise and Fall of Excise*, at 26; 1 Burgh, *Political Disquisitions*, at 182. See also Speech of Thomas Pitt, Commons Debates, 8 May 1780, 21 *Parliamentary History*, at 597; [Rivers,] *Letters*, at 285; Anon., *Æolus*, at 167–69; [Forester,] *Answer to the Question Stated*, at 4; *London Journal* (no. 726), 26 May 1733, at 1, col. 2; Sutherland, "Burke and Members," at 1006. But see Anon., *Advice to a New Member*, at 20.

27. Anon., *Rise and Fall of Excise*, at 27; Speech of John Willes, Commons Debates, 13 March 1734, 9 *Parliamentary History*, at 435. See also Kramnick, *Bolingbroke's Circle*, at 175.

28. [Jebb,] *Address to Freeholders*, at 4, 5n. For a good summary by Arthur Onslow, Middle Temple bencher, recorder of Guildford, and speaker of the Commons for thirty-three years, see Costin and Watson, *Documents*, at 392. For a New Englander who agreed that universal representation precluded the binding force of instructions, see Rusticus, *Good of Community*, at 47. See also Anon., *Advice to a Member*, at 29; Anon., *Æolus*, at 165, 167–168.

29. For some, of course, there was the problem of reelection. Even people admitting that instructions were not binding said that compliance was a legitimate issue for reelection. [Marchmont,] *Serious Exhortation*, at 12–13. Inexplicably, the strongest arguments against the right of the people not to reelect were made by New Englanders. Hobart, *Civil Government*, at 51; Rusticus, *Good of Community*, at 6.

30. Percival: 43 *London Magazine* (1774), at 537; [Mulgrave,] *Letter from a Member*, at 2. See also 37 *Scots Magazine* (1775), at 519.

31. Letter of 27 February 1775, Hope, *Letters*, at 77. For Hope on binding instructions, see 77–78.

32. 2 *Works of Burke*, at 96.

33. 50 *Gentleman's Magazine* (1780), at 619; Anon., *View of North*, at 304n. (quoting Burke). See also Sutherland, "Burke and Members," at 1006–7, 1018–19; Porritt, *Unreformed House*, at 271; Gibbons, *Ideas of Representation*, at 35; Kramnick, "Idea of Representation," at 90–91. By contrast, nine years earlier, another representative of Bristol had announced that he did follow the wishes of his constituents when their wishes were known and that instructions could cause him to change his mind. Letter from Lord Clare to G.G.S., 18 March 1769,

38 *London Magazine* (1769), at 194. See also Letter to Voters of Liverpool, 20 March 1769, *Boston Post-Boy*, 26 June 1769, at 2, col. 2.

34. Barker, *Essays*, at 199; Kenyon, *Revolution Principles*, at 207 (quoting Burke); Speech of Edmund Burke, Commons Debates, 8 May 1780, 21 *Parliamentary History*, at 606.

35. Colley, *Defiance of Oligarchy*, at 166.

36. Anon., *Letter Concerning Home and Abroad*, at 6.

37. Speech of Charles James Fox, Commons Debates, 25 March 1771, 1 Fox, *Speeches*, at 12. See also Gibbons, *Ideas of Representation*, at 36–37.

38. A variation on instructions that some urban forces, especially Wilkesites, attempted to introduce was to have parliamentary candidates pledge to obey instructions or to support certain reforms. Speech of William Beckford to London Livery, 10 February 1769, *Cambridge Magazine*, at 78; Anon., *Letter on Corruption*, at 33–35; 43 *London Magazine* (1774), at 536; 2 *Political Register* (1768), at 396; Anon., *Second Letter to Member*, at 30.

CHAPTER NINE

1. Ellys, *Tracts on Liberty*, at 261.

2. Speech of Chesterfield, 6 *Hibernian Magazine* (1776), at 542 (also printed in 45 *London Magazine* (1776), at 355); [Marchmont,] *Serious Exhortation*, at 10–11.

3. Porritt, *Unreformed House*, at 273; [Cartwright,] *American Independence*, at 81; half: Clark, *British Opinion*, at 218; 36 *London Magazine* (1767), at 407.

4. [Robinson,] *Political Catechism*, at 68.

5. Sawbridge: 10 *Political Register* (1772), at 263. For the American perception, see Bailyn, *Pamphlets*, at 56 (quoting John Dickinson on British electoral corruption); *Essex Result*, at 31–32. For a recent evaluation of corruption, see Phillips, *Electoral Behavior*, at 73–81.

6. 3 Wynne, *Eunomus*, at 89; Hartley, *Address to York*, at 21. See also Hall, *Apology for Freedom*, at 36n. For definitions, see Pocock, *Politics*, at 92–94, and "English Ideologies," at 570; Colley, "Politics of History," at 374–75. A New Yorker explained, "There is a Difference between a Bribe and a Pension; a *Bribe* is given for a particular Jobb; a *Pension* is a constant and continual *Bribe:* So that the Jobber is a Kind of Day-Labourer, the Pensioner a Domestic Servant hired by the Year, to do all the dirty business of the House." Anon., *O Liberty*, at 2.

7. Speech of George Byng, Commons Debates, 28 March 1774, 1 *American Archives*, at 66–67; Cassius: 2 *Hibernian Magazine* (1772), at 575; "A Friend to the Constitution," 11 *Political Register* (1772), at 333. See also 1 Blackstone, *Commentaries*, at 324, 327, 333, 335–36; [Ramsay,] *Historical Essay*, at 131–41; Arbuthnot, *Freeholder's Catechism*, at 19; Kramnick, "Introduction to Writings," at xxii-xxiii.

8. Typical house: Aptheker, *Revolution*, at 142; military officers: [Baillie,] *Appendix to a Letter*, at 24; House of Lords: Clark, *British Opinion*, at 236; [Almon,] *History of the Late Minority*, at 67–68. For 1774 figures, see 1 Valentine, *Lord North*, at 337. See also Anon., *Present State of the Constitution*, at 3–16; 10 *Gentleman's Magazine* (1740), at 449; Clark, *British Opinion*, at 218, 235; O'Gorman, "After Namier," at 104–5.

9. [Priestley,] *Address to Dissenters*, at 11.

10. Anon., *Considerations Upon Rights of Colonists*, at 19n; Turner, *Election Sermon*, at 26.

11. New Yorker: Anon., *O Liberty*, at 2; like Ireland: Anon., *Rights Asserted*, at 18; 30 *London Magazine* (1761), at 13. See also Day, *Two Speeches*, at 5; Watson, *Principles of the Revolution*, at 7; [Priestley,] *Present State of Liberty*, at 18; [Meredith,] *Question Stated*, at 64–65. For colonial comment, see Cooke, *Election Sermon*, at 165; Letter of 10 December 1767, Eliot, "Letters," at 415; "Americanus," *Letter to Freeholders*, at 5–7. For Irish comment, see Anon., *Interposition of the People*, at 21.

12. "A Whig," 8 *Political Register* (1771), at 286; 36 *London Magazine* (1767), at 406; Anon., *Rights Asserted*, at 16; Speech of earl of Chesterfield, Lords Debates, 13 February 1734, 9 *Parliamentary History*, at 343; 4 *Hibernian Magazine* (1774), at 206; 2 *St. Patrick's Anti-Stamp Chronicle* (1774), at 54–55. See also Petition of London, 24 June 1775, 5 *Hibernian Magazine* (1775), at 384; *Remembrancer for 1776: Part III*, at 339; "Brutus," 9 *Political Register* (1771), at 76–77. For the best detailed criticisms of the system, see Resolutions of Supporters of the Bill of Rights, 9 *Political Register* (1771), at 291–92.

13. Bentham, *Fragment on Government*, at 469, n. g; *Eighteenth-Century Constitution*, at 67 (quoting George III); Speech of Henry Pelham, Commons Debates, 29 January 1740, 11 *Parliamentary History*, at 349; [Chalmers,] *Plain Truth*, at 3–4; Julian Letter, 15 November 1776, *Remembrancer for 1776: Part III*, at 46. See also [Douglas,] *Seasonable Hints*, at 37; Carysfort, *Thoughts on Constitution*, at 50–52; *Daily Gazetteer* (no. 42), 16 August 1735, at 1, cols. 1–3; Keir, *Constitutional History*, at 296–97; Kramnick, *Bolingbroke's Circle*, at 123–24. For the theory of David Hume, see Banning, *Jeffersonian Persuasion*, at 132–33; Wills, *Explaining America*, at 82–83, 120; Gunn, "Influence," at 306.

14. Slavery: Estwick, *Letter to Tucker*, at 104; mercenary band: 44 *Gentleman's Magazine* (1774), at 314; [Priestley,] *Address to Dissenters*, at 10; Speech of the duke of Richmond, Lords Debates, 18 November 1777, 19 *Parliamentary History*, at 398; 2 "Junius," *Junius*, at 155; Speech of Lord Chatham, 41 *Gentleman's Magazine* (1771), at 210. See also Abingdon, *Dedication*, at liiin, lxxv; Hartley, *Two Letters*, at 3; [O'Beirne,] *Short History*, at 40; Anon., *Letter to English*, at 2; "Constitutional Observations," 45 *London Magazine* (1776), at 142; Letter from London to Philadelphia, 4 February 1775, 1 *American Archives*, at 1210; Address of Cripplegate Without to Lord Mayor, 23 April 1771, Anon., *Magna Charta Opposed to Privilege*, at 157. For an American view of influence in a colony, see Anon., *To Freeholders of Pennsylvania*, at 1. Contrary, see [Squire,] *Ballance of Power*, at v.

15. "Americus," 45 *Gentleman's Magazine* (1775), at 563. See also "Regulus," *Defence of the Resolutions*, at 82; 2 Anon., *History of North and South America*, at 254. For excellent summaries of the country perspective, see [Miles,] *Political Mirror or Summary Review*, at 5; Langdon, *Government Corrupted*, at 243–44; [Douglas,] *Seasonable Hints*, at 37–38. For an official claim that corruption of representation was a cause for taking up arms, see "An Act for . . . authorizing armed vessels, to defend the sea-coast of America," 7 *Records of Rhode Island*, at 481.

16. 1 Burgh, *Political Disquisitions*, at 226–27.

17. Speech of Alderman Bull, Commons Debates, 6 March 1776, 6 *Hibernian Magazine* (1776), at 628. See also [Carysfort,] *Serious Address*, at 7, 23; Speech of Sawbridge to Kent, 43 *London Magazine* (1774), at 435; 1 "Junius," *Junius*, at vi-vii; "Brutus," 9 *Political Register* (1771), at 74; Anon., *Duty of Freeman*, at 6; [Priestley,] *Present State of Liberty*, at 19. Contrary, see Speech of Sir Thomas Robinson, Commons Debates, 13 March 1734, 9 *Parliamentary History*, at 414. It was natural in the eighteenth century to connect corruption with long parliaments. Irish parliaments sat the length of a reign. Consequently, in 1760, there had not been a general election for thirty-three years.

18. Speech of Lord Noel Somerset, Commons Debates, 13 March 1734, 9 *Parliamentary History*, at 421; Instructions of Oxford, London, and Nottingham, 1756, *Voice of People*, at xi, 40, 47; Anon., *Abuse of Standing Parliaments*, at 18–19; Anon., *Some Reasons*, at 3; Price, *Two Tracts: Tract One*, at 10. For American arguments, see Williams, *Election Sermon*, at 24; Anon., *Letter to Freeholders* (1749), at 3; Memorial from James Logan to House of Representatives, 2 February 1724, 2 *Pennsylvania Archives*, at 1633–34.

19. Anon., *To Electors of New-York* (1776), at 1. See also [Carysfort,] *Serious Address*, at 8–9; [Toland,] *Mercenary Parliaments*. But see the argument that frequent elections would exclude country gentlemen and make the Commons more corruptible. [Almon,] *Free Parliaments*, at 25–26. For an earlier, opposite appraisal, see Pocock, "English Ideologies,", at 564–65.

20. Lichfield Instructions, 11 March 1741, 2 *Britain's Memorial*, at 33. The opposite argument was also made, that place bills pretending to restrict royal power really restricted the right of the people to a free choice of representative. Anon., *Letter Concerning Home and Abroad*, at 9; Anon., *Danger of Incapacities*, at 4; Witmer, *Property Qualifications*, at 68 (quoting Sir Charles Wager).

21. Instructions of Aberdeen, Hereford, and Gloucester, 2 *Britain's Memorial*, at 44, 50, 96; military officers: 17 *Gentleman's Magazine* (1747), at 367–68; lucrative contracts: Speech of Sir Philip Jennings Clerke, Commons Debates, 13 April 1778, 19 *Parliamentary History*, at 1089. For a detailed contemporary discussion of the statutes, resolutions, and arguments, see 2 Burgh, *Political Disquisitions*, at 168–269. See also Kemp, *King and Commons*, at 51–64.

22. "Philo Patria," 11 *Political Register* (1772), at 265, 262; Witmer, *Property Qualifications*, at 64 (quoting 1721/22 Lords' protest expunged from the records).

23. Christopher Gadsden, "Letter to Mr. Timothy," *Freeman Letters*, at 61. It has been claimed that the American sense of corruption was different from the British: they thought of corruption not as threatening the independence of their legislatures but as the avarice of governors and placemen. But they did take pride in the fact that they had the protection of annual elections to ensure legislative independence. Bushman, "Corruption," at 64–91. An American boasted in 1742, "I esteem it a great Happiness, that we have not a great many Posts of Profit among us; and wish we may be always so happy on that Account." Anon., *Letter to Freeholders* (1742), at 2.

24. "To the Editor," 45 *London Magazine* (1776), at 306–7; [Rokeby,] *Further Examination*, at 128. See also Speech of John Wilkes to London's Livery, 4 July 1776, 45 *London Magazine* (1776), at 388; Bailyn, *Pamphlets*, at 65.

CHAPTER TEN

1. Another reason why representation was first to get the reformers' attention was that it was one part of the constitution that people realized was not timeless. It had always been subject to statutory change, and people were aware of population changes, etc. [Rokeby,] *Further Examination*, at 101–2; Speech of John Wilkes, Commons Debates, 21 March 1776, 6 *Hibernian Magazine* (1776), at 781; Meeting of 30 May 1783, *Society for Constitutional Information*, at 8; Kramnick, "Republican Revisionism," at 638 (quoting John Locke).

2. Kramnick, *Bolingbroke's Circle*, at 258–60.

3. Brewer, "English Radicalism," at 356–57; Witmer, *Property Qualifications*, at 91.

4. Address to Merchants, 18 July 1783, *Society for Constitutional Information*, at 25–26.

5. "A Real Friend to the People," *Declaration of those Rights . . . Without which they cannot be Free* (broadside printed in London, ca. 1775, Huntington Library rare book no. 141710). See also Price, *Importance of the Revolution* (1785), reprinted in Peach, *Richard Price*, at 206n; *Essex Result*, at 42; Lofft, *Observations on Wesley's Address*, at 34; Anon., *Reflexions on Representation*, at 6; *Concept of Liberty*, at 109–12.

6. Speech of William Blackstone, Commons Debates, 3 February 1766, Ryder, "Parliamentary Diaries," at 268; every foot: Pulteney, *Thoughts on Present State*, at 17; represent property: [Williams,] *Letters on Liberty*, at 77–78; Declaration of Rights (1782), *Society for Constitutional Information*, at 37. See also [Robinson,] *Political Catechism*, at 64; Cartwright, *Legislative Rights*, at 30.

7. Hall, *Apology for Freedom*, at 29 (see also 64); Anon., *Review of Constitution*, at 6; Carysfort, *Thoughts on Constitution*, at 14. See also Anon., *British Liberties*, at xxii; Day, *Two Speeches*, at 7.

8. Raise qualification: Anon., *Serious and Impartial Observations*, at 85–86; rotten boroughs: Williamson, *American Suffrage*, at 71–72; Dickinson, *Liberty and Property*, at 190–91; equal: Tucker, *Treatise*, at 257.

9. [Towers,] *Letter to Samuel Johnson*, at 20.

10. [Jebb,] *Address to Freeholders*, at 7; Anon., *Plan for Conciliating*, at xi; Sharp, *Legal Means*, at 14–15.

11. Sharp, *Legal Means*, at 67n (Resolves of London Livery, 31 January 1782).

12. Speech of John Wilkes, Commons Debates, 21 March 1776, *Eighteenth-Century Constitution*, at 217; Principles and Resolves of the Constitutional Society of Nottingham, 1780, Wyvill, *Defence of Price*, at 96–97; Bill of Rights Society Resolves, 23 August 1774, 36 *Scots Magazine* (1774), at 440; Jones, *Speech to Middlesex*, at 10–11; Sharp, *Legal Means*, at 12–24; [Cartwright,] *Take Your Choice*, at 19–31; Carlyle, *Political Liberty*, at 190; Kramnick, "Republican Revisionism," at 638.

13. Absurd: Fletcher, *American Patriotism*, at 27; "impractical": [Powis,] *Dialogue on Parliament*, at 26–27; [Basset,] *Equal Representation*, at 19 (also 15, 20); [Almon,] *Free Parliaments*, at 42–43. See also Young, *Example of France*, at 253; Tucker, *Treatise*, at 40; Anon., *Civil Liberty Asserted*, at 27; 50 *Monthly Review* (1774), at 451.

14. Instructions of Boston, May 1776, *Remembrancer for 1776: Part II*, at 232; Wood, *Creation*, at 183.

15. [Keld,] *Polity of England*, at 231; Young, *Example of France*, at 88. See also Jackson Turner Main, "The American States in the Revolutionary Era," in *Sovereign States*, at 26–27; Rakove, *Beginnings*, at 140; Pole, "American Whig," at 233.

16. Young, *Example of France*, at 94; Tucker, *Treatise*, at 290–91; [Almon,] *Free Parliaments*, at 43–44. For a related argument, see Anon., *Sequel to Essay*, at 39–40.

17. Wyvill, *State of Representation*, at 35–40; Tooke, *Letter on Reform*, at 13, 12. One weakness of the equal representation reform was that those promoting it differed as to what form of equality was preferable. Keld, in the minority, wanted districts equal in number of electors. Carysfort favored voting districts equal by taxes paid. Others urged including women in the equality. [Keld,] *Polity of England*, at 242–55, 376–77; [Carysfort,] *Serious Address*, at 16; women: John Wesley, "Some Observations on Liberty," reprinted in Peach, *Richard Price*, at 248. See also plan of Chatham, 2 *Town and Country Magazine* (1770), at 333.

18. [Sinclair,] *Lucubrations*, at 43. On London, see also [Basset,] *Equal Representation*, at 61.

19. David Williams is a good illustration, for he was not a lawyer and, therefore, might have been more original in his ideas. He urged reform of representation so that the will of the people would in actual fact be represented, but his objective was not legislation but to give stability to government. [Williams,] *Letters on Liberty*. It is remarkable the degree to which would-be reformers were locked into traditional ways of looking at the constitution. An Irishman, e.g., proposed a public subscription to purchase seats for independent men. The purpose: the crown's influence would be neutralized, and the House of Commons—independent again—would resume its constitutional role checking arbitrariness and restraining power. [Waller,] *Address to People*, at 15–18.

20. For the rights to "security" and "property," see *Concept of Liberty*. Yet another concept was equality. The argument for equal representation was sometimes put in terms of the right to equality rather than to consent or representation. See, e.g., [Williams,] *Essential Rights*, at 4; Speech of T. Pitt, Commons Debates, 1782, [Almon,] *Free Parliaments*, at 35; Northcote, *Observations on Rights*, at 10; [Rokeby,] *Further Examination*, at 101–3.

21. Abingdon, *Dedication*, at lxxivn. See also Address to Merchants, 18 July 1783, *Society for Constitutional Information*, at 22; Wyvill, *State of Representation*, at 33–34; [Carysfort,] *Serious Address*, at 18–22; Anon., *Letter on Parliamentary Representation*, at 4, 16; [Jebb,] *Address to Freeholders*, at 14–15; Anon., *Reflexions on Representation;* Gibbons, *Ideas of Representation*, at 30, 43–44. For American attitudes, see *Essex Result*, at 22–23, 28, 50–52.

22. Letter from C. Wyvill to Belfast Committee, 1783, *Collection of Irish Letters*, at 31, 26, 32. See also Dinwiddy, *Wyvill*, at 5, n. 28; Foner, *Tom Paine*, at xix.

23. Speech of John Wilkes, Commons Debates, 21 March 1776, 18 *Parliamentary History*, at 1295, 1297, 1294. For a similar property-oriented argument by a radical, see Cartwright, *Legislative Rights*, at 29, 31. See also Somerville, *Observations on the Constitution*, at 34; Anon., *Review of Constitution*, at 6–7; Mac-

coby, *English Radicalism*, at 86; Pole, "American Whig," at 233; Gibbons, *Ideas of Representation*, at 50.

24. 4 *Hibernian Magazine* (1774), at 205, 206.

25. Speech of George Johnstone, Commons Debates, 16 December 1774, 44 *Gentleman's Magazine* (1774), at 596–97.

26. Unpublished Speech of Chatham, 22 January 1770, [Almon,] *Free Parliaments*, at 58; [Powis,] *Dialogue on Parliament*, at 25. See also Batley, *Letter to Wyvill*, at 8. But see the contrary argument that representation was statutory, not constitutional law. Carysfort, *Letter to Huntingdonshire*, at 4. There was some support for the power of Parliament to eliminate rotten boroughs by compensating their owners. Tooke, *Letter of Reform*, at 14–15; [Sinclair,] *Lucubrations*, at 21; Letter from C. Wyvill to Belfast Committee, 1783, *Collection of Irish Letters*, at 35–36. Contrary, see [Carysfort,] *Serious Address*, at 22–23, 29.

27. 3 Wynne, *Eunomus*, at 81–82.

28. Unpublished Speech of Chatham, 22 January 1770, [Almon,] *Free Parliaments*, at 58–59; [Basset,] *Equal Representation*, at 18–19.

CHAPTER ELEVEN

1. Anon., *Usurpations of England*, at 28. The right to consent to taxes was an element of the English concept of representation. In the 1690s, the earl of Warrington told a Chester grand jury that "we can have no *Tax* imposed upon us, but by our Consent in *Parliament*." Warrington, *Works*, at 647. See also "North Briton, No. 135," 27 *Scots Magazine* (1765), at 117.

2. [Raynal,] *Sentiments*, at "Advertisement" iii. See also Hamilton, *Farmer*, at 106–7; 29 *Scots Magazine* (1767), at 144; Letter of 31 May 1764, 1 Lee, *Richard Henry Lee*, at 28–29.

3. Dependent status: Speech of William Blackstone, Commons Debates, 3 February 1766, Ryder, "Parliamentary Diaries," at 268; representation extends: Anon., *Remarks on the New Essay*, at 7; equally represented: Anon., *Civil Liberty Asserted*, at 87. See also [Gray,] *Right of the Legislature*, at 28–29; 50 *Monthly Review* (1774), at 325; [Canning,] *Letter to Hillsborough*, at 29; Richard Jackson's Argument, 1765, *Franklin-Jackson Letters*, at 194. Contrary, see 39 *London Magazine* (1770), at 417; [Goodricke,] *Observations*, at 52.

4. Virginia Instructions, 6 August 1774, 1 *Papers of Jefferson*, at 141–42; 55 *Monthly Review* (1776), at 153. See also [Galloway,] *Historical Reflections*, at 117–18; [Lee,] *Speech Intended*, at 59–60.

5. "Regulus," *Defence of the Resolutions*, at 80; [Dulany,] *Considerations on the Propriety*, at 8. See also To Quebec, 26 October 1774, *Journal of the First Congress*, at 121; New York Resolves, 18 December 1765, Morgan, *Prologue*, at 61–62; [Hopkins,] "Vindication of a Pamphlet," 9 March 1765, at 1, col. 1; "North Briton, No. 135," 27 *Scots Magazine* (1765), at 116.

6. Creasy, *Imperial Constitutions*, at 121.

7. "Vindex Patriae," *New and Impartial Letters*, at 127.

8. Letter of Capel Lofft, 19 September 1782, Young and Lofft, *Enquiry into Legality*, at 13; Cartwright, *People's Barrier*, at 4 (quoting Lord Chatham).

9. Are represented: Anon., *Speech Never Intended*, at 10–11. See also

Fletcher, *Vindication of Wesley*, at 7–33; [Knox,] *Present State*, at 87; [Seabury,] *View of the Controversy*, at 10.

10. Letter of 14 December 1765, Bernard, *Select Letters*, at 39; Declaration of Stamp Act Congress, Morgan, *Prologue*, at 63. See also Maryland Resolves, 28 September 1765, *Maryland Votes and Proceedings* (September 1765), at 10; Massachusetts Resolves, 29 October 1765, South Carolina Resolves, 29 November 1765, and New Jersey Resolves, 30 November 1765, Morgan, *Prologue*, at 57, 58, 60; Resolves of Provincial Congress, 27 August 1774, 9 *North Carolina Colonial Records*, at 1044; [Howard,] *Defence of the Letter*, at 11.

11. Connecticut Resolves, June 1774, 2 *Revolutionary Virginia*, at 117; Delaware Convention Resolves, 2 August 1774, and Hunterdon County (N.J.) Resolves, 8 July 1774, 1 *American Archives*, at 667–68, 524; Westmoreland Petition, Minutes of 2 April 1768, 11 *Journal of Burgesses*, at 146. A loyalist association stated the same constitutional proposition when opposing whig committees and the Continental Congress. Dutchess County (N.Y.) Association, 18 January 1775, 1 *American Archives*, at 1164.

12. Declaration of Rights, 14 October 1774, *Journal of the First Congress*, at 61. See also Address to Quebec, 26 October 1774, *Commemoration Ceremony*, at 121–22.

13. Hartley, *Letters on the War*, at 77; Virginia Petition, 14 April 1766, 11 *Journal of Burgesses*, at 167; Pulteney, *Thoughts on Present State*, at 42–43. See also [Joseph Hawley,] "To Inhabitants," 30 March 1775, 2 *American Archives*, at 248. Contrary, see Carlyle, *Justice and Necessity*, at 8.

14. Johnstone, *Speech on the Question*, at 5; [Bancroft,] *Remarks*, at 95–96; *Boston News-Letter*, 9 March 1775, at 2, col. 1. See also James Wilson, "Parliamentary Authority," 17 August 1774, reprinted in *Commemoration Ceremony*, at 58; New Hampshire "Watchman," 24 December 1774, 1 *American Archives*, at 1064; Salem Instructions, 21 October 1765, Phillips, *Salem*, at 287; Johnstone, "Speech of November, 1775," at 86; "Regulus," *Defence of the Resolutions*, at 11; Anon., *Honor of Parliament*, at 30–31; Anon., *Prospect of the Consequences*, at 17.

15. [Knox,] *Claim of the Colonies*, at 16–17.

16. "L.," *Letter to G[renville]*, at 35.

17. Anon., *Case of Great Britain*, at 3.

18. See, e.g., Maryland Resolves, 28 September 1765, *Prior Documents*, at 23.

19. Quincy, *Observations with Thoughts*, at 399–400. See also *Boston Evening-Post*, 2 December 1765, at 1, col. 1 (quoting *London Gazetter*, 3 September 1765); Anon., *America Vindicated*, at 39–40; Sharp, *Legal Means*, at 44; Letter from Virginia Burgesses to Pennsylvania Assembly, 9 May 1768, and Instructions of Pennsylvania Representations to Agent Richard Jackson, 20 October 1764, 7 *Pennsylvania Archives*, at 6189, 5679; Virginia Petition to Commons, 14 April 1768, 11 *Journal of Burgesses*, at 170; Petition from Pennsylvania Assembly to Commons, 22 September 1768, *Boston Gazette*, 20 February 1769, at 1, col. 2; Petition of Stamp Act Congress to Commons (1765), New York Resolves, 18 December 1765, and New Jersey Resolves, 30 November 1765, Morgan, *Prologue*, at 68, 61, 60; Resolves of Burgesses, 30 May 1765, Virginia Remonstrance to Commons, 18 December 1764, and Virginia Memorial to Lords, 18 December

1764, 10 *Journal of Burgesses*, at 360, 303; Massachusetts Representatives' Letter to Agent Dennys de Berdt, 20 December 1765, 1 Adams, *Writings*, at 67–68; Speech of Lord Chatham, Lords Debates, 18 November 1777, 19 *Parliamentary History*, at 373; [Mitchell,] *The Present State*, at 296n. The 1776 election sermon, preached by a chaplain in Washington's army, highlighted two sides of localism: (1) representatives "who are perfect strangers" lack "that fellow-feeling" for those represented that representatives must have to truly represent; (2) because of "their unacquaintedness with the circumstances of the people over whom they claim the right of jurisdiction, [they] are utterly unable to judge, in a multitude of cases, which is best for them." West, *Election Sermon*, at 280.

20. Paley, *Principles of Philosophy*, at 471–72. For an even stronger claim for *actual* representation, but one saying that it should be a right and perhaps not that it was a right, see Address to Members, 18 July 1783, *Society for Constitutional Information*, at 22.

21. *Boston Evening-Post*, 14 October 1765, at 1, col. 3 (reprinting *New London Gazette*, 20 September 1765); [Dulany,] *Considerations*, at 608; private bills: Anon., *Inquiry into the Nature*, at 44–45.

22. Speech of Sir William Meredith, Commons Debates, 15 February 1765, 2 *Proceedings and Debates*, at 26; New York petition: Letter of 18 March 1769, Hope, *Letters*, at 40. See also 2 *Proceedings and Debates*, at 110–11 (quoting Horace Walpole, 27 January 1766); Speech of Robert Viner, Commons Debates, 16 December 1754, 1 *Parliamentary Debates*, at 30 (refusal to receive Massachusetts petition on a mutiny act). For the right to petition, see *Authority of Rights*, at 21–23.

23. Theory: Evans, *Political Sophistry detected*, at 10–11; Martin, *Familiar Dialogues*, at 22n. For accounts of a vote affecting American interests without American "representation," see 2 *Proceedings and Debates*, at 376–77.

24. 1 [Maseres,] *Canadian Freeholder*, at 467; Campbell v. Hall (1774), 20 *State Trials*, at 239–354.

25. Examples were the game laws and taxes on beer, soap, and candles. Pulteney, *Plan of Reunion*, at 159–61n; [Ramsay,] *Historical Essay*, at 132; Dickinson, "Debate on Sovereignty," at 200.

26. Anon., *Observations of Consequence*, at 18.

CHAPTER TWELVE

1. Anon., *Letter to the Essay Author*, at 16.

2. [Phelps,] *Rights of the Colonies*, at 13.

3. Speech of Joseph Galloway, [Galloway,] *Historical Reflections*, at 76, 78, 79. Galloway also argued that no matter what "might be" Parliament's authority "in law, to bind them" it "was not so competent in reason," which is an entirely different matter. Ibid., at 62.

4. Pole, *Pursuit of Equality*, at 53.

5. New Hampshire Constitution of 1783, Part I, Bill of Rights, Article 12; Massachusetts Constitution of 1780, Declaration of Rights, Article 10.

6. Anon., *Fact Without Fallacy*, at 24; Lowth, *Durham Assize Sermon*, at 11.

7. Anon., *To Electors of New-York* (1776), at 2; Anon., *Observations on Assembly*, at 5. See also *Boston Gazette*, 16 June 1766, at 4, col. 2; Gordon, *History*, at

143; Pole, *Gift*, at 89, 113, 122, 130. One earlier value had been that members of Parliament should not do "any thing that might look like an appeal to their constituents." For discussion, see Commons Debates, 13 April 1738, 10 *Parliamentary History*, at 803–7.

8. London's Address to King, 23 March 1770, 2 *Town and Country Magazine* (1770), at 127; old walls: [Macfarlane,] *George Third*, at 280–81. See also [Lee,] *Junius Americanus*, at 65; Anon., *View of North*, at 79–80; Maccoby, *English Radicalism*, at 174 (see also "engagement" of Wilkes and Townsend's barrister, at 203); Middlesex Petition, 9 April 1770, 2 *Town and Country Magazine* (1770), at 220; London Remonstrance, March 1773, 2 *Correspondence George III*, at 463; Speech of Charles James Fox, Commons Debates, 27 November 1781, 1 Fox, *Speeches*, at 438; Speech of John Wilkes, Commons Debates, 21 March 1776, *Society for Constitutional Information*, at 13, 17; Speech of Edmund Burke, Commons Debates, 19 March 1770, 2 *Burke Writings*, at 241; 1 Burgh, *Political Disquisitions*, at 265–66; 43 *London Magazine* (1774), at 228; Letter of 13 January 1770, Hope, *Letters*, at 61–62; Cartwright, *Constitutional Defence*, at 94–95. In a remarkable argument, Catharine Macauley contended that the Commons was unrepresentative, but to make her case she listed the former, "autonomous," independent reasons for representation. "A vigilant and jealous eye over executory and judicial magistracy, an anxious care of public money, an openness approaching towards facility to public complaint; these seem to be the true characteristicks, of a house of commons." Macaulay, *Observations on a Pamphlet*, at 21n.

9. Anon., *Proposals for Union*, at 25; 44 *London Magazine* (1775), at 315 (reprinting Galloway, *Candid Examination*). See also Letter from Joseph Galloway and Samuel Rhoads to Virginia Committee, 1 July 1774, 2 *Revolutionary Virginia*, at 137–38; Cartwright, *Memorial*, at 11; Sharp, *Declaration of Natural Right*, at 9.

10. Rakove, *Beginnings*, at 66; Letter from Governor John Wentworth to Lord Dartmouth, 2 December 1774, 1 *American Archives*, at 1013; Speech of Sir William Beckford, Commons Debates, 16 December 1754, 1 *Parliamentary Debates*, at 38.

11. Letter from James Simpson to General Sir Henry Clinton, 15 May 1780, Brown, "James Simpson's Reports," at 511, 519, 518; Letters from James Simpson to William Knox, 20 August 1781 and 28 July 1781, 20 *Revolution Documents*, at 218, 203, 202. See also Letters from Governor James Robertson to General Sir Henry Clinton, 29 March 1780 and 25 June 1780, *Twilight*, at 88–89, 121–22; Instructions from Lord George Germain to Governor James Robertson, 9 July 1779, and Letter from Governor Patrick Tonyn to Lord George Germain, 3 July 1779, 17 *Revolution Documents*, at 160, 156. Contrary, see Letter from Tonyn to Germain, 9 December 1780, 18 *Revolution Documents*, at 253.

12. Edmund S. Morgan has argued that the Revolution was caused by the British carrying "the fiction of representation too far from the facts, destroying altogether its local character." Morgan provides a marvelous demonstration of the historian's imagination, but the material, arguments, and evidence presented in this book demonstrate that his conclusions cannot be sustained in law. Morgan, "Government by Fiction," at 337–39.

13. [Cartwright,] *Memorial*, at 28–29.

14. Robinson, *Christian Submission*, at 15; Payson, *Election Sermon*, at 330. See also Young, *Example of France*, at 129; Anon., *Civil Liberty Asserted*, at 21.

15. Late into the nineteenth century, the various editions of Justice Story's *Commentaries* were denying that consent was a basis for authority in American constitutionalism and described consent by the former English concepts of constructive or attenuated consent. Joseph Story, *Commentaries on the Constitution*, bk. 3, chap. 3, secs. 327–30 (1858).

SHORT TITLES

Abingdon, *Dedication*
Willoughby Bertie, earl of Abingdon. *Dedication to the Collective Body of the People of England, in which the Source of our present Political Distractions are pointed out, and a Plan proposed for their Remedy and Redress.* Oxford, England, 1780.

Abingdon, *Thoughts on Burke's Letter*
Willoughby Bertie, earl of Abingdon. *Thoughts on the Letter of Edmund Burke, Esq; to the Sheriffs of Bristol, on the Affairs of America.* 6th ed. Oxford, England, 1777.

Adams, "Novanglus"
John Adams. "Novanglus." Reprinted in *The American Colonial Crisis: The Daniel Leonard–John Adams Letters to the Press, 1774–1775,* edited by Bernard Mason. New York, 1972.

[Adams,] *Thoughts*
[John Adams.] *Thoughts on Government: Applicable to the Present State of the American Colonies. In a Letter from a Gentleman to his Friend.* Philadelphia, 1776.

Adams, *Writings*
The Writings of Samuel Adams. Edited by Harry Alonzo Cushing. 4 vols. New York, 1904–8.

Addresses and Petitions of Common Council
Addresses, Remonstrances, and Petititons; Commencing the 24th of June, 1769, Presented to the King and Parliament, from the Court of Common Council, and the Livery in Common Hall assembled, with his Majesty's Answers: Likewise the Speech to the King, made by the late Mr. Alderman Beckford, When Lord Mayor of the City of London. London, [1778].

Addresses of Common Council
Addresses Presented from the Court of Common Council to the King, On his Majesty's Accession to the Throne, and on various other Occasions, and his Answers. Resolutions of the Court, ... Instructions at different Times to the Representatives of the City in Parliament. Petitions to Parliament for different Purposes. . . . Agreed to between the 23d October, 1760, and the 12th October, 1770. London, [1770].

Allen, *American Crisis*
William Allen. *The American Crisis: A Letter, Addressed by Permission to the Earl Gower, Lord President of the Council, &c. &c. &c. On the present alarming Disturbances in the Colonies.* London, 1774.

Allen, *English Political Thought*
> J. W. Allen. *English Political Thought, 1603–1660.* Vol. 1. London, 1938.

Allen, *In English Ways*
> David Grayson Allen. *In English Ways: The Movement of Societies and the Transferal of English Local Law and Custom to Massachusetts Bay in the Seventeenth Century.* Chapel Hill, N.C., 1981.

[Almon,] *Free Parliaments*
> [John Almon.] *Free Parliaments: or, a Vindication of the Parliamentary Constitution of England; in Answer to Certain visionary Plans of modern Reformers.* London, 1783.

[Almon,] *History of the Late Minority*
> [John Almon.] *The History of the Late Minority. Exhibiting the Conduct, Principles, and Views of that Party, during the Years 1762, 1763, 1764, and 1765.* London, 1766.

American Archives
> *American Archives, Fourth Series. Containing a Documentary History of the English Colonies in North America From the King's Message to Parliament, of March 7, 1774, to the Declaration of Independence by the United States.* Vols. 1 and 2. Washington, D.C., 1837.

American Gazette
> *The American Gazette. Being a Collection of all the Authentic Addresses, Memorials, Letters, &c. Which relate to the Present Disputes Between Great Britain and her Colonies. Containing also Many Original Papers Never Before Published.* London, 1768.

"Americanus," *Letter to Freeholders*
> "Americanus." *A Letter to the Freeholders and other Inhabitants of the Massachusetts-Bay, relating to their approaching Election of Representatives.* [Newport, R.I.,] 1739.

[Anderson], *Free Thoughts*
> [James Anderson.] *Free Thoughts on the American Contest.* Edinburgh, 1776.

Anecdotes of Pitt
> *Anecdotes of the Life of the Right Hon. William Pitt, Earl of Chatham, and of the Principal Events of his Time. With His Speeches in Parliamant, From the Year 1736 to the Year 1778.* 2 vols. Dublin, 1792.

Annual Register 1765
> *The Annual Register, or a View of the History, Politics, and Literature For the Year 1765.* 3d ed. London, 1802.

Annual Register 1766
> *The Annual Register, or a View of the History, Politics, and Literature, For the Year 1766.* 6th ed. London, 1803.

Anon., *Abuse of Standing Parliaments*
> Anonymous. *The Abuse of Standing Parliaments, and the Great Advantage of Frequent Elections in a Letter to a Noble Lord.* London, [1750?].

Anon., *Address to Free*
> Anonymous. *An Address to the Free and Independent Voters of England.* London, 1780.

Anon., *Advice to a Member*
Anonymous. *Advice to a Newly Elected Member of Parliament: With Observations on the Legislative Constitution, and the Contract relating thereto, between the Representatives of the People in Parliament and their Constituents.* Dublin, 1780.

Anon., *Advice to a New Member*
Anonymous. *Advice to a New Member; Containing a Compendious System of such P[arliamentar]y Practice and Political Principle as Every Member must learn, before he can Expect to Derive any Popularity or Preferment from his Senatorial Conduct, Character, or Consequence.* London, 1784.

Anon., *Æolus*
Anonymous. *Æolus: or, the Constitutional Politician. With the Remarks of a Briton on the Trial of the Irish Chairmen; A Gentle Reproof to the Monthly Reviewers; and a free Conversation between an Elector and his Representative.* London, 1770.

Anon., *America Vindicated*
Anonymous. *America Vindicated From the High Charge of Ingratitude and Rebellion: With a Plan of Legislation, Proposed to the Consideration of Both Houses, For Establishing a Permanent and Solid Foundation, For a just constitutional Union Between Great Britain and her Colonies. By a Friend to Both Countries.* London, 1774.

Anon., *American Resistance Indefensible*
Anonymous. *American Resistance Indefensible. A Sermon, Preached on Friday, December 13, 1776, Being a Day appointed for a General Fast.* London, [1776].

Anon., *Animadversions on Discourse*
Anonymous. *Animadversions on a Discourse Entituled, God's Way of Disposing of Kingdoms.* London, 1691.

Anon., *Answer to Foolish Reason*
Anonymous. *Answer to the Foolish Reason that is given for re-choosing the Old Members, to wit, that they passed certain Resolves, agreeable to the Instructions given them by some of their Constituents.* [New York, 1769.]

Anon., *Answer to Pitt's Speech*
Anonymous. *The Answer at Large to Mr. P[i]tt's Speech.* London, 1766.

Anon., *Answer to Sheridan*
Anonymous. *Answer to a Pamphlet, Written by C. F. Sheridan, Esq; Entitled, A Review of the Three Great National Questions . . . Part the First, Declaration of Right.* Dublin, 1782.

Anon., *Appeal to Reason and Justice*
Anonymous. *An Appeal to Reason and Justice, in Behalf of the British Constitution, and the Subjects of the British Empire. In which the present Important Contest with the Revolted Colonies is impartially considered, the Inconsistency of Modern Patriotism is demonstrated, the Supremacy of Parliament is asserted on Revolution Principles, and American Independence is proved to be a manifest Violation of the Rights of British Subjects.* London, 1778.

Anon., *Application of Political Rules*
Anonymous. *An Application of some General Political Rules, to the Present State of Great-Britain, Ireland and America. In a Letter to the Right Honourable Earl Temple.* London, 1766.

Anon., *Argument in Defence*
Anonymous. *An Argument in Defence of the Exclusive Right Claimed by the Colonies to Tax Themselves, with a Review of the Laws of England, Relative to Representation and Taxation. To Which is Added, An Account of the Rise of the Colonies, and the Manner in which the rights of the subjects within the realm were communicated to those that went to America, with the exercise of those rights from their first settlement to the present time.* London, 1774.

Anon., *Arguments in Support of Supremacy*
Anonymous. *A Brief Extract, or Summary of Important Arguments Advanced by Some Late Distinguished Writers, in Support of the Supremacy of the British Legislature, and their Right to Tax the Americans, Addressed to the Freemen and Liverymen of London, And Recommended to the serious Perusal of every Candid and Dispassionate Man.* London, 1775.

Anon., *British Liberties*
Anonymous. *British Liberties, or the Free-born Subject's Inheritance; Containing the Laws that form the Basis of those Liberties, with Observations thereon; also an Introductory Essay on Political Liberty and a Comprehensive View of the Constitution of Great Britain.* London, 1766.

Anon., *Case of Great Britain*
[Gervase Parker Bushe.] *Case of Great Britain and America, Addressed to the King, and Both Houses of Parliament.* 3d ed. Boston, [1769].

Anon., *Cautionary Address*
Anonymous. *A Cautionary Address to the Electors of England: Being a Touchstone between the Constituents and Candidates. With a Word touching John Wilkes, Esq.* London, 1768.

Anon., *Celebrated Speech*
Anonymous. *The Celebrated Speech of a Celebrated Commoner.* New ed., corrected. London, 1766.

Anon., *Civil Liberty Asserted*
Anonymous. *Civil Liberty Asserted, and the Rights of the Subject Defended, Against the Anarchial Principles of the Reverend Dr. Price.* London, 1766.

Anon., *Common Sense Conferences*
Anonymous. *Common Sense: in Nine Conferences, Between a British Merchant and a Candid Merchant of America, in their private capacities as friends; tracing the several causes of the present contests between the mother country and her American subjects; the fallacy of their prepossessions; and the ingratitude and danger of them; the reciprocal benefits of national friendship; and the moral obligations of individuals which enforce it.* London, 1775.

Anon., *Conduct of Livery-Men*
Anonymous. *The Conduct of the Livery-Men at the Late Election of a Lord-Mayor, and their Proceedings in the Common-Hall Justified; with Some Cautions relating to their Future Conduct, and the Present State of the Nation. In an address to the Common-Council and Livery.* London, 1739.

Anon., *Confutation of Sherlock*
Anonymous. *A Confutation of sundry Errors in Dr. Sherlock's Book concerning Allegiance.* [London, 1691.]

Anon., *Considerations on National Independence*
Anonymous. *Considerations on National Independence, Suggested by Mr. Pitt's Speeches on the Irish Union. Addressed to the People of Great Britain and Ireland. By a Member of the Honourable Society of Lincoln's Inn.* London, n.d.

Anon., *Considerations on the Addresses*
Anonymous. *Considerations on the Addresses Lately Presented to His Majesty, on Occasion of the Loss of Minorca. In a Letter to a Member of Parliament.* 2d ed. London, 1756.

Anon., *Considerations Upon Rights of Colonists*
Anonymous. *Considerations Upon the Rights of the Colonists to the Privileges of British Subjects, Introduc'd by a brief Review of the Rise and Progress of English Liberty, and concluded with some Remarks upon our present Alarming Situation.* New York, 1766.

Anon., *Considerations Upon the Act*
Anonymous. *Considerations Upon the Act of Parliament Whereby a Duty is laid of six Pence Sterling per Gallon on Molasses, and five Shillings per Hundred on Sugar of foreign Growth, imported into any of the British Colonies. Shewing, some of the Many Inconveniencies necessarily resulting from the operation of the said Act, not only to those Colonies, but also to the British Sugar Islands, and finally to Great Britain.* Boston, 1764.

Anon., *Constitution*
Anonymous. *The Constitution, or a Full Answer to Mr. Edmund Burke's Anti-Constitutional Plan of Reform.* London, 1781.

Anon., *Constitutional Advocate*
[Richard Goodenough.] *The Constitutional Advocate: By which, From the Evidence of History, and of Records, and from The Principles of the British Government, Every Reader may form his own Judgement concerning the Justice and Policy of the present War with America. Addressed to the People at Large, And humbly submitted to the Consideration of their Representatives.* London, 1776.

Anon., *Constitutional Answer to Wesley*
Anonymous. *A Constitutional Answer to the Rev. Mr. John Wesley's Calm Address to the American Colonies.* London, 1775.

Anon., *Critical Review of Liberties*
Anonymous. *A Critical Review of the Liberties of British Subjects. With a Comparative View of the Proceedings of the H[ous]e of C[ommon]s of I[relan]d, against an unfortunate Exile of that Country; who, in contending for the Rights and Liberties of the Publick, lost his own. By a Gentleman of the Middle-Temple.* 2d ed. London, 1750.

Anon., *Danger of Incapacities*
Anonymous. *An Enquiry into the Danger of Multiplying Incapacities of the Gentlemen of England to sit in Parliament.* London, 1739.

Anon., *Defence of English History*
Anonymous. *A Defence of English History Against the Misrepresentations of M. de Rapin Thoyras, in his History of England, Now Publishing Weekly.* London, 1734.

Anon., *Dialogue on the Constitution*
Anonymous. *A Dialogue on the Principles of the Constitution and Legal Liberty,*

Compared with Despotism; Applied to the American Question; and the Probable Events of the War, with Observations on some important Law Authorities. London, 1776.

Anon., *Divine Rights*
Anonymous. *The Divine Rights of the British Nation and Constitution Vindicated.* London, 1710.

Anon., *Duty of Freeman*
Anonymous. *The Duty of a Freeman, Addressed to the Electors of Great Britain.* n.i., 1780. [Distributed by the Society for Constitutional Information, 1782.]

Anon., *Eclipse*
Anonymous. *The Eclipse.* [Boston,] 1754.

Anon., *Essay on Constitutional Liberty*
Anonymous. *An Essay on Constitutional Liberty: Wherein the Necessity of Frequent Elections of Parliament is shewn to be superseded by the Unity of the Executive Power.* London, 1780.

Anon., *Evidence of Common and Statute Laws*
Anonymous. *The Evidence of the Common and Statute Laws of the Realm; Usage, Records, History with the Greatest and Best Authorities Down to the 3d of George the IIId, in Proof of the Rights of Britons Throughout the British Empire. Addressed to the People.* London, 1775.

Anon., *Experience preferable*
Anonymous. *Experience preferable to Theory. An Answer to Dr. Price's Observations on the Nature of Civil Liberty, and the Justice and Policy of the War with America.* London, 1776.

Anon., *Fact Without Fallacy*
Anonymous. *Fact Without Fallacy: or, Constitutional Principles Contrasted with the Ruinous Effects of Unconstitutional Practices.* London, 1793.

Anon., *Fair Trial*
Anonymous. *A Fair Trial of the Important Question, or the Rights of Election Asserted; Against the Doctrine of Incapacity by Expulsion, or by Resolution: Upon True Constitutional Principles, the Real Law of Parliament, the Common Right of the Subject, and the Determinations of the House of Commons.* London, 1769.

Anon., *First Letter to Grafton*
Anonymous. *A First Letter to the Duke of Grafton.* London, 1770.

Anon., *Free and Candid Remarks*
Anonymous. *Free and Candid Remarks On a late Celebrated Oration; With some few Occasional thoughts On the late Commotions in America.* London, 1765.

Anon., *History of Lord North*
Anonymous. *The History of Lord North's Administration, to the Dissolution of the Thirteenth Parliament of Great-Britain.* London, 1781.

Anon., *History of North and South America*
Anonymous. *The History of North and South America, Containing an Account of the First Discoveries of the New World, the Customs, Genius, and Persons of the Original Inhabitants, and a particular Description of the Air, Soil, natural Productions, Manufacturers and Commerce of each Settlement.* 2 vols. London, 1776.

Anon., *Honor of Parliament*

Anonymous. *The Honor of Parliament and the Justice of the Nation Vindicated. In a Reply to Dr. Price's Observations on the Nature of Civil Liberty.* London, 1776.

Anon., *Inquiry into the Nature*

Anonymous. *An Inquiry into the Nature and Causes of the Present Disputes Between the British Colonies in America and their Mother-Country; and their reciprocal Claims and just Rights impartially examined, and fairly stated.* London, 1769.

Anon., *Interposition of the People*

Anonymous. *Arguments to Prove the Interposition of the People to be Constitutional and Strictly Legal: in which the Necessary of a More Equal Representation of the People in Parliament is also Proved: and a Simple, Unobjectionable Mode of Equalizing the Representation is Suggested.* Dublin, 1783.

Anon., *Judgment of Whole Kingdoms*

[Lord Somers.] *The Judgment of Whole Kingdoms and Nations, Concerning the Rights, Power, and Prerogative of Kings, and the Rights, Privileges, & Properties of the People.* 12th ed. Newport, R.I., 1774.

Anon., *Justice to a Judge*

Anonymous. *Justice to a Judge. An Answer to the Judge's Appeal to Justice, in Proof of the Blessings enjoyed by British Subjects. A Letter to Sir Wm. H. Ashhurst, Knight; in Reply to his Charge to the Grand Jury of Middlesex, in the Court of King's Bench, Nov. 19, 1792.* 2d ed. London, 1793.

Anon., *Letter Concerning Home and Abroad*

Anonymous. *A Letter to a Member of Parliament Concerning the present State of Affairs at Home and Abroad. By a True Lover of the People.* London, 1740.

Anon., *Letter on Corruption*

Anonymous. *A Letter to the People of Great Britain, on the present alarming Crisis. Pointing at the most eligible Means for limiting the Number of Place-Men and Pensioners, in Parliament, and putting an End to Bribery and Corruption; to obviate the Dangers which now threaten this Kingdom.* London, 1771.

Anon., *Letter on Parliamentary Representation*

Anonymous. *A Letter on Parliamentary Representation, in which the Propriety of Trienial and Septennial Parliaments is Considered. Inscribed to John Sinclair, Esq. M.P.* London, 1783.

Anon., *Letter to a Member*

Anonymous. *A Letter to a Member of Parliament on the Present Unhappy Dispute between Great-Britain and her Colonies. Wherein the Supremacy of the Former is Asserted and Proved; and the Necessity of Compelling the Latter to Pay Due Obedience to the Sovereign State, is Enforced upon Principles of Sound Policy, Reason, and Justice.* London, 1774.

Anon., *Letter to Cooper*

Anonymous. *A Letter to the Rev. Dr. Cooper, on the Origin of Civil Government; in Answer to his Sermon, Preached before the University of Oxford, on the Day appointed by Proclamation for a General Fast.* London, 1777.

Anon., *Letter to De Brett*

Anonymous. *A Letter to Mr. De Brett, Being an Answer to "Lucubrations During a Short Recess" which Pamphlet contains a Plan for altering the Representation of the People.* London, 1783.

Anon., *Letter to English*

Anonymous. *A Letter to the English Nation, on the Present War with America; with a Review of our Military Operations in that Country; and a Series of Facts never before published, From which the absolute Impossibility of reducing the Colonies will sufficiently appear, and the Folly of continuing the Contest demonstrated. With a Prefatory Address to Sir George Saville, Bart. By an Officer returned from that Service.* London, 1777.

Anon., *Letter to Freeholders* (1742)
Anonymous. *A Letter to the Freeholders and other Inhabitants of this Province, qualified to vote for Representatives in the ensuing Election.* [Boston, 1742.]

Anon., *Letter to Freeholders* (1749)
Anonymous. *A Letter to the Freeholders and other Inhabitants of the Massachusetts-Bay, Relating to their approaching Election of Representatives.* Boston, [1749].

Anon., *Letter to Freemen of New York*
Anonymous. *A Letter to the Freemen and Freeholders of the Province of New-York, Relating to the Approaching Election of their Representatives.* New York, 1750.

Anon., *Letter to Mansfield*
Anonymous. *A Letter to the Right Honourable Lord M[ansfield], on the Affairs of America: From a Member of Parliament.* London, 1775.

Anon., *Letter to People of Great Britain*
Anonymous. *A Letter to the People of Great-Britain, in Answer to that Published by the American Congress.* London, 1775.

Anon., *Letter to Robert Morris*
Anonymous. *Letter to Robert Morris, Esq. Wherein the Rise and Progress of our Political Disputes are considered. Together with Some Observations on the Power of Judges and Juries As relating to the Cases of Woodfall and Almon.* London, 1771.

Anon., *Letter to the Common Council*
Anonymous. *A Letter to the Common Council of the City of London. With Remarks on Lord Chief Justice Pratt's Letter to the City of Exeter.* London, 1764.

Anon., *Letter to the Essay Author*
Anonymous. *A Letter to the Author of an Essay on the Middlesex Election: In which his Objections to the Power of Expulsion are considered: And the Nature of Representation in Parliament examined.* London, 1770.

Anon., *Letter to those Ladies*
Anonymous. *A Letter to those Ladies whose Husbands Possess a Seat in either House of Parliament.* London, 1775.

Anon., *Liberal Strictures*
Anonymous. *Liberal Strictures on Freedom and Slavery: Occasioned by the Numerous Petitions to Parliament, for the Abolition of the Slave-Trade.* London, 1789.

Anon., *Liberty in Two Parts*
Anonymous. *Liberty in Two Parts.* London, 1754.

Anon., *Magna Charta Opposed to Privilege*
Anonymous. *Magna Charta, Opposed to Assumed Privilege: Being a complete View of the late Interesting Disputes between the House of Commons and the Magistrates of London.* London, 1771.

Anon., *New System of Policy*
Anonymous. *A New System of Patriot Policy. Containing the Genuine Recantation*

of the British Cicero. To which is added, An Abstract of the Reciprocal Duties of Representatives and their Constituents, on Constitutional Principles. London, 1756.

Anon., *North-Country Poll*

Anonymous. *The North-Country Poll; or, an Essay on the New Method of Appointing Members to serve in Parliament.* London, 1768.

Anon., *O Liberty*

Anonymous. *O Liberty, thou Goddess Heavenly Bright.* [New York, 1732.]

Anon., *Observations of Consequence*

Anonymous. *Some Observations of Consequence, In Three Parts. Occasioned by the Stamp-Tax, Lately imposed on the British Colonies.* [Philadelphia,] 1768.

Anon., *Obeservations on Assembly*

Anonymous. *A Few Observations on the Conduct of the General Assembly of New-York, for some Years Past. Addressed to the Freemen and Freeholders of the City and Province.* [New York,] 1768.

Anon., *Observations on Excise Bill*

Anonymous. *Some Observations on the Bill, Intitled, "An Act for granting to His Majesty an Excise upon Wines, and Spirits distilled, sold by Retail or consumed within this Province, and upon Limes, Lemons, and Oranges."* Boston, 1754.

Anon., *Plan for Conciliating*

Anonymous. *A Plan for Conciliating the Jarring Political Interests of Great Britain and her North American Colonies, and for promoting a general Re-union throughout the Whole British Empire.* London, 1775.

Anon., *Plea for Poor*

Anonymous. *A Plea for the Poor and Distressed, Against the Bill for granting an Excise upon Wines, and Spirits distilled, sold by Retail, or consumed within this Province &.c.* Boston, 1754.

Anon., *Political Disquisitions*

Anonymous. *Political Disquisitions Proper for Public Consideration in the Present State of Affairs in a Letter to a Noble Duke.* London, 1763.

Anon., *Power and Grandeur*

Anonymous. *The Power and Grandeur of Great-Britain, Founded on the Liberty of the Colonies, and The Mischiefs attending the Taxing them by Act of Parliament Demonstrated.* New York, 1768.

Anon., *Present State of the Constitution*

Anonymous. *The Present State of the British Constitution, Deduced from Facts. By an Old Whig.* London, 1793.

Anon., *Priviledges of Parliament*

Anonymous. *The Priviledges and Practice of Parliaments in England. Collected out of the Common Lawes of this Land. Seene and allowed by the Learned in the Lawes. Commenced to the High Court of Parliament now Assembled.* [London,] 1628.

Anon., *Proposals for Union*

Anonymous. *Proposals for a Plan Towards a Reconciliation and Re-Union with the Thirteen Provinces of America, and for a Union with the other Colonies.* London, 1778.

Anon., *Prospect of the Consequences*
Anonymous. *A Prospect of the Consequences of the Present Conduct of Great Britain Towards America.* London, 1776.

Anon., *Reasons Against*
Anonymous. *Reasons Against the Renewal of the Sugar Act, As it will be prejudicial to the Trade, Not Only Of the Northern Colonies, but to that of Great-Britain Also.* Boston, 1764.

Anon., *Reflections on the Contest*
Anonymous. *Reflections on the American Contest: In which the Consequence of a Formal Submission, and the Means of a Lasting Reconciliation are pointed out, Communicated by Letter to a Member of Parliament, Some Time Since, and now Addressed to Edmund Burke, Esq.* London, 1776.

Anon., *Reflections on Wilkes*
Anonymous. *Reflections on the Case of Mr. Wilkes, and on the Right of the People to Elect their own Representatives. To which is added, The Case of Mr. Walpole.* London, 1768.

Anon., *Reflexions on Representation*
Anonymous. *Reflexions on Representation in Parliament: Being an Attempt to shew the Equity and Practicability, not only of establishing a more equal Representation throughout Great Britain, but also of admitting the Americans to a Share in the Legislature. With Enumeration of the principal Benefits which would result from these Measures, both to the Colonies and the Mother-Country.* London, 1766.

Anon., *Relapse*
Anonymous. *The Relapse.* [Boston, 1754.]

Anon., *Remarks on the New Essay*
Anonymous. *Remarks on the New Essay of the Pen[n]sylvanian Farmer; and on the Resolves and Instructions Prefixed to that Essay; By the Author of the Right of the British Legislature Vindicated.* London, 1775.

Anon., *Representative of London*
Anonymous. *The Representative of London and Westminster in Parliament Examined and Consider'd. Wherein Appears the Antiquity of the Borroughs in England; with the Proportions whereby every County is over or under Represented, according to a Scale from the Royal Aid Assessments; by which appears that Middlesex is found to be Represented but one Tenth part of it's due Proportion; unto which a Remedy is proposed, and several Reasons offer'd to prove the same, of universal Benefit to the Kingdom.* London, 1702.

Anon., *Review*
Anonymous. *The Review.* [Boston, 1754.]

Anon., *Review of Constitution*
Anonymous. *A Review of the Constitution of Great Britain: Being the Substance of a Speech Delivered in a Numerous Assembly on the following Question: "Is the Petition of Mr. Horne Tooke a Libel on the House of Commons, or a just Statement of public Grievances arising from an unfair Representation of the People?"* London, 1791.

Anon., *Right to Petition*
Anonymous. *The Right of British Subjects, to Petition and Apply to their Representatives, Asserted and Vindicated.* London, 1733.

Anon., *Rights Asserted*
   Anonymous. *The Rights of the People Asserted, and the Necessity of a More Equal Representation in Parliament Stated and Proved.* Dublin, 1783.
Anon, *Rights of Parliament*
   Anonymous. *The Rights of Parliament Vindicated, On Occasion of the late Stamp-Act. In which is exposed the Conduct of the American Colonists. Addressed to all the People of Great Britain.* London, 1766.
Anon., *Rise and Fall of Excise*
   Anonymous. *The Rise and Fall of the late Projected Excise, Impartially Consider'd.* London, 1733.
Anon., *Scandalous Paper*
   Anonymous. *As a Scandalous Paper has Appeared, Stiled an Answer to the foolish Reason for re-choosing the old Members, &c.* [New York, 1769.]
Anon., *Seasonable Expostulations*
   Anonymous. *Seasonable Expostulations with the Worthy Citizens of London; Upon their late Instructions to their Representatives.* London, 1742.
Anon., *Second Letter to Member*
   Anonymous. *A Second Letter to a Member of Parliament Concerning the Present State of Affairs. Wherein all that has been written against the former is fully refuted; and the Positions therein laid down with respect to the Right of Instructing Members, &c. are further explained and supported from, Reason, Law, and History.* London, 1741.
Anon., "Second Part"
   Anonymous. "The Second Part of an Argument against Excises; In Answer to the Objections of Several Writers." 10 *Craftsman* (1737) [Printed as an appendix.].
Anon., *Sequel to Essay*
   Anonymous. *Sequel to an Essay on the Orgin and Progress of Government.* London, 1783.
Anon., *Serious Address to Electors*
   Anonymous. *A Serious Address to the Electors of Great-Britain on the Subject of Short Parliaments, and an Equal Representation.* London, 1782.
Anon., *Serious and Impartial Observations*
   Anonymous. *Serious and Impartial Observations on the Blessings of Liberty and Peace. Addressed to Persons of all Parties. Inviting them also to enter into that Grand ASSOCIATION, which is able to secure the Safety and Happiness of the British Empire.* London, 1776.
Anon., *Serious Considerations*
   Anonymous. *Serious Considerations on a Late Very Important Decision of the House of Commons.* London, 1769.
Anon., *Serious Reflections*
   Anonymous. *Serious Reflections upon some late important Determinations in a Certain Assembly.* London, 1770.
Anon., *Some Few Observations*
   Anonymous. *Some Few Observations on the present Publication of the Speech of a Right Honourable Gentleman, against the Expulsion of Mr. Wilkes, on the 3d of February, 1769. In a Letter to a Friend in Buckinghamshire.* London, 1769.

Anon., *Some Reasons*
Anoymous. *Some Reasons for Annual Parliaments, in a Letter to a Friend.* n.i., [1699?].
Anon., *Speech Never Intended*
Anonymous. *A Speech Never Intended to be Spoken, In Answer to a Speech Intended to have been Spoken on the Bill for Altering the Charter of the Colony of Massachuset's Bay. Dedicated to the Right Reverend the Lord Bishop of St. A——.* London, 1774.
Anon., *Supremacy of Legislature*
Anonymous. *The Supremacy of the British Legislature over Colonies, Candidly Discussed.* London, 1775.
Anon., *Taxation, Tyranny*
Anonymous. *Taxation, Tyranny. Addressed to Samuel Johnson, L.L.D.* London, 1775.
Anon., *Thoughts on Quebec Act*
Anonymous. *Thoughts on the Act for making more Effectual Provision for the Government of the Province of Quebec.* London, 1774.
Anon., *Three Letters*
Anonymous. *Three Letters to a Member of Parliament, On the Subject of the Present Dispute With Our American Colonies.* London, 1775.
Anon., *To Committee of London Merchants*
Anonymous. *A Letter To the Gentlemen of the Committee of London Merchants, Trading to North America: Shewing In what Manner, it is apprehended, that the Trade and Manufactures of Britain may be affected by some late Restrictions on the American Commerce, and by the Operation of the Act for the Stamp Duty in America; as also how far the Freedom and Liberty of the Subjects residing in Britain, are supposed to be interested in the Preservation of the Rights of the Provinces, and in what Manner those Rights appear to be abridged by that Statute.* London, 1766.
Anon., *To Electors of New-York* (1776)
Anonymous. *To the Electors of New-York.* [New York, 1776.]
Anon., *To Freeholders of New York* (1768a)
Anonymous. *To the Freeholders and Freemen of the City and County of New-York. This Vindication, of the Professors of the Law, in Answer to the Remarks on the 17 Queries, is humbly submitted by a sincere Friend to the Cause of Liberty, and this Colony.* [New York, 1768.]
Anon., *To Freeholders of New York* (1768b)
Anonymous. *To the Freeholders and Freemen of the City and County of New-York.* [New York, 1768.] (Evans 11088.)
Anon., *To Freeholders of New York* (1768c)
Anonymous. *To the Freeholders and Freemen of the City and County of New-York.* [New York, 1768.] (Evans 11040.)
Anon., *To Freeholders of Pennsylvania*
Anonymous. *To the Freeholders of the Province of Pennsylvania.* [Philadelphia, 1743?].
Anon., *To Tax Themselves*
Anonymous. *An Argument in Defence of the Exclusive Right Claimed by the Colonies to Tax Themselves; With A Review of the Laws of England, Relative to Rep-*

resentation and Taxation. To which is Added, an Account of the Rise of the Colonies, and the Manner in which the Rights of the Subjects within the realm were communicated to those that went to America, with the Exercise of those Rights from the First Settlement to the Present Time. London, 1774.

Anon., *Triumphs of Justice*
Anonymous. *The Triumphs of Justice over Unjust Judges.* London, 1681.

Anon., *Tyranny Unmasked*
Anonymous. *Tyranny Unmasked. An Answer to a Late Pamphlet, Entitled Taxation no Tyranny.* London, 1775.

Anon., *Usurpations of England*
Anonymous. *The Usurpations of England the chief Sources of the Miseries of Ireland; and the Legislative Independence of this Kingdom, the only Means of securing and perpetuating the Commercial Advantages lately recovered.* Dublin, 1780.

Anon., *View of North*
Anonymous. *A View of the History of Great-Britain, During the Administration of Lord North, to the Second Session of the Fifteenth Parliament.* London, 1782.

Anon., *Voice of People* (Boston)
Anonymous. *The Voice of the People.* [Boston, 1754.]

Anon., *Voice of People* (London)
Anonymous. *The Voice of the People: A Collection of Addresses to His Majesty, and Instructions to Members of Parliament by their Constituents, Upon the Unsuccessful Management of the present War both at Land and Sea; and the Establishment of a National Militia.* London, 1756.

Anon., *Whigs and Jacobites*
Anonymous. *The Spirit and Principles of the Whigs and Jacobites Compared. Being the Substance of a Discourse delivered to an Audience of Gentlemen at Edinburgh, December 22, 1745.* London, 1746.

Anon., *With Respect to America*
Anonymous. *Reflections on Goverment, With Respect to America. To which is Added, Carmen Latinum.* London, 1776.

Aptheker, *Revolution*
Herbert Aptheker. *The American Revolution, 1763–1783.* New York, 1969.

Arbuthnot, *Freeholder's Catechism*
[John] Arbuthnot. *The Freeholder's Political Catechism. Written by Dr. Arbuthnot.* [London,] 1769.

Atkyns, *Enquiry into Power*
Sir Robert Atkyns. *An Enquiry into the Power of Dispensing with Penal Statutes. Together with some Animadversions upon a Book writ by Sir Edn. Herbert, Lord Chief Justice of the Court of Common Pleas, Entituled, A Short Account of the Authorities in Law, upon which Judgement was given in Sir Edward Hale's Case.* London, 1689.

[Atkyns,] *Treatise of Jurisdiction*
[Sir Robert Atkyns.] *A Treatise of the True and Ancient Jurisdiction of the House of Peers.* London, 1699.

Authority of Rights
John Phillip Reid. *Constitutional History of the American Revolution: The Authority of Rights.* Madison, Wis., 1986.

Authority to Tax
  John Phillip Reid. *Constitutional History of the American Revolution: The Authority to Tax.* Madison, Wis., 1987.
[Baillie,] *Appendix to a Letter*
  [Hugh Baillie.] *An Appendix to a Letter to Dr. Shebbeare. To which are added, Some Observations on a Pamphlet, Entitled, Taxation no Tyranny; In which the Sophistry of the Author's Reasoning is Detected.* London, 1775.
Bailyn, *Origins of Politics*
  Bernard Bailyn. *The Origins of American Politics.* New York, 1968.
Bailyn, *Pamphlets*
  Pamphlets of the American Revolution, 1750–1776. Edited by Bernard Bailyn. Vol. 1. Cambridge, Mass., 1965.
Bainbrigg, *Seasonable Reflections*
  Thomas Bainbrigg. *Seasonable Reflections, on a late Pamphlet, Entituled, a History of Passive Obedience Since the Reformation: Wherein the true Notion of Passive Obedience is Settled and Secured from the Malicious Interpretations of ill-designing Men.* London, 1689/90.
Baldwin, *New England Clergy*
  Alice M. Baldwin. *The New England Clergy and the American Revolution.* New York, 1958.
Ball, *Power of Kings*
  William Ball. *The Power of King's discussed; or, an Examen of the Fundamental Constitution of the Free-born People of England, in Answer to several Tenets of Mr. David Jenkins.* 1649. Reprinted in 5 *Somers' Tracts,* at 132–39.
[Bancroft,] *Remarks*
  [Edward Bancroft.] *Remarks on the Review of the Controversy Between Great Britain and her Colonies. In which the Errors of its Author are exposed, and the Claims of the Colonies vindicated, Upon the Evidence of Historical Facts and authentic records.* London, 1769.
Banning, *Jeffersonian Persuasion*
  Lance Banning. *The Jeffersonian Persuasion: Evolution of a Party Ideology.* Ithaca, N.Y., 1978.
Barker, *Essays*
  Ernest Barker. *Essays on Government.* Oxford, England, 1945.
Barker, "Natural Law"
  Sir Ernest Barker. "Natural Law and the American Revolution." In *Traditions of Civility: Eight Essays,* at 263–355. Cambridge, England, 1948.
Barnard, *Election Sermon*
  Thomas Barnard. *A Sermon Preached before his Excellency Francis Bernard, Esq.; Governor and Commander in Chief, the Honourable His Majesty's Council, and the Honourable House of Representatives, of the Province of the Massachusetts-Bay in New-England, May 25th. 1763. Being the Anniversary for the Election of His Majesty's Council for said Province.* Boston, 1763.
Barnes, *Dominion of New England*
  Viola Florence Barnes. *The Dominion of New England: A Study in British Colonial Policy.* New Haven, Conn., 1923.
[Barrington,] *Revolution Principles*

[John Shute Barrington, first Viscount Barrington.] *The Revolution and Anti-Revolution Principles Stated and Compar'd, the Constitution Explain'd and Vindicated, And the Justice and Necessity of Excluding the Pretender, Maintain'd against the Book Entituled, Hereditary Right of the Crown of England Asserted.* 3d ed. London, 1714.

[Basset,] *Equal Representation*
[Francis Basset, Baron Basset.] *Thoughts on Equal Representation.* London, 1783.

[Bath,] *Review of Excise*
[William Pulteney, earl of Bath.] *A Review of the Excise-Scheme; In Answer to a Pamphlet, intitled The Rise and Fall of the late projected Excise, impartially considered. With some Proper Hints to the Electors of Great Britain.* London, 1733.

Batley, *Letter to Wyvill*
Jeremiah Batley. *A Letter to the Rev. Christopher Wyvill, Chairman of the Committee of the Yorkshire Association.* London, 1782.

Becker, *Declaration*
Carl L. Becker. *The Declaration of Independence: A Study in the History of Political Ideas.* Vintage ed. New York, 1958.

Bellamy, *Sermon*
Joseph Bellamy. *A Sermon Delivered before the General Assembly of the Colony of Connecticut, at Hartford, on the Day of the Anniversary Election, May 13, 1762.* New London, Conn., 1762.

Bentham, *Comment on Commentaries*
Jeremy Bentham. *A Comment on the Commentaries.* Reprinted in *The Collected Works of Jeremy Bentham,* edited by J. H. Burns and H. L. A. Hart, at 1–389. London, 1977.

Bentham, *Fragment on Government*
Jeremy Bentham. *A Fragment on Government.* 1776. Reprinted in *The Collected Works of Jeremy Bentham: Principles of Legislation—A Comment on the Commentaries and a Fragment on Government,* edited by J. H. Burns and H. L. A. Hart, at 391–551. London, 1977.

Bernard, *Select Letters*
Francis Bernard. *Select Letters on the Trade and Government of America; and the Principle of Law and Polity, Applied to the American Colonies. Written by Governor Bernard at Boston, In the Years 1763, 4, 5, 6, 7, and 8. To which are added the Petition of the Assembly of Massachuset's Bay against the Governor, his Answer thereto, and the Order of the King in Council thereon.* London, 1774.

[Blacklock,] *Remarks on Liberty*
[Thomas Blacklock.] *Remarks on the Nature and Extent of Liberty, as compatible with the Genius of Civil Societies; On the Principles of Government and the proper Limits of its Powers in Free States; And, on the Justice and Policy of the American War. Occasioned by Perusing the Observations of Dr. Price on these Subjects. In a Letter to a Friend.* Edinburgh, 1776.

Blackstone, *Commentaries*
William Blackstone. *Commentaries on the Laws of England.* 4 vols. Oxford, England, 1765–69.

Blackstone, *Tracts*
William Blackstone. *Tracts, Chiefly Relating to the Antiquities and Laws of England.* 3d ed. Oxford, England, 1771.
[Bland,] *Colonel Dismounted*
[Richard Bland.] *The Colonel Dismounted: Or the Rector Vindicated. In a Letter addressed to His Reverence: Containing A Dissertation Upon the Constitution of the Colony.* Williamsburg, Va., 1764.
Bolingbroke, *Craftsman*
Lord Bolingbroke. *Contributions to the Craftsman.* Edited by Simon Varey. Oxford, England, 1982.
[Bolingbroke,] *Dissertation*
[Henry Saint John, first Viscount Bolingbroke.] *A Dissertation Upon Parties; In Several Letters to Caleb D'Anvers, Esq.* 3d ed. London, 1735.
Bolingbroke, *Political Writings*
Viscount Bolingbroke. *Political Writings.* Edited by Isaac Kramnick. New York, 1970.
[Bollan,] *Freedom of Speech*
[William Bollan.] *The Freedom of Speech and Writing upon Public Affairs, Considered.* London, 1766.
Bonomi, *Factious People*
Patrica U. Bonomi. *A Factious People: Politics and Society in Colonial New York.* New York, 1971.
Bonwick, *English Radicals*
Colin Bonwick. *English Radicals and the American Revolution.* Chapel Hill, N.C., 1977.
Boorstin, *Mysterious Science of Law*
Daniel J. Boorstin. *The Mysterious Science of the Law: An Essay on Blackstone's* COMMENTARIES *Showing How Blackstone, Employing Eighteenth-Century Ideas of Science, Religion, History, Aesthetics, and Philosophy, Made of the Law at Once a Conservative and a Mysterious Science.* Cambridge, Mass., 1941.
Boston Chronicle
The Boston Chronicle. [Weekly newspaper.]
Boston Evening-Post
The Boston Evening-Post. [Weekly newspaper.]
Boston Gazette
The Boston Gazette and Country Journal. [Weekly newspaper.]
Boston News-Letter
The Massachusetts Gazette and Boston News-Letter. [Weekly newspaper, also sometimes *The Massachusetts Gazette and the Boston Weekly News-Letter* or *The Boston News-Letter.*]
Boston Post-Boy
The Boston Post-Boy & Advertiser. [Weekly newspaper.]
Boston Town Records
A Report of the Record Commissioners of the City of Boston, Containing the Boston Town Records, 1758 to 1769. 16th report. Boston, 1886. [Listed by the Library of Congress in library catalogs as: BOSTON. *Registry dept.* "Records relating to the early history of Boston."]

Boucher, *Causes and Consequences*
    Jonathan Boucher. *A View of the Causes and Consequences of the American Rev-
    olution; in Thirteen Discourses, Preached in North America between the Years 1763
    and 1775: With an Historical Preface.* London, 1797.
Boyer, "Borrowed Rhetoric"
    Paul S. Boyer. "Borrowed Rhetoric: The Massachusetts Excise Controversy
    of 1754." 21 *William and Mary Quarterly* 328–51 (1964).
Bracton, *Laws and Customs*
    Henry de Bracton. *On the Laws and Customs of England.* Translated and ed-
    ited by Samuel E. Thorne. 5 vols. Cambridge, Mass., 1968–77.
[Brecknock,] *Droit le Roy*
    [Timothy Brecknock.] *Droit le Roy. Or a Digest of the Rights and Prerogatives of
    the Imperial Crown of Great-Britain.* London, 1764.
Breen, *Good Ruler*
    T. H. Breen. *The Character of the Good Ruler: A Study of Puritan Political Ideas
    in New England, 1630–1730.* New Haven, Conn., 1970.
Brewer, "English Radicalism"
    John Brewer. "English Radicalism in the Age of George III." In *Three British
    Revolutions: 1641, 1688, 1776,* edited by J. G. A. Pocock, at 323–67. Prince-
    ton, N.J., 1980.
Brewer, *Party Ideology*
    John Brewer. *Party Ideology and Popular Politics at the Accession of George III.*
    New York, 1976.
Briefs of Revolution
    *The Briefs of the American Revolution: Constitutional Arguments between Thomas
    Hutchinson, Governor of Massachusetts Bay, and James Bowdoin for the Council
    and John Adams for the House of Representatives.* Edited by John Phillip Reid.
    New York, 1981.
Britain's Memorial
    *Great-Britain's Memorial. Containing a Collection of the Instructions, Representa-
    tions, &c. &c. of the Freeholders and other Electors of Great-Britain, to their Rep-
    resentatives in Parliament, for these Two Years past.* London, 1741. *The Second
    Part of Great-Britain's Memorial Containing a Collection of the Instructions, Rep-
    resentations, &c. &c. of the Freeholders and other Electors of Great-Britain, to their
    Representatives in Parliament, since the late Election.* London, 1742.
[Brooke,] *Liberty and Common Sense*
    [Henry Brooke.] *Liberty and Common Sense to the People of Ireland, Greeting.*
    London, 1760.
[Brooke,] *Liberty and Common Sense: Letter II*
    [Henry Brooke.] *Liberty and Common Sense to the People of Ireland, Greeting:
    Letter II.* Dublin, [1759].
Brown, *Estimate of Manners*
    John Brown. *An Estimate of the Manners and Principles of the Times.* 7th ed.
    Boston, 1758.
Brown, "James Simpson's Reports"
    Alan S. Brown. "James Simpson's Reports on the Carolina Loyalists, 1779–
    1780." 21 *Journal of Southern History* 513–19 (1955).

Brown, *Middle-Class Democracy*
    Robert E. Brown. *Middle-Class Democracy and the Revolution in Massachusetts, 1691–1780*. Ithaca, N.Y., 1955.
Brown, *Revolutionary Politics*
    Richard D. Brown. *Revolutionary Politics in Massachusetts: The Boston Committee of Correspondence and the Towns, 1772–1774*. New York, 1976.
Browning, *Court Whigs*
    Reed Browning. *Political and Constitutional Ideas of the Court Whigs*. Baton Rouge, La., 1982.
[Brydall,] *New-Years-Gift*
    [John Brydall.] *A New-Years-Gift for the Anti-Prerogative-Men: Or, A Lawyer's Opinion, in Defence of His Majesties Power-Royal, of granting Pardons, as he pleases*. London, 1682.
Burgh, *Political Disquisitions*
    J. Burgh. *Political Disquisitions; or, An Enquiry into public Errors, Defects, and Abuses. Illustrated by, and established upon Facts and Remarks, extracted from a Variety of Authors, Ancient and Modern*. 3 vols. Philadelphia, 1775.
Burke, *Letter to Sheriffs*
    Edmund Burke. *A Letter from Edmund Burke, Esq; One of the Representatives in Parliament for the City of Bristol, to John Farr and John Harris, Esqrs. Sheriffs of that City, on the Affairs of America*. 3d ed. London, 1777.
Burke Writings
    The Writings and Speeches of Edmund Burke. Vol. 2, *Party, Parliament, and the American Crisis*. Edited by Paul Langford. Oxford, 1981.
Burlamaqui, *Politic Law*
    J. J. Burlamaqui. *The Principles of Politic Law: Being a Sequel to the Principles of Natural Law*. London, 1752.
Bushman, "Corruption"
    Richard L. Bushman. "Corruption and Power in Provincial America." In *The Development of a Revolutionary Mentality*, at 64–91. Library of Congress Symposia on the American Revolution. Washington, D.C., 1972.
Butterfield, *George III and People*
    H. Butterfield. *George III, Lord North, and the People, 1779–80*. London, 1949.
Cambridge Magazine
    The Cambridge Magazine: or Universal Repository of Arts, Sciences, and the Belles Letters. For the Year MDCCLXIX. London, 1769.
Camden, "Speech on American Taxation"
    Lord Camden. "Speech on American taxation, House of Lords, 24 February 1766." Reprinted in *The Debate on the American Revolution, 1761–1783*, edited by Max Beloff, at 119–24. 2d ed. London, 1960.
Campbell, *Duty of Allegiance*
    George Campbell. *The Nature, Extent, and Importance, of the Duty of Allegiance: A Sermon Preached at Aberdeen, December 12, 1776, Being the Fast Day Appointed by the King, on Account of the Rebellion in America*. Aberdeen, Scotland, 1778.
Candidus, *Two Letters*
    Mystagogus Candidus. *Two Letters: viz. I. A Letter to the Earl of Abingdon, in*

which his Grace of York's Notions of Civil Liberty are examined by Liberalis; published in the London Evening Post, November 6th, 1777. II. Vera Icon; or a Vindication of his Grace of York's Sermon, preached on February 21st, 1777. Proving it to Contain a severe Satire against the Ministry, and a Defence of Civil and Religious Liberty, upon the well-known Principles of Whiggism. In Answer to a Letter from Liberalis, to the Earl of Abingdon. London, 1777.

Canning, Letter to Hillsborough
George Canning. A Letter to the Right Honourable Wills Earl of Hillsborough, on the Connection Between Great Britain and her American Colonies. Dublin, 1768.

[Care,] English Liberties First Edition
[Henry Care.] English Liberties: or, the Free-Born Subject's Inheritance, Containing I. MAGNA CHARTA, The Petition of Right, The Habeas Corpus Act; and divers other most Useful Statutes: With Large Comments upon each of them. London, [ca. 1690].

Carlyle, Justice and Necessity
Alexander Carlyle. The Justice and Necessity of the War with our American Colonies Examined. A Sermon, Preached at Inveresk, December 12, 1776, Being the Fast-Day Appointed by the King, on account of the American Rebellion. Edinburgh, 1777.

Carlyle, Political Liberty
A. J. Carlyle. Political Liberty: A History of the Conception in the Middle Ages and Modern Times. Oxford, 1941.

Carroll, "First Citizen"
Charles Carroll. "First Citizen." Reprinted in Maryland and the Empire, 1773: The Antilon–First Citizen Letters, edited by Peter S. Onuf. Baltimore, 1974.

[Cartwright,] American Independence
[John Cartwright.] American Independence the Interest and Glory of Great Britain; Containing Arguments which prove, that not only in Taxation, but in Trade, Manufactures, and Government, the Colonies are entitled to an entire Independency on the British Legislature; and that it can only be by a formal Declaration of these Rights, and forming thereupon a friendly League with them, that the true and lasting Welfare of both Countries can be promoted. In a Series of Letters to the Legislature. Philadelphia, 1776.

Cartwright, Appeal on Constitution
John Cartwright. An Appeal, Civil and Military, on the Subject of the English Constitution. 2d ed. Boston, England, 1799.

Cartwright, Constitutional Defence
John Cartwright. The Constitutional Defence of England, Internal and External. London, 1796.

Cartwright, Legislative Rights
John Cartwright. The Legislative Rights of the Commonalty Vindicated; or, Take Your Choice! Representation and Respect: Imposition and Contempt: Annual Parliaments and Liberty: Long Parliaments and Slavery. 2d ed. London, 1777.

Cartwright, Letter to Abingdon
John Cartwright. A Letter to the Earl of Abingdon: Discussing a Position Relative to a Fundamental Right of the Constitution: Contained in his Lordship's Thoughts on the Letter of Edmund Burke, Esq. to the Sheriffs of Bristol. London, 1778.

Cartwright, *Letters to Deputies*
John Cartwright. *Letters to the Deputies of the Associated and Petitioning Counties, Cities, and Towns; on the Means Necessary to a Reformation of Parliament.* London, 1781.

[Cartwright,] *Memorial*
[John Cartwright.] *The Memorial of Common-Sense, Upon the Present Crisis Between Great-Britain and America.* London, 1778.

Cartwright, *People's Barrier*
John Cartwright. *The People's Barrier Against Undue Influence and Corruption: Or the Commons' House of Parliament According to the Constitution. In which the Objections to an equal Representation and new Parliaments once in every year at least are answered: And a digested Plan of the Whole is submitted to the Public.* London, 1780.

Cartwright, *Postscript*
John Cartwright. *The Postscript to Major Cartwright's Reply to Soame Jenyns, Esq; Humbly Recommended to the Perusal of Lord North's Admirers, Previous to His Lordship's Next Speech Against a Parliamentary Reform.* London, 1785.

[Cartwright,] *Take Your Choice*
[John Cartwright.] *Take Your Choice! Representation and Respect: Imposition and Contempt: Annual Parliaments and Liberty: Long Parliaments and Slavery.* London, 1776.

[Cary,] *Answer to Molyneux*
[John Cary.] *An Answer to Mr. Molyneux His Case of Ireland's being bound by Acts of Parliament in England, Stated: and His Dangerous Notion of Ireland's being under no Subordination to the Parliamentary Authority of England* REFUTED; *By Reasoning from his own Arguments and Authorities.* London, 1698.

Carysfort, *Letter to Huntingdonshire*
John Joshua Proby, first earl of Carysfort. *A Letter from the Right Honourable Lord Carysfort, to the Huntingdonshire Committee.* London, 1780.

[Carysfort,] *Serious Address*
[John Joshua Proby, first earl of Carysfort.] *A Serious Address to the Electors of Great-Britain, on the Subject of Short Parliaments and an Equal Representation.* London, 1782.

Carysfort, *Thoughts on Constitution*
Lord Carysfort [John Joshua Proby, first earl of Carysfort.] *Thoughts on the Constitution, with a View to the Proposed Reform in the Representation of the People, and Duration of Parliaments.* London, 1783.

Cato's Letters
Cato's Letters: or, Essays on Liberty, Civil and Religious, And other Important Subjects. In Four Volumes. 6th ed. London, 1755. Reprint. (4 vols. in 2). New York, 1971.

"Cato's Letters"
John Trenchard and Thomas Gordon. "Cato's Letters." Reprinted in *The English Libertarian Heritage from the Writings of John Trenchard and Thomas Gordon in the Independent Whig and Cato's Letters,* edited by David L. Jacobson. Indianapolis, Ind., 1965.

[Chalmers,] *Plain Truth*
   [James Chalmers.] *Plain Truth; Addressed to the Inhabitants of America, Containing, Remarks on a late Pamphlet, entitled Common Sense. Wherein are shewn, that
   the Scheme of Independence is Ruinous, Delusive, and Impractical: That were the
   Author's Asseverations, Respecting the Power of America, as Real as Nugatory; Rec-
   onciliation on liberal Principles with Great Britain, would be exalted Policy: And that
   circumstanced as we are, Permanent Liberty, and True Happiness, can only be ob-
   tained by Reconciliation with that Kingdom.* Philadelphia, 1776.
Champagne, "New York Elections"
   Roger Champagne. "Family Politics versus Constitutional Principles: The
   New York Assembly Elections of 1768 and 1769." 20 *William and Mary Quar-
   terly* 57–79 (1963).
Chandler, *Representation in Virginia*
   Julian A. C. Chandler. *Representation in Virginia.* Johns Hopkins University
   Studies in Historical and Political Science, 14th ser., nos. 6–7. Baltimore,
   1896.
Chapman, *Burke*
   Gerald W. Chapman. *Edmund Burke: The Practical Imagination.* Cambridge,
   Mass., 1967.
Charles I, *Several Speeches*
   Charles I. *Several Speeches Delivered By His Majesty to the two Houses of Westmin-
   ster, And at other places, since the beginning of this Parliament. Contained in Reli-
   quiae Sacrae Carolinae: The Works of that Great Monarch and Glorious Martyr
   King Charles I. both Civil and Sacred with a short View of the Life and Reign of
   that Most blessed Prince from his Birth to his Buriall.* The Hague, n.d.
Chatham, *Genuine Abstracts*
   *Genuine Abstracts from Two Speeches of the Late Earl of Chatham: And his Reply to
   the Earl of Suffolk.* London, 1779.
Chatham, *Speech of 20 January*
   William Pitt, earl of Chatham. *The Speech of the Right Honourable the Earl of
   Chatham, in the House of Lords, Jan. 20, 1775.* n.i., [1775].
Checkley, *Election Sermon*
   Samuel Checkley. *A Day of Darkness. A Sermon Preach'd before His Excellency
   William Shirley, Esq; The Honorable His Majesty's Council, and House of Repre-
   sentatives, of the Province of the Massachusetts-Bay, in New-England: May 28th,
   1755. Being the Anniversary for the Election of His Majesty's Council for said Prov-
   ince.* Boston, 1755.
Chrimes, "Introduction"
   S. B. Chrimes. "Introduction" to *Kingship and Law in the Middle Ages,* by Fritz
   Kern, at ix–xxxi. Torchbook ed. New York, 1970.
Christie and Labaree, *Empire*
   Ian R. Christie and Benjamin W. Labaree. *Empire or Independence, 1760–
   1776: A British-American Dialogue on the Coming of the American Revolution.*
   New York, 1976.
[Claridge,] *Defence of Government*
   [Richard Claridge.] *A Defence of the Present Government under King William &*

Queen Mary. Shewing the Miseries of England under the Arbitrary Reign of the Late King James II. London, 1689.

Clark, *British Opinion*

Dora Mae Clark. *British Opinion and the American Revolution.* New Haven, Conn., 1930.

Clarke, *Representation and Consent*

M. V. Clarke. *Medieval Representation and Consent: A Study of Early Parliaments in England and Ireland, with Special Reference to the Modus Tenendi Parliamentum.* New York, 1936.

Colegrove, "Town Mandates"

Kenneth Colegrove. "New England Town Mandates." 21 *Publications of the Colonial Society of Massachusetts* 411–49 (1920).

Collection of Irish Letters

A Collection of the Letters which have been addressed to the Volunteers of Ireland, on the subject of a Parliamentary Reform. London, 1783.

Collection on Salaries

A Collection of the Proceedings of the Great and General Court or Assembly of His Majesty's Province of the Massachusetts-Bay, in New England; Containing several Instructions from the Crown, to the Council and Assembly of that Province, for fixing a Salary on the Governour, and their Determination thereon. As also, The Methods taken by the Court for Supporting the several Governours, since the Arrival of the present Charter. Printed by Order of the House of Representatives. Boston, 1729.

Colley, *Defiance of Oligarchy*

Linda Colley. *In Defiance of Oligarchy: The Tory Party, 1714–60.* Cambridge, England, 1982.

Colley, "Politics of History"

Linda Colley. "The Politics of Eighteenth-Century British History." 25 *Journal of British Studies* 359–79 (1986).

Commemoration Ceremony

Commemoration Ceremony in Honor of the Two Hundredth Anniversary of the First Continental Congress in the United States House of Representatives. 93d Cong., 2d sess., 1975. H. Doc. 93-413.

Commons Debates 1628

Commons Debates, 1628. Edited by Robert C. Johnson, Mary Frear Keeler, Maija Jansson Cole, and William B. Bidwell. 6 vols. New Haven, Conn., 1977–83.

Concept of Liberty

John Phillip Reid. *The Concept of Liberty in the Age of the American Revolution.* Chicago, 1988.

Cook, *King Charls his Case*

John Cook. *King Charl[e]s his Case, or an Appeal to all Rational Men, Concerning his Tryal at the High Court of Justice. Being for the most part that which was intended to have been delivered at the Bar, if the King had Pleaded to the Charge, and put himself upon a fair Tryal. With an additional Opinion concerning the Death of King James, the loss of Rochel, and the Blood of Ireland.* London, 1649.

Cooke, *Election Sermon*

Samuel Cooke. *A Sermon Preached at Cambridge in the Audience of his Honor*

Thomas Hutchinson, Esq; Lietenant-Governor and Commander in Chief; The Honorable His Majesty's Council, and the Honorable House of Representatives, of the Province of the Massachusetts-Bay in New-England, May 30th, 1770. Being the Anniversay of the Election of His Majesty's Council for the Said Province. Boston, 1770. Reprinted in *Pulpit of the American Revolution: or, the Political Sermons of the period of 1776,* edited by John Wingate Thornton, at 147–86. Boston, 1860.

Correspondence George III
The Correspondence of King George the Third from 1760 to December 1783. Vol. 2, 1768–June 1773. London, 1967.

Costin and Watson, *Documents*
W. C. Costin and J. Steven Watson. *The Law and Working of the Constitution: Documents, 1660–1914.* Vol. 1. London, 1952.

Cotton, *Election Sermon*
John Cotton. *Wisdom, Knowledge, and the Fear of God recommended to Rulers & People. A Sermon Preach'd in the Audience of His Honour Spencer Phips, Esq; Lieutenant-Governour and Commander in Chief, the Honourable His Majesty's Council, and House of Representatives, of the Province of the Massachusetts-Bay, in New-England. May 30th. 1753. Being the Day for the Election of His Majesty's Council for the Province.* Boston, 1753.

Courtney, *Montesquieu and Burke*
C. P. Courtney. *Montesquieu and Burke.* Oxford, England, 1963.

Craftsman
The Craftsman. Vols. 2, 5, 11, 14. London, 1737.

Cragg, *Freedom and Authority*
Gerald R. Cragg. *Freedom and Authority: A Study of English Thought in the Early Seventeenth Century.* Philadelphia, 1975.

Creasy, *Imperial Constitutions*
Sir Edward Creasy. *The Imperial and Colonial Constitutions of the Britannic Empire, Including Indian Institutions.* London, 1872.

Daily Gazetteer
The Daily Gazetteer, no. 30, 2 August 1735, and no. 42, 16 August 1735. [London daily newspaper.]

Dalrymple, *Feudal Property*
John Dalrymple. *An Essay Towards a General History of Feudal Property in Great Britain.* 4th ed. London, 1757.

Dargo, *Roots*
George Dargo. *Roots of the Republic: A New Perspective on Early American Contitutionalism.* New York, 1974.

Davis, *Reports*
Sir John Davis [Davies]. *Les Reports Des Cases & Matters en Ley, Resolves & Adjudges en les Courts del Roy en Ireland.* London, 1674.

Day, *Two Speeches*
Thomas Day. *Two Speeches of Thomas Day, Esq. at the General Meetings of the Counties of Cambridge and Essex, Held March 25, and April 25, 1780.* n.i., 1780.

[Defoe,] *A Speech Without Doors*
[Daniel Defoe.] *A Speech Without Doors.* London, 1710.

De Lolme, *Constitution: New Edition*
> J. L. De Lolme. *The Constitution of England; or, an Account of the English Government; in which it is Compared Both with the Republican Form of Government, and the Other Monarchies in Europe.* New ed. London, 1817.

Derry, *Fox*
> John W. Derry. *Charles James Fox.* New York, 1972.

Dickinson, *Connecticut Election Sermon*
> Moses Dickinson. *A Sermon Preached before the General Assembly of the Colony of Connecticut, at Hartford on the Day of the Anniversary Election, May 8th, 1755.* New London, Conn., 1755.

Dickinson, "Debate on Sovereignty"
> H. T. Dickinson. "The Eighteenth Century Debate on the Sovereignty of Parliament." 26 (5th ser.) *Transactions of the Royal Historical Society* 189–218 (1976).

Dickinson, *Letter to Merchants*
> John Dickinson. *Letter to the Philadelphia Merchants Concerning Non-Importation, July, 1768.* Reprinted in Dickinson, *Writings*, at 439–45.

Dickinson, *Liberty and Property*
> H. T. Dickinson. *Liberty and Property: Political Ideology in Eighteenth-Century Britian.* New York, 1977.

[Dickinson,] *New Essay*
> [John Dickinson.] *An Essay [by the Pennsylvania Farmer] on the Constitutional Power of Great-Britain over the Colonies in America; with the Resolves of the Committee For the Province of Pennsylvania, and their Instructions to their Representatives in Assembly.* Philadelphia, 1774.

Dickinson, *Speech Delivered*
> John Dickinson. *A Speech Delivered in the House of Assembly of the Province of Pennsylvania, May 24th, 1764.* 2d ed. Philadelphia, 1764.

Dickinson, *Writings*
> *The Writings of John Dickinson: Political Writings, 1764–1774.* Edited by Paul Leicester Ford. Philadelphia, 1895.

Dinwiddy, *Wyvill*
> J. R. Dinwiddy. *Christopher Wyvill and Reform, 1790–1820.* Borthwick Papers, no. 39. York, England, 1971.

Dobbs, *Letter to North*
> Francis Dobbs. *A Letter to the Right Honourable Lord North on his Propositions in Favour of Ireland.* Dublin, 1780.

[Douglas,] *Seasonable Hints*
> [John Douglas.] *Seasonable Hints From an Honest Man On the Present Important Crisis of a New Reign and a New Parliament.* London, 1761.

[Downer,] *Discourse in Providence*
> [Silas Downer.] *A Discourse Delivered in Providence, in the Colony of Rhode-Island, upon the 25th Day of July 1768. At the Dedication of the Tree of Liberty, From the Summer House in the Tree. By a Son of Liberty.* Providence, R.I., 1768.

[Downley,] *Sentiments*
> [—— Downley.] *The Sentiments of an English Freeholder, on the Late Decision of the Middlesex Election.* London, 1769.

[Dulany,] *Considerations*
  [Daniel Dulany.] *Considerations on the Propriety of Imposing Taxes in the British Colonies, For the Purpose of raising a Revenue, by Act of Parliament.* 1765. Reprinted in 1 Bailyn, *Pamphlets,* at 608–58.
[Dulany,] *Considerations on the Propriety*
  [Daniel Dulany.] *Considerations on the Propriety of Imposing Taxes in the British Colonies, For the Purpose of raising a Revenue, by Act of Parliament.* 2d ed. Annapolis, Md., 1765.
[Dyson,] *Case of Middlesex*
  [Jeremiah Dyson.] *The Case of the Late Election for the County of Middlesex, Considered on the Principles of the Constitution, and the Authorities of Law.* London, 1769.
Eccleshall, *Order and Reason*
  Robert Eccleshall. *Order and Reason in Politics: Theories of Absolute and Limited Monarchy in Early Modern England.* New York, 1978.
Egerton, *Discourse*
  A Discourse upon the Exposicion & Understandinge of Statutes With Sir Thomas Egerton's Additions. Edited by Samuel E. Thorne. San Marino, Calif., 1942.
Eighteenth-Century Constitution
  E. Neville Williams. *The Eighteenth-Century Constitution, 1688–1815: Documents and Commentary.* Cambridge, England, 1965.
Eliot, *Give Cesar his Due*
  Jared Eliot. *Give Cesar his Due. Or, the Obligation that Subjects are under to their Civil Rulers, As was shewed in a Sermon Preach'd before the General Assembly of the Colony of Connecticut at Hartford, May the 11th, 1738. The Day for the Election of the Honourable the Governour, the Deputy-Governour, and the Worshipful Assistants.* New London, Conn., 1738.
Eliot, "Letters"
  "Letters from Andrew Eliot to Thomas Hollis." 4 *Collections of the Massachusetts Historical Society* 398–461 (1858).
Ellys, *Tracts on Liberty*
  Anthony Ellys. *Tracts on the Liberty, Spiritual and Temporal, of the Subjects in England. Addressed to J. N. Esq; at Aix-la-Chapelle. Part II. [Of the Temporal Liberty of Subjects in England.]* London, 1765.
[Erskine,] *Reflections on the Rise*
  [John Erskine.] *Reflections on the Rise, Progress, and Probable Consequences, of the Present Contentions with the Colonies. By a Freeholder.* Edinburgh, 1776.
Essex Result
  Result of the Convention of Delegates Holden at Ipswich in the County of Essex, who were Deputed to take into Consideration the Constitution and form of Government, Proposed by the Convention of the State of Massachusetts-Bay. Newburyport, Mass., 1778.
Estwick, *Letter to Tucker*
  Samuel Estwick. *A Letter to the Reverend Josiah Tucker, D. D. Dean of Glocester, in Answer to His Humble Address and Earnest Appeal, &c. with a Postscript, in which the present War against America is shewn to be the Effect, not the Causes assigned by Him and Others. But of a Fixed Plan of Administration, Founded in*

System: The Landed opposed to the Commercial Interest of the State, Being as the Means in order to the End. London, 1776.

[Evans,] *Letter to John Wesley*
[Caleb Evans.] *A Letter to the Rev. Mr. John Wesley, Occasioned by his Calm Address to the American Colonies.* Bristol, England, 1775.

Evans, *Political Sophistry detected*
Caleb Evans. *Political Sophistry detected, or, Brief Remarks on the Rev. Mr. Fletcher's late Tract, entitled "American Patriotism." In a Letter to a Friend.* Bristol, England, 1776.

Evans, *Reply to Fletcher*
Caleb Evans. *A Reply to the Rev. Mr. Fletcher's Vindication of Mr. Wesley's Calm Address to Our American Colonies.* Bristol, England, [1776].

Extracts from the Votes and Proceedings
Extracts from the Votes and Proceedings of the American Continental Congress, Held at Philadelphia, Sept. 5, 1774. Containing, the Bill of Rights, & List of Grievances, Occasional Resolves, the Association, an Address to the People of Great-Britain, and a Memorial to the Inhabitants of the British Colonies. Philadelphia, 1774.

[Ferguson,] *Remarks on Dr. Price*
[Adam Ferguson.] *Remarks on a Pamphlet Lately Published by Dr. Price, Intitled, Observations on the Nature of Civil Liberty, the Principles of Government, and the Justice and Policy of the War with America, &c. in a Letter from a Gentleman in the Country to a Member of Parliament.* London, 1776.

Filmer, *Necessity of Absolute Power*
Robert Filmer. *The Necessity of the Absolute Power of all Kings: And in particular of the King of England by John Bodin a Protestant according to the Church of Geneva.* 1648. Reprinted in Filmer, *Patriarcha,* at 315–26.

Filmer, *Observations upon Aristotle*
Robert Filmer. *Observations Upon Aristotles Politiques Touching Forms of Government Together with Directions for Obedience to Governours in dangerous and doubtfull Times.* 1652. Reprinted in Filmer, *Patriarcha,* at 185–229.

Filmer, *Patriarcha*
Patriarcha and Other Political Works of Sir Robert Filmer. Edited by Peter Laslett. Oxford, 1949.

Fish, *Connecticut Election Sermon*
Joseph Fish. *Christ Jesus the Physician, and his Blood the recommended for the Healing of a Diseased People. In a Sermon Preach'd before the General Assembly of the Colony of Connecticut, at Hartford, on the Day of their Anniversary Election, May 8, 1760.* New London, Conn., 1760.

[Fitch et al.,] *Reasons Why*
[Thomas Fitch, Jared Ingersoll, Ebenezer Silliman, and George Wyllys.] *Reasons Why the British Colonies, in America, Should not be Charged with Internal Taxes, by Authority of Parliament; Humbly offered, For Consideration, In Behalf of the Colony of Connecticut.* New Haven, Conn., 1764.

Fletcher, *American Patriotism*
J[ohn William] Fletcher. *American Patriotism Farther confronted with Reason, Scripture, and the Constitution: Being Observations on the Dangerous Politicks*

Taught by the Rev. Mr. Evans, M. A. and the Rev. Dr. Price. With a Scriptual Plea for the Revolted Colonies. Shrewsbury, England, 1776.

Fletcher, *Vindication of Wesley*
    John Fletcher. *A Vindication of the Rev. Mr. Wesley's "Calm Address to our American Colonies:" In Some Letters to Mr. Caleb Evans.* London, [1776].

Foner, *Tom Paine*
    Eric Foner. *Tom Paine and Revolutionary America.* New York, 1976.

[Forester,] *Answer to the Question Stated*
    [Nathaniel Forester]. *An Answer to a Pamphlet Entitled, "The Question Stated, Whether the Freeholders of Middlesex forfeited their Right by Voting for Mr. Wilkes at the last Election? In a Letter from a Member of Parliament to one of his Constituents."* London, 1769.

[Fowle,] *Appendix to Eclipse*
    [Daniel Fowle.] *An Appendix to the late Total Eclipse of Liberty. Being some Thoughts on the End and Design of Civil Government; also the inherent Power of the People asserted and maintained; that it is not given up to their Representatives; this confirmed and acknowledged by Kings or Emperors, and prov'd from Scripture and Reason.* Boston, 1756.

Fowle, *Total Eclipse*
    Daniel Fowle. *A Total Eclipse of Liberty: Being a true and faithful Account of the Arraignment, and Examination of Daniel Fowle before the Honourable House of Representatives of the Province of the Massachusetts-Bay in New-England, Octob. 24th, 1754. Barely on Suspicion of his being concern'd in Printing and Publishing a Pamphlet, intitled, The Monster of Monsters.* Boston, 1755.

Fox, *Speeches*
    The Speeches of the Right Honourable Charles James Fox in the House of Commons. Vols. 1 and 2. London, 1815.

Franklin-Jackson Letters
    Letters and Papers of Benjamin Franklin and Richard Jackson, 1753–1785. Edited by Carl Van Doren. Memoirs of the American Philosophical Society, vol. 24. Philadelphia, 1947.

Franklin's Letters to the Press
    Benjamin Franklin's Letters to the Press, 1758–1775. Edited by Verner W. Crane. Chapel Hill, N.C., 1950.

Free, *Speech of John Free*
    John Free. *The Speech of Dr. John Free, Containing A concise and clear Account of the English Constitution, both Old and New: And of the Rise and Progress of the modern Part of that Assembly, which we now call the Parliament.* London, 1753.

Freeman Letters
    The Letters of Freeman, Etc.: Essays on the Nonimportation Movement in South Carolina Collected by Wiliam Henry Drayton. Edited by Robert M. Weir. Columbia, S.C., 1977.

Frink, *Election Sermon*
    Thomas Frink. *A King reigning in Righteousness, and Princes ruling in Judgment. A Sermon Preached before His Excellency Thomas Pownall, Esq.; Governour, the Honourable His Majesty's Council, and House of Representatives, of the Province*

of the Massachusetts-Bay, in New-England, May 31. 1758. Being the Anniversary for the Election of His Majesty's Council, for said Province. Boston, 1758.

Gadsden, *Writings*

The Writings of Christopher Gadsden, 1746–1805. Edited by Richard Walsh. Columbia, S.C., 1966.

Gallaway, *Sermon at St. Mary's*

John Cole Gallaway. *Christianity the true Foundation of Civil Liberty: A Sermon Preached at St. Mary's Church in Leicester, at the Assizes held there, August 12, 1778.* London, 1779.

[Galloway,] *Candid Examination*

[Joseph Galloway.] *A Candid Examination of the Mutual Claims of Great-Britain, and the Colonies: with a Plan of Accomodation, on Constitutional Principles.* New York, 1775.

[Galloway,] *Historical Reflections*

[Joseph Galloway.] *Historical and Political Reflections on the Rise and Progress of the American Rebellion. In which the Causes of that Rebellion are pointed out, and the Policy and Necessity of offering to the* AMERICANS *a System of Government founded in the Principles of the British Constitution, are clearly demonstrated.* London, 1780.

Galloway, *Speech in Answer*

Joseph Galloway. *The Speech of Joseph Galloway, Esq; One of the Members for Philadelphia County: In Answer to the Speech of John Dickinson, Esq.; Delivered in the House of Assembly, of the Province of Pennsylvania, May 24, 1764. On Occasion of a Petition drawn up by Order, and then under the Consideration of the House; praying his Majesty for a Royal, in lieu of a Proprietary Government.* Philadelphia, 1764.

[Galloway,] *True and Impartial State*

[Joseph Galloway.] *A True and Impartial State of the Province of Pennsylvania.* Philadelphia, 1759.

Garth, "Letter"

"Letter from Charles Garth to South Carolina, 19 January 1766." 26 *South Carolina Historical and Genealogical Magazine* 68–92 (1925).

Gazette and Post-Boy

The Massachusetts Gazette and Boston Post-Boy and the Advertiser.

Gentleman's Magazine

The Gentleman's Magazine and Historical Chronicle. [Monthly magazine, London.]

Georgia House Journal

The Colonial Records of the State of Georgia. Vol. 15, *Journal of the Commons House of Assembly October 30, 1769, to June 16, 1782, Inclusive.* New York, 1970.

Gerard, *Liberty Cloke of Maliciousness*

Alexander Gerard. *Liberty the Cloke of Maliciousness, both in the American Rebellion, and in the Manners of the Times. A Sermon Preached at Old Aberdeen, February 26, 1778, Being the Fast-Day appointed by Proclamation on account of the Rebellion in America.* Aberdeen, Scotland, 1778.

Gibbons, *Ideas of Representation*

Philip Arnold Gibbons. *Ideas of Political Representation in Parliament, 1660–1832.* Oxford, England, 1914.

Gipson, "Debate on Repeal"
Lawrence Henry Gipson. "The Great Debate in the Committee of the Whole House of Commons on the Stamp Act, 1766, as Reported by Nathaniel Ryder." 86 *Pennsylvania Magazine of History and Biography* 10–41 (1962).

Glanville, *Reports*
John Glanville. *Reports of Certain Cases, Determined and Adjudged by the Commons in Parliament, in the Twenty-first and Twenty-second Years of the Reign of King James the First.* London, 1775.

Gonson, *Charges*
Sir John Gonson's Five Charges to Several Grand Juries.... 4th ed. London, n.d.

Gooch, *English Democratic Ideas*
G. P. Gooch. *English Democratic Ideas in the Seventeenth Century: Second Edition with Supplementary Notes and Appendices by H. J. Laski.* Cambridge, England, 1954.

[Goodricke,] *Observations*
[Henry Goodricke.] *Observations on Dr. Price's Theory and Principles of Civil Liberty and Government, Preceded by a Letter to a Friend on the Pretensions of the American Colonies, in respect to Right and Equity.* York, England, 1776.

Gordon, *History*
William Gordon. *The History of the Rise, Progress, and Establishment of the Independence of the United States of America.* 3d American ed. Vol. 1. New York, 1801.

Gough, *Locke's Political Philosophy*
J. W. Gough. *John Locke's Political Philosophy: Eight Studies by J. W. Gough.* 2d ed. Oxford, England, 1973.

[Grange,] *Late Excise*
[James Erskine, Lord Grange.] *The Late Excise Scheme Dissected: Or, an Exact Copy of the Late Bill, for Repealing several Subsidies, and an Impost, Now Payable on Tocabbo, &c.* London, 1734.

[Gray,] *Right of the Legislature*
[John Gray.] *The Right of the British Legislature to Tax the American Colonies Vindicated; and the Means of Asserting that Right Proposed.* 2d ed. London, 1775.

Greenberg, "Representation"
Kenneth S. Greenberg. "Representation and the Isolation of South Carolina, 1776–1860." 64 *Journal of American History* 723–43 (1977).

Greene, *Quest*
Jack P. Greene. *The Quest for Power: The Lower Houses of Assembly in the Southern Royal Colonies, 1689–1776.* Norton Library ed. New York, 1972.

Grenville, *Papers*
The Grenville Papers: Being the Correspondence of Richard Grenville Earl Temple, K.G., and The Right Hon: George Grenville their Friends and Contemporaries. Edited by William James Smith. 4 vols. London, 1852–53.

[Grenville,] *Speech on Wilkes*

[George Grenville.] *The Speech of a Right Honourable Gentleman, on the Motion for Expelling Mr. Wilkes, Friday, February 3, 1769.* London, 1769.

Grenville Letterbooks
Letterbooks of George Grenville. ST 7, Huntington Library, San Marino, Calif.

Guide to Rights
A Guide to the Knowledge of the Rights and Privileges of Englishmen. London, 1757.

Gunn, "Influence"
J. A. W. Gunn. "Influence, Parties and the Constitution: Changing Attitudes, 1783–1832." 17 *Historical Journal* 301–28 (1974).

Guttridge, *English Whiggism*
G. H. Guttridge. *English Whiggism and the American Revolution.* Berkeley, Calif., 1966.

[Hale,] *History*
[Matthew Hale.] *The History of the Common Law of England.* 2d ed., corrected. London, 1716.

Hale, "Reflections"
Matthew Hale. "Reflections by the Lrd. Chiefe Justice Hale on Mr. Hobbes His Dialogue of the Lawe." Printed in W. S. Holdsworth, *A History of English Law,* vol. 5, at 500–13. London, 1924.

Hall, *Apology for Freedom*
Robert Hall. *An Apology for the Freedom of the Press, and for General Liberty. To which are Prefixed Remarks on Bishop Horsley's Sermon, Preached on the Thirtieth of January Last.* London, 1793.

Hamilton, *Duty of Obedience to Laws*
Hugh Hamilton. *The Duty of Obedience to the Laws and of Submission to Magistrates. A Sermon Occasioned by the Late Disturbances in the North of Ireland, Preached before the Judges of Assize in the Cathedral Church of Armagh, on Sunday, April 12, 1772.* London, 1772.

Hamilton, *Farmer*
Alexander Hamilton. *The Farmer Refuted: or A more impartial and comprehensive View of the Dispute between Great-Britain and the Colonies, Intended as a Further Vindication of the Congress.* 1775. Reprinted in *The Papers of Alexander Hamilton,* edited by Harold C. Syrett, vol. 1, at 81–165. New York, 1961.

Handlin and Handlin, "James Burgh"
Oscar Handlin and Mary Handlin. "James Burgh and American Revolutionary Theory." 73 *Proceedings of the Massachusetts Historical Society* 38–57 (1963).

Harris, *Eighteenth-Century England*
R. W. Harris. *England in the Eighteenth Century, 1689–1793: A Balanced Constitution and New Horizons.* London, 1963.

Hartley, *Address to York*
David Hartley. *An Address to the Committee of Association of the County of York, on the State of Public Affairs.* York, England, 1781.

Hartley, *Letters on the War*
David Hartley. *Letters on the American War. Addressed to the Right Worshipful the*

Mayor and Corporation, to the Worshipful the Wardens and Corporation of the Trinity-House, and to the Worthy Burgesses of the Town of Kingston-Upon-Hull. 8th ed. London, 1779.

Hartley, *Two Letters*

David Hartley. *Two Letters from D. Hartley, Esq. M.P. Addressed to the Committee of the County of York.* London, 1780.

Harskins, "Rule of Law"

George L. Haskins. "Executive Justice and the Rule of Law: Some Reflections on Thirteenth-Century England." 30 *Speculum* 529–38 (1955).

Haven, *Election Sermon*

Jason Haven. *A Sermon Preached before His Excellency Sir Francis Bernard, Baronet, Governor: His Honor Thomas Hutchinson, Esq.; Lieutenant-Governor, The Honorable His Majesty's Council, and the Honorable the House of Representatives, of the Province of the Massachusetts-Bay in New-England. May 31st. 1769. Being the Anniversary of the Election of His Majesty's Council for said Province.* Boston, 1769.

Hawkins, *Life of Johnson*

Sir John Hawkins. *The Life of Samuel Johnson, LL.D.* New York, 1961.

Head, *Carlisle Assize Sermon*

Erasmus Head. *Loyalty recommended on the proper Princples. A Sermon Preached in the Cathedral Church of Carlisle, during the Special Assizes held there, for the Trial of the Rebels, before the Right Honourable Lord Chief Baron Parker, the Honourable Mr. Justice Burnet, Mr. Justice Dennison, Mr. Baron Clarke, on Sunday, September 14, 1746.* London, 1747.

[Heath,] *Case of Devon to Excise*

[B. Heath.] *The Case of the County of Devon, With Respect to the Consequences of the New Excise Duty on Cyder and Perry. Published by the Direction of the Committee appointed at a General Meeting of that County to superintend the Application for the Repeal of that Duty.* London, 1763.

Hibernian Magazine

The Hibernian Magazine or Compendium of Entertaining Knowledge Containing The Greatest Variety of the most Curious & useful Subjects in every Branch of Polite Literature. [Monthly magazine, Dublin.]

[Hicks,] *Nature of Parliamentary Power*

[William Hicks.] *The Nature and Extent of Parliamentary Power Considered; In some Remarks upon Mr. Pitt's Speech in the House of Commons, previous to the Repeal of the Stamp-Act: With an Introduction, Applicable to the present Situation of the Colonies.* Philadelphia, 1768.

His Majesties Declaration

His Majesties Declaration to all His Loving Subjects. Occasioned by a false and scandalous Imputation laid upon His Majestie of an Intention of Raysing or Leavying War against His Parliament. Published at his Court at Yorke, the 16. day of June, 1642. London, 1642.

Hoadly, *Works*

The Works of Benjamin Hoadly, D.D. Successively Bishop of Bangor, Hereford, Salisbury, and Winchester. 3 vols. London, 1773.

Hobart, *Civil Government*

Noah Hobart. *Civil Government the Foundation of Social Happiness. A Sermon Preached before the General Assembly of the Colony of Connecticut, at Hartford, on the Day of their Anniversary Election, May 10th, 1750.* New London, Conn., 1751.

Hobbes, *De Cive*

Thomas Hobbes. *De Cive or the Citizen.* Edited by Sterling P. Lamprecht. New York, 1949.

Holliday, *Life of Mansfield*

John Holliday. *The Life of William Late Earl of Mansfield.* London, 1797.

Hooker, *Laws of Ecclesiastical Polity*

Richard Hooker. *Of the Laws of Ecclesiastical Polity.* Reprinted in *The Works of that Learned and Judicious Divine Mr. Richard Hooker With an Account of His Life and Death by Isaac Walton.* "Arranged" by John Keble. 7th ed. Oxford, England 1888.

Hope, *Letters*

John Hope. *Letters on Certain proceedings in Parliament, During the Sessions of the Years 1769 and 1770.* London, 1772.

[Hopkins,] "Vindication of a Pamphlet"

[Stephen Hopkins.] "A Vindication of a Late Pamphlet, entitled, The Rights of Colonies examined, from the Censures and Remarks contained in a *Letter* from a Gentleman in Halifax, to his friend in Rhode-Island, just published at Newport." *Providence Gazette and Country Journal,* 23 February, 2 March, and 9 March 1765.

Hosmer, *Adams*

James K. Hosmer. *Samuel Adams.* Boston, 1899.

[Howard,] *Defence of the Letter*

[Martin Howard.] *A Defence of the Letter from a Gentleman at Halifax, to His Friend in Rhode-Island.* Newport, R.I., 1765.

Howard, *Election Sermon*

Simeon Howard. *A Sermon Preached before the Honorable Council and the Honorable House of Representatives of the State of Massachusetts-Bay, in New-England, May 31, 1780. Being the Anniversary for the Election of the Honorable Council.* 1780. Reprinted in *The Pulpit of the American Revolution: or, the Political Sermons of the Period of 1776,* edited by John Wingate Thornton, at 359–96. Boston, 1860.

Hume, *Essays*

David Hume. *Essays and Treatises on Several Subjects.* New ed. 4 vols. Edinburgh, 1866.

[Hurd,] *Moral and Political Dialogues*

[Richard Hurd.] *Moral and Political Dialogues Between Divers Eminent Persons of the Past and Present Age; with Critical and Explanatory Notes.* 2d ed. London, 1760.

Hutson, "County, Court, and Constitution"

James H. Hutson. "Country, Court, and Constitution: Antifederalism and the Historians." 38 *William and Mary Quarterly* 337–68 (1981).

[Ibbetson,] *National Assemblies*

[James Ibbetson.] *A Dissertation on the National Assemblies Under the Saxon and Norman Governments*. London, 1781.

In a Defiant Stance
John Phillip Reid. *In a Defiant Stance: The Conditions of Law in Massachusetts Bay, the Irish Comparison, and the Coming of the American Revolution*. University Park, Pa., 1977.

"Ingersoll Correspondence"
"A Selection from the Correspondence and Miscellaneous Papers of Jared Ingersoll." Edited by Franklin B. Dexter. 9 *Papers of the New Haven Colony Historical Society* 201–472 (1918).

Interesting Letters
A New and Impartial Collection of Interesting Letters from the Public Papers; Many of them Written by Persons of Eminence. Vol. 2. London, 1767.

Jackson, *Grounds of Government*
John Jackson. *The Grounds of Civil and Ecclesiastical Government Briefly Consider'd*. London, 1718.

[Jebb,] *Address to Freeholders*
[John Jebb.] *An Address to the Freeholders of Middlesex, Assembled at Free Masons Tavern, in Great Queen Street, Upon Monday the 20th of December 1779, Being the Day appointed for a Meeting of the Freeholders, For the Purpose of Establishing Meetings to Maintain and Support the Freedom of Election*. 3d ed. [London, 1779.]

Jensen, *Revolution Within*
Merrill Jensen. *The American Revolution within America*. New York, 1974.

Jezierski, "Parliament or People"
John V. Jezierski. "Parliament or People: James Wilson and Blackstone on the Nature and Location of Sovereignty." 32 *Journal of the History of Ideas* 95–106 (1971).

Johnson, *Argument Proving*
Samuel Johnson. *An Argument Proving, That the Abrogation of King James by the People of England from the Regal Throne, and the Promotion of the Prince of Orange, one of the Royal Family, to the Throne of the Kingdom in his stead, was according to the Constitution of the English Government, and Prescribed by it*. 4th ed. London, 1692.

[Johnson,] *Defence of Magna Charta*
[Samuel Johnson.] *A History and Defence of Magna Charta. Containing a Copy of the Original Charter at large with an English Translation; The Manner of its being Obtained from King John, with its Preservation and Final Establishment in the Succeeding Reigns; with an Introductory Discourse*. London, 1769.

Johnson, *Notes on Pastoral*
Samuel Johnson. *Notes Upon the Phoenix Edition of the Pastoral Letter. Part I*. London, 1694.

Johnson, *Remarks on Sherlock*
Samuel Johnson. *Remarks Upon Dr. Sherlock's Book, Intituled the Case of Resistance of the Supreme Powers Stated and Resolved, according to the Doctrine of the Holy Scriptures*. London, 1689.

Johnstone, "Speech of November, 1775"
   William [*sic* George] Johnstone. "Governor Johnstone's Speech to the House
   of Commons, November 1775." In *The American Revolution: The Anglo-
   American Relation, 1763–1794*, edited by Charles R. Ritcheson, at 85–91.
   Reading, Mass., 1969.
Johnstone, *Speech on the Question*
   George Johnstone. *Governor Johnstone's Speech on the Question of Recommitting
   the address declaring the Colony of Massachuset[t]s Bay in Rebellion: To which is
   added the two Most Masterly Letters of Junius to the people of England in favour of
   the Americans.* London, [1776].
[Jones], *Constitutional Criterion*
   [William Jones.] *The Constitutional Criterion: By a Member of the University of
   Cambridge.* London, 1768.
Jones, *Country and Court*
   J. R. Jones. *Country and Court: England, 1658–1717.* Cambridge, Mass.,
   1978.
Jones, *Speech to Middlesex*
   William Jones. *A Speech of William Jones, Esq. to the Assembled Inhabitants of the
   Counties of Middlesex and Surry, the Cities of London and Westminster, and the
   Borough of Southwark. 28 May 1782.* London, 1782.
Journal of Burgesses
   *Journals of the House of Burgesses of Virginia [Vol. 10] 1761–1765, [Vol. 11]
   1766–1769, [Vol. 12] 1770–1772, [Vol. 13] 1773–1776, Including the records of
   the Committee of Correspondence.* Edited by John Pendleton Kennedy. Rich-
   mond, Va., 1905–7.
Journal of the First Congress
   *Journal of the Proceedings of the Congress, Held at Philadelphia, September 5,
   1774.* Philadelphia, 1774.
Journal of the Times
   Boston under Military Rule, 1768–1769 as Revealed in a Journal of the Times.
   Compiled by Oliver Morton Dickerson. Boston, 1936.
Judson, *Crisis*
   Margaret Atwood Judson. *The Crisis of the Constitution: An Essay in Constitu-
   tional and Political Thought in England, 1603–1645.* New York, 1949.
"Junius," *Junius*
   ["Junius."] *Junius.* 2 vols. London, [1794].
Kammen, *Deputyes & Libertyes*
   Michael Kammen. *Deputyes & Libertyes: The Origins of Representative Govern-
   ment in Colonial America.* New York, 1969.
Kammen, *Empire and Interest*
   Michael Kammen. *Empire and Interest: The American Colonies and the Politics of
   Mercantilism.* Philadelphia, 1970.
Keir, *Constitutional History*
   Sir David Lindsay Keir. *The Constitutional History of Modern Britain since 1485.*
   8th ed. Princeton, N.J., 1966.
[Keld,] *Polity of England*
   [Christopher Keld.] *An Essay on the Polity of England.* London, 1785.

Kelly, "Constituents' Instructions"
    Paul Kelly. "Constituents' Instructions to Members of Parliament in the Eighteenth Century." In *Party and Management in Parliament, 1660–1784*, edited by Clyve Jones. Leicester, England, 1984.
Kemp, *King and Commons*
    Betty Kemp. *King and Commons, 1660–1832*. London, 1957.
Kemp. "Parliamentary Sovereignty"
    Betty Kemp. "Parliamentary Sovereignty." *London Review of Books*, 18 January 1984, at 12–14.
Kenyon, "Ideological Origins"
    Cecelia Kenyon. "Ideological Origins of the First Continental Congress." In *Commemoration Ceremony*, at 6–10.
Kenyon, *Revolution Principles*
    J. P. Kenyon. *Revolution Principles: The Politics of Party, 1689–1720*. Cambridge, England, 1977.
Kern, *Kingship*.
    Fritz Kern. *Kingship and Law in the Middle Ages*. Translated by S. B. Chrimes. Harper Torchbook ed. New York, 1970.
[Knox,] *Claim of the Colonies*
    [William Knox.] *The Claim of the Colonies to an Exemption from Internal Taxes Imposed By Authority of Parliament, Examined: In a Letter from a Gentleman in London, to his Friend in America*. London, 1765.
[Knox,] *Controversy*
    [William Knox.] *The Controversy Between Great Britain and her Colonies Reviewed; The Several Pleas of the Colonies, In Support of their Right to all the Liberties and Privileges of British Subjects, and to Exemption from the Legislative Authority of Parliament, Stated and Considered; and the Nature of their Connection with, and Dependence on, Great Britain, Shewn, Upon the Evidence of Historical Facts and Authentic Records*. London, 1769.
[Knox,] *Extra Official Papers*
    [William Knox.] *Extra Official State Papers. Addressed to the Right Hon. Lord Rawdon, and the Other Members of the Two Houses of Parliament, Associated for the Preservation of the Constitution and Promoting the Prosperity of the British Empire. By a Late Under Secretary of State. Volume the Second*. London, 1789.
[Knox,] *Letter to a Member*
    [William Knox.] *A Letter to a Member of Parliament, Wherein the Power of the British Legislature, And the Case of the Colonists, Are briefly and impartially considered*. London, 1765.
[Knox,] *Present State*
    [William Knox.] *The Present State of the Nation: Particularly with respect to its Trade, Finances, &c. &c. Addressed to the King and both Houses of Parliament*. 4th ed. London, 1769.
Kramnick, "Augustan Reply"
    Isaac Kramnick. "An Augustan Reply to Locke: Bolingbroke on Natural Law and the Origin of Government." 82 *Political Science Quarterly* 571–94 (1967).
Kramnick, *Bolingbroke's Circle*

Isaac Kramnick. *Bolingbroke and His Circle: The Politics of Nostalgia in the Age of Walpole.* Cambridge, Mass., 1968.

Kramnick, "Idea of Representation"
Isaac Kramnick. "An Augustan Debate: Notes on the History of the Idea of Representation." In *Representation,* edited by J. Roland Pennock and John W. Chapman. *Nomos,* vol. 10. New York, 1968.

Kramnick, "Introduction to Writings"
Isaac Kramnick. "Introduction." In Bolingbroke, *Political Writings.*

Kramnick, "Republican Revisionism"
Isaac Kramnick. "Republican Revisionism Revisited." 87 *American Historical Review* 629–64 (1982).

"L.," *Letter to G[renville]*
"L." *A Letter to G. G. Stiff in Opinions, always in the wrong.* London, 1767.

Langdon, *Government Corrupted*
Samuel Langdon. *Government corrupted by Vice, and recovered by Righteousness. A Sermon Preached Before the Honorable Congress of the Colony of the Massachusetts-Bay in New-England, Assembled at Watertown, on Wednesday the 31st Day of May, 1775. Being the Anniversary fixed by Charter for the Election of Counsellors* (1775). Reprinted in *Pulpit of American Revolution: or, the Political Sermons of the Period of 1776,* edited by John Wingate Thornton, at 233–58. Boston, 1860.

Langford, *Excise Crisis*
Paul Langford. *The Excise Crisis: Society and Politics in the Age of Walpole.* Oxford, England, 1975.

Langford, "Old Whigs"
Paul Langford. "Old Whigs, Old Tories, and the American Revolution." 8 *Journal of Imperial and Commonwealth History* 106–30 (1980).

Lawson, *Politica Sacra*
George Lawson. *Politica Sacra & Civilis: Or, a Model of Civil and Ecclesiastical Government.* 2d ed. London, 1689.

Lediard, *Charge to Westminster Jury*
Thomas Lediard. *A Charge Delivered to the Grand Jury, at the Sessions of the Peace Held for the City and Liberty of Westminster, On Wednesday the 16th of October, 1754.* London, 1754.

[Lee,] *Junius Americanus*
[Arthur Lee.] *The Political Detection; or, the Treachery and Tyranny of Administration, both at Home and Abroad; Displayed in a Series of Letters, signed Junius Americanus.* London, 1770.

Lee, *Richard Henry Lee*
Richard Henry Lee. *Memoir of the Life of Richard Henry Lee, and His Correspondence with the Most Distinguished Men in America and Europe, Illustrative of their Characters, and of the Events of the American Revolution.* 2 vols. Philadelphia, 1825.

[Lee,] *Speech Intended*
[Arthur Lee.] *A Speech, Intended to have been Delivered in the House of Commons, in Support of the Petition from the General Congress at Philadelphia.* London, 1775.

Lemisch, "New York Petitions"
L. Jesse Lemisch. "New York's Petitions and Resolves of December 1765: Liberals vs. Radicals." 49 *New-York Historical Society Quarterly* 313–26 (1965).
Letters and Papers of Pendleton
The Letters and Papers of Edmund Pendleton, 1734–1803. Edited by David John Mays. Vol. 1. Charlottesville, Va., 1967.
Letters of Delegates to Congress
Letters of Delegates to Congress: August 1774–August 1775. Edited by Paul H. Smith. 14 vols. Washington, D.C., 1976–87.
[Lind,] *Englishman's Answer*
[John Lind.] *An Englishman's Answer, To the Address, From the Delegates, To the People of Great Britain, in a Letter to the Several Colonies, which were Represented in the Late Continental Congress.* New York, [1775].
[Lind,] *Letters to Price*
[John Lind.] *Three Letters to Dr. Price, Containing Remarks on his Observations on the Nature of Civil Liberty, the Principles of Government, and the Justice and Policy of the War with America.* London, 1776.
[Lind,] *Thirteenth Parliament*
[John Lind.] *Remarks on the Principal Acts of the Thirteenth Parliament of Great Britain. By the Author of "Letters concerning the Present State of Poland."* Vol. I. *Containing Remarks on the Acts relating to the Colonies. With a Plan of Reconciliation.* London, 1775.
[Livingston,] *The Other Side*
[Philip Livingston.] *The Other Side of the Question; or, A Defence of the Liberties of North-America. In Answer to a Late Friendly Address to all Reasonable Americans on the Subject of our Political Confusions.* 1774. Reprinted in *Extra Number 52 of the Magazine of History with Notes and Queries* 225–51 (1916).
Lloyd, *Legislative Power*
David Lloyd. *A Vindication of the Legislative Power. Submitted to the Representatives of all the Free-men of the Province of Pennsylvania, now sitting in Assembly.* [Philadelphia, 1725.]
Locke, *Two Treatises*
John Locke. *Two Treatises of Government: A Critical Edition with an Introduction and Apparatus Criticus.* Edited by Peter Laslett. 2d ed. Cambridge, England, 1967.
Lofft, *Observations on Publication*
Capel Lofft. *Observations on a late Publication, entitled "A Dialogue on the Actual State of Parliament," and also on a Treatise Entitled "Free Parliaments."* London, 1783.
Lofft, *Observations on Wesley's Address*
Capel Lofft. *Observations on Mr. Wesley's Second Calm Address, and Incidently on other Writings upon the American Question. Together with Thoughts on Toleration, and on the Point how Far the Conscience of the Subject is Concerned in a War; Remarks on Constitution in General, and that of England in Particular; on the Nature of Colonial Government, and a Recommendation of a Plan of Peace.* London, 1777.
Logan, *Antidote*

James Logan. *The Antidote. In some Remarks on a Paper of David Lloyd's, called a Vindication of the Legislative Power. Submitted to the Representatives of all the Freemen of Pennsylvania.* [Philadelphia, 1725]

London Journal
[Weekly newspaper, London.]

London Magazine
The London Magazine or Gentleman's Monthly Intelligencer. [Monthly magazine, London.]

"Lords Debate on Declaratory Act"
"Debate on the Conway Resolutions. House of Lords, 10 February 1766." In *The Debate on the American Revolution,* edited by Max Beloff, at 106–18. 2d ed. London, 1960.

Lowth, *Durham Assize Sermon*
Robert Lowth. *A Sermon Preached Before the Honourable and Right Reverend Richard, Lord Bishop of Durham, the Honourable Henry Bathurst, One of the Justices of the Court of Common Pleas, and the Honourable Sir Joseph Yates, One of the Justices of the Court of King's Bench; at the Assizes Holden at Durham, August 15, 1764.* Newcastle, England, 1764.

Lutz, *Popular Consent and Control*
Donald S. Lutz. *Popular Consent and Popular Control: Whig Political Theory in the Early State Constitutions.* Baton Rouge, La., 1980.

McAdam, *Johnson and Law*
E. L. McAdam, Jr. *Dr. Johnson and the English Law.* Syracuse, N.Y., 1951.

Macaulay, *History of England*
Thomas Babington, Lord Macaulay. *The History of England from the Accession of James the Second.* Vol. 1. Philadelphia, n.d.

Macaulay, *Observations on a Pamphlet*
Catharine Macaulay. *Observations on a Pamphlet, Entitled, Thoughts on the Cause of the Present Discontents.* 3d ed., corrected. London, 1770.

Maccoby, *English Radicalism*
S. Maccoby. *English Radicalism, 1762–1785: The Origins.* London, 1955.

McCulloh, *General Thoughts*
Henry McCulloh. *General Thoughts, endeavouring to demonstrate that the Legislature here, in all Cases of a public and General Concern, have a Right to Tax the British Colonies; But that, with respect to the late American Stamp Duty Bill, there are several Clauses inserted therein which are very Exceptionable, and have, as humbly Conceived, passed upon wrong Information.* HM 1480, Huntington Library, San Marino, Calif.

[Macfarlane,] *George Third*
[Robert Macfarlane.] *The History of the First Ten Years of the Reign of George the Third, King of Great Britain, &c. From his Accession to the Throne, in 1760, to the Conclusion of the Third Session of the Thirteenth Parliament of Great Britain, in 1770; To which is prefixed, a Review of the War, which was terminated by the Peace of Paris, in 1783.* 2d ed. London, 1783.

[Macfarlane,] *Second Ten Years*
[Robert Macfarlane.] *The History of the Second Ten Years of the Reign of George the Third, King of Great-Britain, &c. From the Conclusion of the Third Session of*

the Thirteenth Parliament, in 1770, to the end of the Last Session of the Fourteenth Parliament of Great Britain, in 1780. London, 1782.

[Macpherson,] *Rights of Great Britain*
[James Macpherson.] *The Rights of Great Britain Asserted against the Claims of America: Being an Answer to the Declaration of the General Congress.* 6th ed. London, 1776.

Manning, "Levellers"
Brian Manning. "The Levellers." In *The English Revolution, 1600–1660,* edited by E. W. Ives, at 144–57. London, 1968.

Manning, "Puritanism and Democracy"
Brian Manning. "Puritanism and Democracy, 1640–1642." In *Puritans and Revolutionaries: Essays in Seventeenth-Century History Presented to Christopher Hill,* edited by Donald Pennington and Keith Thomas, at 139–60. Oxford, 1978.

[Mantell,] *Short Treatise of the Lawes*
[Walter Mantell.] *A Short Treatise of the Lawes of England: With the jurisdiction of the High Court of Parliament, With the Liberties and Freedomes of the Subjects.* London, 1644.

[Marat,] *Chains of Slavery*
[John Paul Marat.] *The Chains of Slavery. A Work Wherein the Clandestine and Villainous Attempts of Princes to Ruin Liberty are Pointed Out, and the Dreadful Scenes of Depotism Disclosed. To which is prefixed, An Address to the Electors of Great Britain, in order to draw their timely Attention to the Choice of proper Representatives in the next Parliament.* London, 1774.

[Marchmont,] *Serious Exhortation*
[Hugh Hume, third Earl Marchmont.] *A Serious Exhortation to the Electors of Great Britain: Wherein the Importance of the Approaching Elections is particularly proved from our present Situation both at Home and Abroad.* London, 1740.

Martin, *Familiar Dialogues*
John Martin. *Familiar Dialogues Between Americus and Britannicus; in which the Right of Private Judgment; the exploded Doctrines of Infallibility, Passive Obedience, and Non-Resistance; with the leading Sentiments of Dr. Price, on the Nature of Civil Liberty, &c. are Particularly Considered.* London, 1776.

Maryland Gazette
[Weekly newspaper.]

Maryland Votes and Proceedings (September 1765)
Votes and Proceedings of the Lower House of Assembly of the Province of Maryland. September Session, 1765. Being the First Session of this Assembly. Annapolis, Md., n.d.

[Maseres,] *Canadian Freeholder*
[Francis Maseres.] *The Canadian Freeholder: In Two Dialogues Between an Englishman and a Frenchman Settled in Canada.* 3 vols. London, 1777–79.

[Maseres,] *Considerations on Admitting Representatives*
[Francis Maseres.] *Considerations on the Expediency of Admitting Representatives From the American Colonies into the British House of Commons.* London, 1770.

Massachusetts Representative Journal (1754)
Journal of the Honourable House of Representatives, of His Majesty's Province of

the Massachusetts-Bay in New-England. Begun and Held at Boston, in the County of Suffolk, on Wednesday the Twenty-ninth of May, Annoque Domini, 1754. Boston, 1754.

Massacre Orations

Orations Delivered at the Request of the Town of Boston to Commemorate the Evening of the Fifth of March, 1770; When a Number of Citizens were Killed by a Party of British Troops, Quartered Among them, in a Time of Peace. Boston, [1785].

[Mauduit,] *Northern Colonies*

[Israel Mauduit.] *Some Thoughts on the Method of Improving and Securing the Advantages which Accrue to Great-Britain from the Northern Colonies.* London, 1765.

May, *Parliamentary Practice*

Sir Thomas Erskine May. *A Treatise on the Law, Privileges, Proceedings and Usages of Parliament.* Edited by Sir Gilbert Campion. 14th ed. London, 1946.

Mayhew, *Election Sermon*

Jonathan Mayhew. *A Sermon Preach'd in the Audience of His Excellency William Shirley, Esq.; Captain General, Governour and Commander in Chief, the Honourable His Majesty's Council, and the Honourable House of Representatives, of the Province of the Massachusetts-Bay, in New-England. May 29th, 1754. Being the Anniversary for the Election of His Majesty's Council for the Province.* Boston, 1754.

[Meredith] *Question Stated*

[Sir William Meredith.] *The Question Stated, Whether the Freeholders of Middlesex lost their Right, by voting for Mr. Wilkes at the last Election? In a letter from a Member of Parliament to one of his Constituents.* London, [1769].

[Miles,] *Political Mirror or Summary Review*

[William Augustus Miles.] *A Political Mirror; or, a Summary Review of the Present Reign. With Notes, Explanatory and Historical, and an Authentic List of the Ships and Vessels of War, Taken and Destroyed, Since the Commencement of Hostilities.* London, 1779.

Missing, *Letter to Mansfield on Instructions*

John Missing. *A Letter to the Right Honourable William Lord Mansfield, Lord Chief Justice of the Court of King's Bench: Proving that the Subjects of England, lawfully assembled to Petition their King, or to Elect or Instruct their Representatives, are intitled to Freedom of Debate; and that all Suits and Prosecutions for exerting that Right, are Unconstitutional and Illegal.* London, 1770.

[Mitchell,] *The Present State*

[John Mitchell.] *The Present State of Great Britain and North America, with Regard to Agriculture, Population, Trade, and Manufactures, impartially considered.* London, 1767.

Molesworth, *Principles of a Real Whig*

The Principles of a Real Whig; Contained in a Preface to the Famous Hotoman's Franco-Gallia, Written by the late Lord-Viscount Molesworth; And now Reprinted at the Request of the London Association. To which are added their Resolutions and Circular Letter. London, 1775.

Monthly Review

The Monthly Review; or, Liberty Journal: by Several Hands. [Monthly magazine, London.]

Moore, "Comment"
James Moore. "A Comment on Pocock." In *Theories of Property: Aristotle to the Present,* edited by Anthony Parel and Thomas Flanagan, at 167–75. Waterloo, Ont., 1979.

Moore, *Taxing Colonies*
Maurice Moore. *The Justice and Policy of Taxing the American Colonies, in Great-Britain, considered.* 1765. Reprinted in *Not a Conquered People: Two Carolinians View Parliamentary Taxation,* edited by William S. Pierce, at 37–48. Raleigh, N.C., 1975.

Morgan, "Government by Fiction"
Edmund S. Morgan. "Government by Fiction: The Idea of Representation." 72 *Yale Review* 321–39 (1983).

Morgan, *Prologue*
Prologue to Revolution: Sources and Documents on the Stamp Act Crisis, 1764–1766. Edited by Edmund S. Morgan. New York, 1973.

Moss, *Connecticut Election Sermon*
Joseph Moss. *An Election Sermon, Preached Before the General Assembly of the Colony of Connecticut, at Hartford, May the 12th. 1715. The Discourse sheweth, that frequent Reading and Studying the Scriptures and the Civil Law of the Common Wealth, is Needful and Profitable for Rulers.* New London, Conn., 1715.

Mountagu, *Wiltshire Grand Jury Charge*
The Charge of James Mountague, Esq; to the Grand Jury, and the other Jurys of the County of Wilts: At the General Quarter-Sessions of the Peace, held at the Devizes, April 26. 1720. London, 1720.

[Mulgrave,] *Letter from a Member*
[Constance John Phipps, second Baron Mulgrave.] *A Letter from a Member of Parliament to One of his Constituents, on the Late Proceedings of the House of Commons in the Middlesex Elections. With a Postscript, Containing Some Observations on a Pamphlet entitled, "The Case of the late Election for the County of Middlesex Considered."* London, 1769.

[Nedham,] *Excellencie of Free State*
[Marchamont Nedham.] *The Excellencie of a Free State.* London, 1767.

[Neville,] *Plato Redivivus*
[Henry Neville.] *Plato Redivivus: or, a Dialogue Concerning Government.* London, 1681.

New and Impartial Letters
A New and Impartial Collection of Interesting Letters, from the Public Papers; Many of them Written by Persons of Eminence, on a great Variety of Important Subjects, which have occasionally engaged the Public Attention: From the Accession of his present Majesty, in September 1760, to May 1767. Vol. 2. London, 1767.

New York Journal of Votes
Journal of the Votes and Proceedings of the General Assembly of the Colony of New-York. Began the 8th Day of November, 1743; and Ended the 23th of December, 1765. Vol. II. *Published by Order of the General Assembly.* New York, 1766.

North, *Argument in Soames Case*
    [Francis North.] *The late Lord Chief Justice North's Argument. In the Case between Sir William Soames, Sheriff of Suffolk, and Sir Sam. Barnardiston, Bar. Adjudged in the Court of Exchequer-Chamber.* London, 1689.
North Carolina Colonial Records
    The Colonial Records of North Carolina, Published Under the Supervision of the Trustees of the Public Libraries, By Order of the General Assembly. Edited by William L. Saunders. Vols. 7, 8, 9, 10. Raleigh, N.C., 1890.
Northcote, *Observations on Rights*
    Thomas Northcote. *Observations on the Natural and Civil Rights of Mankind, the Prerogatives of Princes, and the Powers of Government.* London, 1781.
[O'Beirne,] *Short History*
    [Thomas L. O'Beirne.] *A Short History of the Last Session of Parliament, with Remarks.* London, 1780.
O'Gorman, "After Namier"
    Frank O'Gorman. "Fifty Years After Namier: The Eighteenth Century in British Historical Writing." 20 *Eighteenth Century: Theory and Interpretation* 99–120 (1979).
[Oldfield,] *History of the Boroughs*
    [J. H. B. Oldfield.] *An Entire and Complete History, Political and Personal, of the Boroughs of Great Britain; to which is Prefixed, an Original Sketch of Constitutional Rights, from the Earliest Period Until the Present Time; and the Principles of our Ancient Representation Traced from the Most Authentic Records, Supported by Undeniable Testimonies, and Illustrated by a Variety of Notes and References, Collected from the Most Respectable, Legal, Political, and Historical Authorities.* 2 vols. London, 1792.
[Otis,] *Vindication*
    [James Otis.] *A Vindication of the British Colonies, against the Aspersions of the Halifax Gentleman, in His Letter to a Rhode Island Friend.* 1765. Reprinted in 1 Bailyn, *Pamphlets*, at 554–79.
Paley, *Principles of Philosophy*
    William Paley. *The Principles of Moral and Political Philosophy.* London, 1785.
Papers of Iredell
    The Papers of James Iredell. Vol. 1, *1767–1777.* Edited by Don Higginbotham. Raleigh, N.C., 1976.
Papers of Jefferson
    The Papers of Thomas Jefferson. Edited by Julian P. Boyd. 22 vols. Princeton, N.J., 1950–86.
Parliament Debates
    Proceedings and Debates of the British Parliaments Respecting North America, 1754–1783. Edited by R. C. Simmons and P. D. G. Thomas. 6 vols. Millwood, N.Y., 1982–87.
Parliamentary History
    The Parliamentary History of England, From the Earliest Period to the Year 1803. 36 vols. London, 1808–20.
Patten, *Discourse at Hallifax*

William Patten. *A Discourse Delivered at Hallifax in the County of Plymouth, July 24th 1766. On the Day of Thanks-giving to Almighty God, throughout the Province of the Massachusetts-Bay in New England, for the Repeal of the* STAMP-ACT. Boston, 1766.

Payson, *Election Sermon*
> Phillips Payson. *A Sermon Preached before the Honorable Council, and the Honorable House of Representatives, of the State of Massachusetts-Bay, in New-England, at Boston, May 27, 1778. Being the Anniversary for the Election of the Honorable Council.* 1778. Reprinted in *The Pulpit of the American Revolution: or, The Political Sermons of the Period of 1776,* edited by John Wingate Thornton, at 329–53. Boston, 1860.

Peach, *Richard Price*
> Bernard Peach. *Richard Price and the Ethical Foundations of the American Revolution.* Durham, N.C., 1979.

Pencak, *War, Politics, and Revolution*
> William Pencak. *War, Politics, and Revolution in Provincial Massachusetts.* Boston, 1981.

Pennsylvania Archives
> *Pennsylvania Archives: Eighth Series [Votes and Proceedings of the House of Representatives].* 8 vols. [Harrisburg, Pa.,] 1931–35.

Perry, *Connecticut Election Sermon*
> Joseph Perry. *A Sermon Preached before the General Assembly of the Colony of Connecticut, at Hartford, on the Day of their Anniversary Election, May 11, 1775.* Hartford, 1775.

Petyt, *Antient Right*
> William Petyt. *The Antient Right of the Commons of England Asserted; or, a Discourse Proving by Records and the best Historians, that the Commons of England were ever an Essential part of Parliament.* London, 1680.

Petyt, *Jus Parliamentarium*
> William Petyt. *Jus Parliamentarium: or, the Ancient Power, Jurisdiction, Rights and Liberties, of the Most High Court of Parliament, Revived and Asserted.* London, 1739.

Petyt, *Lex Parliamentaria*
> G[eorge] P[etyt]. *Lex Parliamentaria: or, a Treatise of the Law and Custom of the Parliaments of England. With an Appendix of a Case in Parliament between Sir Francis Goodwyn and Sir John Fortescue, for the Knights Place for the County of Bucks. I Jac. I. From an Original French Manuscript, Translated into English.* London, 1690.

[Phelps,] *Rights of the Colonies*
> [Richard Phelps.] *The Rights of the Colonies, And the Extent of the Legislative Authority of Great-Britain, Briefly Stated and Considered.* London, 1769.

Phillips, *Electoral Behavior*
> John A. Phillips. *Electoral Behavior in Unreformed England: Plumpers, Splitters, and Straights.* Princeton, N.J., 1982.

Phillips, *Salem*
> James Duncan Phillips. *Salem in the Eighteenth Century.* Boston, 1937.

Pitkin, "Obligation and Consent"
Hanna Pitkin. "Obligation and Consent. I." 59 *American Political Science Review* 990–99 (1965).

Plowden, *Friendly and Constitutional*
Francis Plowden. *A Friendly and Constitutional Address to the People of Great Britain.* London, 1794.

Pocock, *Ancient Constitution*
J. G. A. Pocock. *The Ancient Constitution and the Feudal Law: A Study of English Historical Thought in the Seventeenth Century.* New York, 1967.

Pocock, "Classical Deference"
J. G. A. Pocock. "The Classical Theory of Deference." 81 *American Historical Review* 516–23 (1976).

Pocock, "English Ideologies"
J. G. A. Pocock. "Machiavelli, Harrington and English Political Ideologies in the Eighteenth Century." 22 *William and Mary Quarterly* 549–83 (1965).

Pocock, "Mobility of Property"
J. G. A. Pocock. "The Mobility of Property and the Rise of Eighteenth-Century Sociology." In *Theories of Property: Aristotle to the Present,* edited by Anthony Parel and Thomas Flanagan, at 141–64. Waterloo, Ont., 1979.

Pocock, *Politics*
J. G. A. Pocock. *Politics, Language and Time: Essays on Political Thought and History.* New York, 1971.

Pole, "American Whig"
J. R. Pole. "An Anatomy of the American Whig." 9 *Historical Journal* 229–36 (1966).

Pole, *Gift*
J. R. Pole. *The Gift of Government: Political Responsibility from the English Restoration to American Independence.* Athens, Ga., 1983.

Pole, *Legislative Power*
J. R. Pole. *The Seventeenth Century: The Sources of Legislative Power.* Jamestown Essays on Representation. Charlottesville, Va., 1969.

Pole, *Pursuit of Equality*
J. R. Pole. *Pursuit of Equality in American History.* Berkeley, Calif., 1978.

Pole, *Representation*
J. R. Pole. *Political Representation in England and the Origins of the American Republic.* Berkeley, Calif., 1971.

Political Register
The Political Register, and Impartial Review of New Books. [Monthly magazine, London.]

Pollock, "Sovereignty in English Law"
Frederick Pollock. "Sovereignty in English Law." 8 *Harvard Law Review* 243–51 (1894).

Porritt, *Unreformed House*
Edward Porritt. *The Unreformed House of Commons—Parliamentary Representation before 1832.* Vol. 1, *England and Wales.* Cambridge, England, 1909.

[Powis,] *Dialogue on Parliament*
[M. Powis.] *A Dialogue of the Actual State of Parliament.* Dublin, 1783.

Pownall, *Adminstration*
Thomas Pownall. *The Administration of the Colonies. Wherein their Rights and Constitution are Discussed and Stated.* 4th ed. London, 1768.

[Pownall,] *Considerations*
[Thomas Pownall.] *Considerations on the Points lately brought into Question as to the Parliament's Right of Taxing the Colonies, And of the Measures necessary to be taken at the Crisis. Being an Appendix, Section III, to the Administration of the Colonies.* London, 1766.

Price, *Two Tracts*
Richard Price. *Two Tracts on Civil Liberty, the War with America, and the Debts and Finances of the Kingdom: with a General Introduction and Supplement.* London, 1778. Reprint. New York, 1972.

Price, *Two Tracts: Tract One*
Richard Price. *Observations on the Nature of Civil Liberty, the Principles of Government, and the Justice and Policy of the War with America.* 8th ed. London, 1778. Reprinted in Price, *Two Tracts,* at i–xxvi, 1–112.

Price, *Two Tracts: Tract Two*
Richard Price. *Additional Observations on the Nature and Value of Civil Liberty, and the War with America: Also Observations on Schemes for raising Money by Public Loans; An Historical Deduction and Analysis of the National Debt; And a brief Account of the Debts and Resources of France.* [3d ed. 1778.] Reprinted in Price, *Two Tracts,* at vii–xiv, 1–216.

[Priestley,] *Address to Dissenters*
[Joseph Priestley.] *An Address to Protestant Dissenters of all Denominations, on the Approaching Election of Members of Parliament, With Respect to the State of Public Liberty in General, and of American Affairs in Particular.* Philadelphia, 1774.

Priestley, *First Principles* (1768)
Joseph Priestley. *An Essay on the First Principles of Government; and on the Nature of Political, Civil, and Religious Liberty.* London, 1768.

Priestley, *First Principles* (1771)
Joseph Priestley. *An Essay on the First Principles of Government, and on the Nature of Political, Civil, and Religious Liberty, Including Remarks on Dr. Brown's Code of Education, and on Dr. Balguy's Sermon on Church Authority.* 2d ed. London, 1771.

[Priestley,] *Present State of Liberty*
[Joseph Priestly.] *The Present State of Liberty in Great Britain and Her Colonies.* London, 1769.

Prior Documents
A Collection of Interesting, Authentic Papers, Relative to the Dispute Between Great Britain and America; Shewing the Causes and Progress of that Misunderstanding From 1764 to 1775. London, 1777.

Proceedings and Debates
Proceedings and Debates of the British Parliaments respecting North America. Edited by Leo Francis Stock. 5 vols. Washington, D.C., 1924–41.

"Proceedings Committee of Correspondence"
"Proceedings of the Virginia Committee of Correspondence." 12 *Vir-*

ginia Magazine of History and Biography 1–14, 157–69, 225–40, 353–64 (1904–5).

Providence Gazette
The Providence Gazette and Country Journal. [Weekly newpaper, Providence, R.I.]

Pulteney, *Effects from East India Bill*
William Pulteney. *The Effects to be Expected from the East India Bill, Upon the Constitution of Great Britain, if passed into a Law.* 4th ed. London, 1784.

Pulteney, *Plan of Reunion*
William Pulteney. *Plan of Re-Union Between Great Britain and Her Colonies.* London, 1778.

[Pulteney,] *Reflections on Domestic Policy*
[William Pulteney.] *Reflections on the Domestic Policy, Proper to be observed on the Conclusion of a Peace.* London, 1763.

Pulteney, *Thoughts on Present State*
William Pulteney. *Thoughts on the Present State of Affairs with America, and the Means of Conciliation.* 5th ed. London, 1778.

"Putney Debates"
"The Putney Debates: At the General Council of Officers, 1647." Printed in *Puritanism and Liberty: Being the Army Debates (1647–9) from the Clarke Manuscripts with Supplementary Documents,* edited by A. S. P. Woodhouse, at 1–124. Chicago, 1965.

Pym, *Speech of summing up*
John Pym. *The Speech or Declaration of John Pym, Esquire: After the Recapitulation or summing up of the Charge of High-Treason, Against Thomas, Earle of Strafford, 12 April, 1641.* London, 1641.

Quincy, *Observations with Thoughts*
Josiah Quincy, Jun'r. *Observations on the Act of Parliament Commonly Called the Boston Port-Bill; with Thoughts on Civil Society and Standing Armies.* Boston 1774. Reprinted in *Memoir of the Life of Josiah Quincy Jun. of Massachusetts: By his Son, Josiah Quincy,* at 355–469. Boston, 1825.

Rakove, *Beginnings*
Jack N. Rakove. *The Beginnings of National Politics: An Interpretive History of the Continental Congress.* New York, 1979.

[Ramsay,] *Historical Essay*
[Allan Ramsay.] *An Historical Essay on the English Constitution: Or, An impartial Inquiry into the Elective Power of the People, from the first Establishment of the Saxons in this Kingdom. Wherein the Right of Parliament, to Tax our distant Provinces, is explained, and justified, upon such constitutional Principles as will afford an equal Security to the Colonists, as to their Brethren at Home.* London, 1771.

[Ramsay,] *Letters on Present Disturbances*
[Allan Ramsay.] *Letters on the Present Disturbances in Great Britain and her American Provinces.* London, 1777.

[Ramsay,] *Origin and Nature*
[Allan Ramsay.] *Thoughts on the Origin and Nature of Government. Occasioned*

by The late Disputes between Great Britain and her American Colonies. Written in the Year 1766. London, 1769.

[Rawson,] *Revolution in New England*

[Edward Rawson.] *Revolution in New England Justified, And the People there Vindicated From the Aspersions cast upon them by Mr. John Palmer, In his Pretended Answer to the Declaration, Published by the Inhabitants of Boston, and the Country adjacent, on the day when they secured their late Oppressors, who acted by an Illegal and Arbitrary Commission from the Late King JAMES.* Boston, 1691.

[Raynal.] *Sentiments*

[Guillaume Thomas F. Raynal.] *The Sentiments of a Foreigner on the Disputes of Great-Britain with America. Translated from the French.* Philadelphia, 1775.

Records of Rhode Island

Records of the Colony of Rhode Island & Providence Plantations in New England. Edited by John Russell Bartlett. 10 vols. Providence, 1862.

"Regulus," *Defence of the Resolutions*

"Regulus." *A Defence of the Resolutions and Address of the American Congress, in Reply to Taxation no Tyranny. By the Author of Regulus. To which are added, General Remarks on the Leading Principles of that Work, as Published in The London Evening Post on the 2d and 4th of May; and a Short Chain of Deductions From One Clear Position of Common Sense and Experience.* London, [1775].

Reliquiae Sacrae Carolinae

Reliquiae Sacrae Carolinae: The Pourtraicture of His Sacred Majestie in his Solitudes and Sufferings: Together with Severall additionals relating to the Death of that most Religious and Blessed Prince. The Hague, [ca. 1648].

Remembrancer for 1776: Part II

The Remembrance; or, Impartial Repository of Public Events: Part II. For the Year 1776. London, 1776.

Remembrancer for 1776: Part III

The Remembrancer; or, Impartial Repository of Public Events. Part III. For the Year 1776. London, 1777.

Remonstrance of the Cities (1659)

The Remonstrance and Protestation of the Well-affected People of the Cities of London, Westminster, and other the Cities, Counties and Places within the Commonwealth of England, against those Officers of the Army, who put force upon, and interrupted the Parliament; the 13th of Octob. 1659, and against all pretended Powers or Authoritys that they have or shall set up, to Rule or Govern this Common-Wealth that is not established by Parliament. London, 1659.

Revolution Documents

Documents of the American Revolution, 1770–1783. Edited by K. G. Davies. Vols. 1–21. Dublin, 1972–81.

Revolutionary Virginia

Revolutionary Virginia: The Road to Independence. Vol. 1, *Forming Thunderclouds and the First Convention, 1763–1774: A Documentary Record,* compiled by William J. Van Schreeven, edited by Robert L. Scribner. Vol. 2, *The Committees and the Second Convention, 1773–1775: A Documentary Record,* compiled by William J. Van Schreeven and Robert L. Scribner. Vol. 3, *The Breaking Storm and the Third Convention, 1775: A Documentrary Record,* compiled and edited by Robert L. Scribner. Vol. 4, *The Committee of Safety and the Balance of Forces, 1775: A Documentary Record,* compiled and edited by Robert L. Scribner and Brent Tarter. Vol. 5, *The Clash of Arms and the Fourth Convention, 1775–1776: A Documentary Record,* compiled and edited by Robert L. Scribner and Brent Tarter. Vol. 6, *The Time for Decision, 1776: A Documentary Record,* compiled and edited by Robert L. Scribner and Brent Tarter. [Charlottesville, Va.,] 1973–81.

[Rivers,] *Letters*

[George Pitt, Baron Rivers of Stratfieldsaye.] *Letters to a Young Nobleman, upon Various Subjects, Particularly on Government and Civil Liberty. Wherein Occasion is taken to Remark on the Writings of some Eminent Authors upon these Subjects; And, in the First Place, upon those of the Reverend Dr. Price. With some Thoughts on the English Constitution, and the heads of a plan of Parliamentary Reform.* London, 1784.

Robbins, "Republicanism"

Caroline Robbins. "European Republicanism in the Century and a Half before 1776." In *The Development of a Revolutionary Mentality,* at 31–55. Library of Congress Symposia on the American Revolution. Washington, D.C., 1972.

Robinson, *Christian Submission*

Robert Robinson. *Christian Submission to Civil Government. A Discourse Preached on January 30, 1780, at the Meeting-House in St. Andrew's, Cambridge.* Cambridge, England, 1780.

Robinson, *Political Catechism*

Robert Robinson. *A Political Catechism. Intended to Convey, in a Familiar Manner, Just Ideas of Good Civil Government, and the British Constitution.* 2d ed. London, 1782.

[Rokeby,] *Further Examination*

[Matthew Robinson-Morris, second Baron Rokeby.] *A Further Examination of our Present American Measures and of the Reasons and the Principles on which they are founded.* Bath, England, 1776.

Rossiter, *Political Thought*

Clinton Rossiter. *The Political Thought of the American Revolution.* New York, 1953.

Rossiter, *Six Characters*

Clinton Rossiter. *Six Characters in Search of a Republic: Studies in the Political Thought of the American Colonies.* New York, 1964.

Rous, *Thoughts on Government*

George Rous. *Thoughts on Government; Occasioned by Mr. Burke's Reflections, &c. in a Letter to a Friend. To which is added a Postscript in Reply to a Vindication of Mr. Burke's Reflections.* 4th ed. London, 1791.

Rushworth, *Historical Collections: Third Part*

John Rushworth. *Historical Collections: The Third Part; in Two Volumes.* Vol. 1. London, 1692.

Rusticus, *Good of Community*

Rusticus. *The Good of the Community Impartially Considered. In a Letter to a Merchant in Boston; In Answer to one Received respecting the Excise Bill. Wherein an Attempt is made, First, to Show that it is for the Interest of the Community to Excise all* LUXURIES *of Life; that this* EXCISE *ought to Extend to Every Man within the Province; and that this is the most Equitable Method of paying the Charges of the Government. Secondly, To answer all the Objections that have been raised, both against Excises, and the present Method proposed for Collecting the same. By a true Friend to Liberty.* Boston, 1754.

Rutherforth, *Natural Law*
  T. Rutherforth. *Institutes of Natural Law Being the substance of a Course of Lectures on Grotius de Jure Belli et Pacis Read in S. Johns College Cambridge.* 2 vols. Cambridge, England, 1754.

Ryder, "Parliamentary Diaries"
  "Parliamentary Diaries of Nathaniel Ryder, 1764–7." Edited by P. D. G. Thomas. In *Camden Miscellany Vol. XXIII.* Camden Society, 4th ser., vol. 7. London, [1969].

St. Amand, *Historical Essay*
  George St. Amand. *An Historical Essay on the Legislative Power of England.* London, 1725.

St. Patrick's Anti-Stamp Chronicle
  St. Patrick's Anti-Stamp Chronicle: Or, Independent Magazine, of News, Politics, and Literary Entertainment. Number II, Friday, June 24th, 1774. Dublin.

Salkeld Reports
  William Salkeld. *Reports of Cases Adjudged in the Court of King's Bench: with some special cases in the Courts of Chancery, Commons Pleas, and Exchequer, Alphabetically digested under proper heads: From the First Year of K. William and Q. Mary to the Tenth Year of Q. Anne.* 6th ed. Vol. 1. Dublin, 1791.

Schutz, *Shirley*
  John A. Schutz. *William Shirley: King's Governor of Massachusetts.* Chapel Hill, N.C., 1961.

Schwoerer, "Bill of Rights"
  Lois G. Schwoerer. "The Bill of Rights: Epitome of the Revolution of 1688–89." In *Three British Revolutions: 1641, 1688, 1776,* edited by J. G. A. Pocock, at 224–43. Princeton, N.J., 1980.

Scots Magazine
  The Scots Magazine. [Monthly magazine, Edinburgh.]

[Scott,] *Remarks on the Patriot*
  [John Scott.] *Remarks on the Patriot. Including some Hints Respecting the Americans: with an Address to the Electors of Great Britain.* London, 1775.

[Seabury,] *View of the Controversy*
  [Samuel Seabury.] *A View of the Controversy Between Great Britain and her Colonies: Including a Mode of Determining their present Disputes, Finally and Effectually; and of Preventing all Future Contentions. In a Letter to the Author of a Full Vindication of the Measures of the Congress, from the Calumnies of their Enemies.* New York, 1774.

[Serle,] *Americans against Liberty*

[Ambrose Serle.] *Americans against Liberty: or, an Essay on the Nature and Principles of True Freedom, Shewing that the Design and Conduct of the Americans tend only to Tyranny and Slavery.* 3d ed. London, 1776.

Sharp, *Declaration of Natural Right*

Granville Sharp. *A Declaration of the People's Natural Right to a Share in the Legislature, which is the Fundamental Principle of the British Constitution of State.* Philadelphia, 1774.

Sharp, *Legal Means*

Granville Sharp. *The Legal Means of Political Reformation, Proposed in Two Small Tracts.* 8th ed. London, 1797.

Shebbeare, *Essay on National Society*

J. Shebbeare. *An Essay on the Origin, Progress and Establishment of National Society; in which the Principles of Government, the Definitions of physicial, moral, civil, and religious Liberty, contained in Dr. Price's Observations, &c. are fairly examined and fully refuted: Together with a Justification of the Legislature, in reducing America to Obedience by Force.* London, 1776.

Shelton, *Charge to Suffolk Grand Jury*

Maurice Shelton. *A Charge Given to the Grand-Jury, at the General Quarter-Sessions of the Peace, Holden at St. Edmunds-Bury for the Liberty thereof; In the County of Suffolk: On the 11th of October, An. Dom. 1725.* London, 1726.

Shelton, *Suffolk Grand Jury Charge*

Maurice Shelton. *A Charge Given to the Grand-Jury, at the General Quarter Sessions of the Peace, Holden at St. Edmunds-Bury for the Liberty thereof; in the County Suffolk: On the 16th of July, An. Dom. 1716.* London, 1716.

[Sheridan,] *Review of Three Questions*

[Charles Francis Sheridan.] *A Review of the Three Great National Questions Relative to Declaration of Right, Poynings' Law, and the Mutiny Bill.* Dublin, 1781.

Sherlock, *Present Majesties Government*

William Sherlock. *Their Present Majesties Government Proved to be Throughly Settled, and that we may Submit to it, without Asserting the Principles of Mr. Hobbs. Shewing also, That Allegiance was not Due to the Usurpers after the late Civil War.* London, 1691.

Shirley, *Richard Hooker*

F. J. Shirley. *Richard Hooker and Contemporary Political Ideas.* London, 1949.

[Short,] *Rights*

[John Short.] *The Rights and Principles of an Englishman Considered and Asserted, on a Review of the late Motion at the Hotel, for a County Meeting in Devonshire.* Exeter, England, 1780.

Shute, *Election Sermon*

Daniel Shute. *A Sermon Preached before his Excellency Francis Bernard, Esq.; Governor, his Honor Thomas Hutchinson, Esq; Lieutenant-Governor, the Honourable His Majesty's Council, and the Honourable House of Representatives, of the Province of the Massachusetts-Bay in New-England, May 25th, 1768. Being the Aniversary [sic] for the Election of His Majesty's Council for said Province.* Boston, 1768.

[Sinclair,] *Lucubrations*

[Sir John Sinclair.] *Lucubrations During a Short Recess.* London, 1782.

Skeel, "Influence of Fortescue"
  Caroline Skeel. "The Influence of the Writings of Sir John Fortescue." 10
  (3d ser.) *Transactions of the Royal Historical Society* 77–114 (1916).

Society for Constitutional Information
  [Two publications distributed by the Society for Constitutional Information
  without title, imprint, or binding. The copies at the Huntington Library,
  San Marino, Calif., are numbered for 1782 rare book 310802 and for 1783
  rare book 305204.]

[Somers,] *Brief History*
  [John Somers.] *A Brief History of the Succession, Collected out of the Records, and
  the most Authentick Historians.* London, [ca. 1682].

Somers, *Security of Englishmen's Lives*
  John Lord Somers. *The Security of Englishmen's Lives: Or, the Trust, Power and
  Duty of Grand Juries of England Explained according to the Fundamentals of the
  English Government, and the Declaration of the same made in Parliament by many
  Statutes. First printed in the Year 1681.* London, 1766.

Somers' Tracts
  *A Collection of Scarce and Valuable Tracts, on the Most Interesting and Entertaining
  Subjects: But Chiefly such as Relate to the History and Constitution of these King-
  doms. Selected from an Infinite Number in Print and Manuscript, in the Royal,
  Cotton, Sion, and other Public, as well as Private, Libraries; Particularly that of the
  Late Lord Somers.* Edited by Walter Scott. 2d ed. Vols. 4 and 5. London,
  1809–15.

Somerville, *Observations on the Constitution*
  Thomas Somerville. *Observations on the Constitution and Present State of Britain.*
  Edinburgh, 1793.

South-Carolina Gazette
  [Weekly newspaper, Charles Town, S.C.]

Sovereign States
  Sovereign States in an Age of Uncertainty. Edited by Ronald Hoffman and Peter
  J. Albert. Charlottesville, Va., 1981.

Speeches
  *Speeches of the Governors of Massachusetts, From 1765 to 1775; And the Answers
  of the House of Representatives, to the Same; with their Resolutions and Addresses
  for that Period. And Other Public Papers, Relating to the Dispute Between this Country and Great Britain, which led to the Independence of the United States.* Boston,
  1818.

Speeches of John Wilkes in Parliament
  *The Speeches of John Wilkes, One of the Knights of the Shire for the County
  of Middlesex, In the Parliament appointed to meet at Westminster the 29th day of November 1774, to the Prorogation the 6th day of June 1777.* 2 vols. London, 1777.

[Squire,] *Ballance of Power*
  [Samuel Squire.] *Historical Essay Upon the Ballance of Civil Power in England,
  From its first Conquest by the Anglo-Saxons, to the Time of the Revolution; in which
  is introduced a new Dissertation Upon Parties. With a proper Dedication to the Freeholders and Burgesses of Great Britain.* London, 1748.

"Stamp Act Debates"

"Debates on the Declaratory Act and the Repeal of the Stamp Act, 1766."
17 *American Historical Review* 563–86 (1912).

Stanlis, *Burke and Natural Law*
Peter J. Stanlis. *Edmund Burke and the Natural Law.* Ann Arbor, Mich. 1965.

Stark, *Loyalists*
James H. Stark. *The Loyalists of Massachusetts and the Other Side of the American Revolution.* Boston, 1910.

State Trials
A Complete Collection of State Trials and Proceedings for High Treason and Other Crimes and Misdemeanors From the Earliest Period to the Year 1783, With Notes and Other Illustrations. Compiled by T. B. Howell. 34 vols. London, 1816–28.

[Steuart,] *Jus Populi*
[Sir James Steuart.] *Jus Populi Vindicatum or the Peoples Right, to defend themselves and their Covenanted Religion, vindicated.* n.i., [1669].

[Stevens,] *Discourse on Constitution*
[William Stevens.] *A Discourse on the English Constitution; Extracted from a Late Eminent Writer, and Applicable to the Present Times.* London, 1776.

[Stillingfleet,] *Discourse*
[Edward Stillingfleet.] *A Discourse Concerning the Unreasonableness of a New Separation, on account of the Oaths. With an Answer to the History of Passive Obedience so far as it relates to Them.* London, 1689.

Sutherland, "Burke and Members"
Lucy S. Sutherland. "Edmund Burke and the Relations between the Members of Parliament and Their Constituents: An Examination of the Eighteenth-Century Theory and Practice in Instructions to Representatives." 10 *Studies in Burke and His Time* 1006–21 (1968).

Sutherland, "City of London"
Lucy Sutherland. "The City of London in Eighteenth-Century Politics." In *Essays Presented to Sir Lewis Namier,* edited by Richard Pares and A. J. P. Taylor, at 49–74. New York, 1956.

Sydney, *Discourses Concerning Government*
Algernon Sydney. *Discourses Concerning Government.* Reprinted in *The Works of Algernon Sydney,* at 1–542. New ed. London, 1772.

Sykes, *Winchester Rebellion Sermon*
Arthur Ashley Sykes. *A Sermon Preached in the Cathedral Church of Winchester, on the 9th Day of October, 1746. Being the Day appointed, for a General Thanksgiving, to Almighty God, for the Suppression of the late unnatural Rebellion.* London, 1746.

Tanner, *Constitutional Conflicts*
J. R. Tanner. *English Constitutional Conflicts of the Seventeenth Century: 1603–1689.* Cambridge, England, 1971.

They Preached Liberty
They Preached Liberty: With an Introductory Essay and Biographical Sketches by Franklin P. Cole. Indianapolis, Ind., 1977.

Thomson, *Constitutional History*
Mark A. Thomson. *A Constitutional History of England, 1642 to 1801.* London, 1938.

Thorne, "Introduction"
   Samuel E. Thorne. "Introduction." In Egerton, *Discourse,* at 3–100.
Tierney, *Religion, Law, and Growth*
   Brian Tierney. *Religion, Law, and the Growth of Constitutional Thought, 1150–1650.* Cambridge, England, 1982.
[Tod,] *Good Humour*
   [Nicholas Tod.] *Good Humour: or, a Way with the Colonies. Wherein is occasionally enquired into Mr. P[it]t's Claim to Popularity; And the Principles of Virtuous Liberty, as Taught in the School of Mr. Wilkes, and other Peripatetics.* London, 1766.
[Toland,] *Mercenary Parliaments*
   [John Toland.] *The Danger of Mercenary Parliaments: With a Preface Shewing the infinite Mischiefs of Long and Pack'd Parliaments.* London, 1722.
Toohey, *Liberty and Empire*
   Robert E. Toohey. *Liberty and Empire: British Radical Solutions to the American Problem, 1774–1776.* Lexington, Ky., 1978.
Tooke, *Letter on Reform*
   John Horne Tooke. *A Letter on Parliamentary Reform; Containing the Sketch of a Plan.* 2d ed. London, [1783].
[Towers,] *Letter to Samuel Johnson*
   [Joseph Towers.] *A Letter to Dr. Samuel Johnson: Occasioned by his late Political Publications. With an Appendix, Containing Some Observations on a Pamphlet Lately Published by Dr. Shebbeare.* London, 1775.
[Towers,] *Letter to Wesley*
   [Joseph Towers.] *A Letter to the Rev. Mr. John Wesley; In Answer to his late Pamphlet, Entitled, "Free Thoughts on the Present State of Public Affairs."* London, 1771.
[Towers,] *Observations on Liberty*
   [Joseph Towers.] *Observations on Public Liberty, Patriotism, Ministerial Despotism, and National Grievances. With Some Remarks on Riots, Petitions, Loyal Addresses, and Military Execution.* London, 1769.
Towers, *Vindication of Locke*
   Joseph Towers. *A Vindication of the Political Principles of Mr. Locke: In Answer to the Objections of the Rev. Dr. Tucker, Dean of Glocester.* London, 1782.
Town and County Magazine
   The Town and Country Magazine; or Universal Repository of Knowledge, Instruction, and Entertainment. [Monthly magazine, London.]
Trumbull, *Discourse at New Haven*
   Benjamin Trumbull. *Discourse, Delivered at the Anniversary Meeting of the Freemen of the Town of New-Haven, April 12, 1773.* New Haven, Conn., 1773.
Trial of Sacheverell
   The Tryal of Dr. Henry Sacheverell, before the House of Peers, For High Crimes and Misdemeanors; Upon an Impeachment by the Knights, Citizens and Burgesses in Parliament Assembled, in the Name of themselves, and of all the Commons of Great Britain: Begun in Westminster Hall the 27th Day of February, 1709/10; and from thence continu'd by several Adjournments until the 23d Day of March following. London, 1710.
A True Copy

A True Copy of the Journal of the High Court of Justice, for the Tryal of K. Charles I. as it was Read in the House of Commons, and Attested under the hand of PHELPS, *Clerk to that Infamous Court.* Edited by J. Nalson. London, 1684.

Tucker, *Election Sermon*

John Tucker. *A Sermon Preached at Cambridge, Before his Excellency Thomas Hutchinson, Esq; Governor: His Honor Andrew Oliver, Esq; Lieutenant-Governor, the Honorable His Majesty's Council, and the Honorable House of Representatives, of the Province of the Massachsuetts-Bay in New England, May 29th, 1771. Being the Anniversary for the Election of His Majesty's Council for the said Province.* Boston, 1771.

Tucker, *Four Letters to Shelburne*

[Josiah Tucker.] *Four Letters on Important National Subjects, Addressed to the Right Honourable the Earl of Shelburne, His Majesty's First Lord Commissioner of the Treasury.* 2d ed. London, 1783.

Tucker, *Treatise*

Josiah Tucker. *A Treatise Concerning Civil Government, In Three Parts.* London, 1781.

Tucker and Hendrickson, *Fall*

Robert W. Tucker and David C. Hendrickson. *The Fall of the First British Empire: Origins of the War of American Independence.* Baltimore, 1982.

Turner, *Election Sermon*

Charles Turner. *A Sermon Preached Before His Excellency Thomas Hutchinson, Esq; Governor: The Honourable His Majesty's Council, and the Honourable House of Representatives, of the Province of the Massachusetts-Bay in New-England, May 26th, 1773. Being the Anniversary of the Election of His Majesty's Council for the said Province.* Boston, 1773.

Twilight

The Twilight of British Rule in Revolutionary America: The New York Letter Book of General James Robertson, 1780–1783. Edited by Milton M. Klein and Roland W. Howard. Cooperstown, N.Y., 1983.

[Tyrrell,] *Brief Enquiry*

[James Tyrrell.] *A Brief Enquiry into the Ancient Constitution and Government of England.* London, 1695.

Tyrrell, *Politica*

James Tyrrell. *Bibliotheca Politica: Or, An Enquiry into the Antient Constitution of the English Government, With Respect to the Just Extent of the Regal Power, and the Rights and Liberties of the Subject. Wherein all the Chief Arguments both for and against the Late Revolution, are Impartially Represented and Consider'd. In Fourteen Dialogues. Collected out of the best Authors, Antient and Modern.* 2d ed. London, 1727.

Valentine, *Lord North*

Alan Valentine. *Lord North.* 2 vols. Norman, Okla., 1967.

Voice of People

The Voice of the People: A Collection of Addresses to His Majesty, and Instructions to Members of Parliament by Constituents, Upon the Unsuccessful Management of the present War both at Land and Sea; And the Establishment of a National Militia. London, 1756.

von Mehren, "Legislation in Tudor England"
    Arthur von Mehren. "The Judicial Conception of Legislation in Tudor En-
gland." In *Interpretations of Modern Legal Philosophies: Essays in Honor of Roscoe
Pound*, edited by Paul Sayre, at 751–66. New York, 1947.

[Waller,] *Address to People*
    [J. G. Waller.] *An Address to the People of England and Ireland. In which is sub-
mitted to their Consideration a Plan for restoring the Freedom and Vigour of our
Constitution, the Independence of Parliament, and the Happiness of the People.*
Dublin, [1782].

Warrington, *Grand Jury Charge*
    Henry Booth, second Baron Delamere. *The Charge of the Right Honourable
Henry Earl of Warrington, to the Grand Jury at the Quarter Sessions Held for the
County of Chester, On the 25th Day of April, 1693.* London, 1694.

Warrington, *Works*
    Henry Booth, earl of Warrington. *The Works of the Right Honourable Henry
late L[ord] Delamer and Earl Warrington.* London, 1694.

Watson, *Assize Sermon*
    Richard Watson. *A Sermon Preached at the University Church in Cambridge, at
the Assizes, before the Honourable Sir Richard Adams, Knt. One of the Barons of his
Majesty's Court of Exchequer; on Thursday, March 9, 1769.* Cambridge, England, 1769.

Watson, *Principles of the Revolution*
    Richard Watson. *The Principles of the Revolution vindicated in a Sermon Preached
Before the University of Cambridge, on Wednesday, May 29, 1776.* Cambridge,
England, 1776.

Welsteed, *Dignity and Duty*
    William Welsteed. *The Dignity and Duty of the Civil Magistrate. A Sermon
Preached in the Audience of His Honour, Spencer Phips, Esq; Lieutenant Governour
and Commander in Chief, the Honourable His Majesty's Council, and the Honour-
able House of Representatives, of the Province of the Massachusetts-Bay, in New-
England, May 29th 1751. Being the Anniversary for the Election of His Majesty's
Council for the said Province.* Boston, 1751.

Wesley, *Calm Address*
    John Wesley. *A Calm Address to our American Colonies. A New Edition corrected
and enlarged. To which is added, "A Calm Address to Americans. By a Native of
America."* London, 1775.

West, *Election Sermon*
    Samuel West. *A Sermon Preached before the Honorable Council, and the Honorable
House of Representatives, of the Colony of the Massachusetts-Bay, in New-England.
May 29th, 1776. Being the Anniversary for the Election of the Honorable Council
for the Colony.* Boston, 1776.

[Whately,] *Regulations*
    [Thomas Whately.] *The Regulations Lately Made Concerning the Colonies, and
the Taxes Imposed Upon Them, Considered.* London, 1765.

[Wheelock,] *Reflections*
    [Matthew Wheelock.] *Reflections Moral and Political on Great Britain and her
Colonies.* London, 1770.

Whitaker, *Manchester*
John Whitaker. *The History of Manchester.* Vol. 2. London, 1775.
White, *Connecticut Election Sermon*
Stephen White. *Civil Rulers Gods by Office, and the Duties of such Considered and Enforced. A Sermon Preached before the General Assembly of the Colony of Connect-icut, at Hartford, on the Day of their Anniversary Election, May the 12th, 1763.* New London, Conn., 1763.
[Whitelocke.] *Concerning Impositions*
[Sir James Whitelocke.] *The Rights of the People Concerning Impositions, Stated in a learned Argument; With a Remonstrance presented to the Kings most excellent Majesty, by the Honorable House of Commons, in the Parliament, An. Dom. 1610. Annoq; Regis Jac. 7.* London, 1658.
Wilkes, *English Liberty*
John Wilkes. *English Liberty: Being a Collection of Interesting Tracts, From the Year 1762 to 1769. Containing the Private Correspondence, Public Letters, Speeches, and Addresses, of John Wilkes, Esq. Humbly Dedicated to the King.* London, [1770].
Williams, *Election Sermon*
Abraham Williams. *A Sermon Preach'd at Boston, Before the Great and General Court or Assembly of the Province of the Massachusetts-Bay in New-England, May 26, 1762. Being the Day appointed by Royal Charter, for the Election of His Majesty's Council for the said Province.* Boston, 1762.
[Williams,] *Essential Rights*
[Elisha Williams.] *The Essential Rights and Liberties of Protestants. A Seasonable Plea for the Liberty of Conscience, and the Right of private Judgment, In Matters of Religion, Without any Controul from human Authority. Being a Letter from a Gentleman in the Massachusetts-Bay to his Friend in Connecticut. Wherein Some Thoughts on the Origin, End, and Extent of the Civil Power, with Brief Considerations on several late Laws in Connecticut, are humbly offered. By a Lover of Truth and Liberty.* Boston, 1744.
[Williams,] *Letters on Liberty*
[David Williams.] *Letters on Political Liberty. Addressed to a Member of the English House of Commons, on his being Chosen into the Committee of an Associating County.* London, 1782.
Williams, *Parliamentary Reformation*
Joseph Williams. *Parliamentary Reformation: Examined Under the Following Articles: Extending the Right of Election. Abolition of Boroughs. Qualification of Members. Abridging the Duration of Parliament.* London, 1782.
Williamson, *American Suffrage*
Chilton Williamson. *American Suffrage: From Property to Democracy, 1760–1860.* Princeton, N.J., 1960.
Williamson, "Imperial Policy"
J. A. Williamson. "The Beginnings of an Imperial Policy, 1649–1660." In *The Cambridge History of the British Empire,* vol. 1, *The Old Empire from the Beginnings to 1783,* edited by J. Holland Rose, A. P. Newton, and E. A. Benians, at 207–38. Cambridge, England, 1929.

Wills, *Explaining America*
   Garry Wills. *Explaining America: The Federalist*. Garden City, N.Y., 1981.
Wills, *Inventing America*
   Garry Wills. *Inventing America: Jefferson's Declaration of Independence*. Garden
   City, N.Y., 1978.
Wilson, *Considerations*
   James Wilson. *Considerations on the Nature and Extent of the Legislative Authority
   of the British Parliament*. 1774. Reprinted in *The Works of James Wilson*, edited
   by Robert Green McCloskey, vol. 2, at 721–46. Cambridge, Mass., 1967.
Wiltse, *Jeffersonian Tradition*
   Charles Maurice Wiltse. *The Jeffersonian Tradition in American Democracy*. New
   York, 1960.
Witmer, *Property Qualifications*
   Helen Elizabeth Witmer. *The Property Qualifications of Members of Parliament*.
   New York, 1943.
Wood, *Creation*
   Gordon S. Wood. *The Creation of the American Republic, 1776–1787*. Chapel
   Hill, N.C. 1969.
[Wood,] *Institute of the Laws*
   [Thomas Wood.] *A New Institute of the Imperial or Civil Law. With Notes, Shew-
   ing in some Principal Cases, amongest other Observations, How the Canon Law, the
   Laws of England, and the Laws and Customs of other Nations differ from it. In Four
   Books Composed for the Use of Some Persons of Quality*. 4th ed. London, 1730.
Woodbridge, *Connecticut Election Sermon*
   Ashbel Woodbridge. *A Sermon Delivered before the General Assembly of the Col-
   ony of Connecticut, on the Anniversary Election at Hartford, May 14th, 1752*. New
   London, Conn., 1753.
Wooddeson, *Jurisprudence*
   Richard Wooddeson. *Elements of Jurisprudence Treated of in the Preliminary Part
   of a Course of Lectures on the Law of England*. Dublin, 1792.
Wooddeson, *Laws of England*
   Richard Wooddeson. *A Systematical View of the Laws of England; as Treated of
   in a Course of Vinerian Lectures, Read at Oxford, During a Series of Years, Com-
   mencing in Michaelmas Term, 1777*. Vol. 1. Dublin, 1792.
Worcester Charges
   *Charges to Grand Juries, Delivered at the Quarter Sessions of the Peace for the
   County of Worcester, from the Year 1760 to 1776*. Worcester, 1780.
Works of Burke
   The Works of the Right Honourable Edmund Burke. 6th ed. 12 vols. Boston,
   1880.
Wynne, *Eunomus*
   Edward Wynne. *Eunomus: or, Dialogues Concerning the Law and Constitution of
   England with an Essay on Dialogue*. 2d ed. 4 vols. London, 1785.
Wyvill, *Defence of Price*
   Christopher Wyvill. *A Defence of Dr. Price and the Reformers of England*. Lon-
   don, 1792.

Wyvill, *State of Representation*
Christopher Wyvill. *A State of the Representation of the People of England, on the Principles of Mr. Pitt in 1785; with an Annexed State of Additional Propositions.* York, England, 1793.

Yale, "Hobbes and Hale"
D. E. C. Yale. "Hobbes and Hale on Law, Legislation and the Sovereign." 31 *Cambridge Law Journal* 121–56 (1973).

Young, *Example of France*
Arthur Young. *The Example of France, A Warning to Britain.* 4th ed. London, 1794.

[Young,] *Political Essays*
[Arthur Young.] *Political Essays Concerning the Present State of the British Empire. Particularily Respecting I. Natural Advantages and Disadvantages. II. Constitution. III. Agriculture. IV. Manufactures. V. The Colonies. and VI. Commerce.* London, 1772.

Young and Lofft, *Enquiry into Legality*
An Enquiry into the Legality and Expediency of Increasing the Royal Navy by Subscriptions for Building County Ships. Being the Correspondence on that Subject between Arthur Young & Capel Lofft, Esqrs. With a list of the Subscribers to the Suffolk Man of War. To which are added, Observations on the State of the Taxes and Resources of the Kingdom on Conclusion of the Peace. Bury St. Edmund's, England, 1783.

INDEX